Those Who Can, Teach

 McMaster Divinity College Press
McMaster General Series 3

Those Who Can, Teach

Teaching as Christian Vocation

EDITED BY
STANLEY E. PORTER

☙PICKWICK *Publications* · Eugene, Oregon

THOSE WHO CAN, TEACH
Teaching as Christian Vocation

McMaster Divinity College General Series

Copyright © 2013 Wipf and Stock Publishers. All rights reserved. Except for brief quotations in critical publications or reviews, no part of this book may be reproduced in any manner without prior written permission from the publisher. Write: Permissions, Wipf and Stock Publishers, 199 W. 8th Ave., Suite 3, Eugene, OR 97401.

McMaster Divinity College Press
1280 Main Street West
Hamilton, Ontario, Canada
L8S 4K1

Pickwick Publications
An Imprint of Wipf and Stock Publishers
199 W. 8th Ave., Suite 3
Eugene, OR 97401

ISBN 13: 978-1-62032-936-8

www.wipfandstock.com

Cataloging-in-Publication data:

Those Who Can, Teach / edited by Stanley E. Porter.

viii + 218 p. ; 23 cm. Includes bibliographical references and index.

McMaster Divinity College Press General Series

ISBN 13: 978-1-62032-936-8

1. I. II. III. IV.

CALL NUMBER

Manufactured in the U.S.A.

Contents

List of Contributors / vii

Introduction: Teaching as Theological Vocation / 1
Stanley E. Porter

1 Developing a Philosophy of Education / 9
Stanley E. Porter

2 Pedagogy and Course Objectives / 38
Michael P. Knowles

3 Designing and Evaluating Learning Experiences for Courses / 56
Mark J. Boda

4 Developing a Syllabus / 89
Cynthia Long Westfall

5 Sculpting a Lesson: The Art of Preparing a Classroom Learning Experience / 107
Lee Beach

6 Teaching Introductory New Testament Greek / 123
Lois K. Fuller Dow

7 Teaching Biblical Hebrew: Practical Strategies for Introductory Courses / 135
Paul Evans

8 Leading Intentional Theological Reflection in the Classroom: The Merging of Mind and Heart / 158
Wendy J. Porter

9 From Doctoral Program to Classroom / 177
Steven M. Studebaker

10 The Upside-Down Professor: The Professor in a Christian Institution / 192
    Gordon L. Heath

11 Spirituality of Teaching and Theological Integration / 206
    Phil C. Zylla

Modern Authors Index / 215

Contributors

Lee Beach, Assistant Professor of Christian Ministry, Director of Ministry Formation, and Garbutt F. Smith Chair of Ministry Formation, McMaster Divinity College, Hamilton, Ontario

Mark J. Boda, Professor of Old Testament, McMaster Divinity College, Hamilton, Ontario

Lois K. Fuller Dow, Assistant Professor of Greek, and Managing Editor of McMaster Divinity College Press, McMaster Divinity College, Hamilton, Ontario

Paul Evans, Assistant Professor of Old Testament, McMaster Divinity College, Hamilton, Ontario

Gordon L. Heath, Associate Professor of Christian History, and Centenary Chair in World Christianity, McMaster Divinity College, Hamilton, Ontario

Michael P. Knowles, George F. Hurlburt Professor of Preaching, McMaster Divinity College, Hamilton, Ontario

Stanley E. Porter, President and Dean, Professor of New Testament, and Roy A. Hope Chair in Christian Worldview, McMaster Divinity College, Hamilton, Ontario

Wendy J. Porter, Director of Music and Worship, McMaster Divinity College, Hamilton, Ontario

Steven M. Studebaker, Associate Professor of Systematic and Historical Theology, and Howard and Shirley Bentall Chair in Evangelical Thought, McMaster Divinity College, Hamilton, Ontario

Cynthia Long Westfall, Assistant Professor of New Testament, McMaster Divinity College, Hamilton, Ontario

Phil C. Zylla, Associate Professor of Pastoral Theology, Academic Dean, and J. Gordon and Margaret Warnock Jones Chair in Church Ministry, McMaster Divinity College, Hamilton, Ontario

Introduction

Teaching as Theological Vocation

STANLEY E. PORTER

In George Bernard Shaw's play, *Man and Superman*, one of the characters is discouraged because his teacher has told him that the play he wrote is not very good. In response, another character tells him not to be upset, because, as we all have heard, "Remember, those who can, do; those who can't, teach." Although this statement has come to be used as a means of disparaging teachers by equating them with those who are incapable of "doing," the reality is something quite different. Teaching is a unique vocation, because it involves the teacher in fundamental intellectual, character, and behavior formation of the student. If this is not "doing," I am bewildered as to what it means to "do" anything of importance. And if this is true of teaching generally conceived, it is even more true (if such a thing can in fact be) of teaching within a theological context, whether that means undergraduate or graduate teaching, or at a Christian college, university, or seminary. The vocation of being a theological educator—and I believe that it is a true vocation, at least the equal of any other vocation, and to be included within the valued vocations of the church—is not one that should be entered into lightly. It is worth investing in learning to do it well at least as rigorously as we have invested in the educational endeavors that have equipped us intellectually to become teachers. This book of essays, each of them by an experienced theological educator who has devoted years to the practice of this vocation and much effort to contemplating it, is designed to help others to learn the craft of becoming a theological educator.

The chapters in this book arose out of a very practical context—the professors at McMaster Divinity College were concerned that the graduates of their PhD program in Christian Theology be well-equipped to enter into the ranks of the professoriate. One of the reasons that we instigated our PhD program at McMaster Divinity College was out of concern that teachers at Christian colleges, universities, and seminaries were not adequately prepared by their graduate institutions for the task of being Christian teachers. In other words, we were concerned that they had not been given the opportunity to think about what it means to be a theological educator, what the responsibilities are, not only intellectually but emotionally, theologically, and spiritually as well, and what it means to be able to integrate the latest in theological thought with deep reflection upon the Scriptures and our Christian theological traditions. We willingly acknowledged that there were many fine PhD programs in theology and related areas that did more than adequate jobs of instilling appropriate knowledge in their graduates, but we were concerned about what happened next. We wanted our students to be able to enter the classroom having already contemplated and even possibly confronted the kinds of issues that they as newly minted members of the teaching guild would encounter.

As a result, we conceived the idea of a teaching colloquy, which all of our PhD students, as well as any interested MA students, would attend and participate in. When we investigated what other, similar PhD programs were doing to prepare their students in this way, we were surprised at how few of them had any kind of sustained or coordinated program in place. I am sure that individual professors probably took it upon themselves to impart their wisdom to their own students or their teaching assistants, but few institutions had a rigorous program that drew upon the collective wisdom of an entire faculty.

The papers in this volume contain a selection of papers from our teaching colloquies held in 2010 and 2012 at McMaster Divinity College. In planning these colloquies, we endeavored to address many, if not most, of the major issues that a new professor would face. This guided our planning and the kinds of papers and seminars that our professors delivered and led. We also tried to arrange the two days of each colloquy so that we would guide our students through the process of reflecting upon their vocational calling as teachers. The papers presented in this volume roughly reflect that ordering. There is inevitably some overlap among the papers—we did not try to eliminate this, because we realize that teaching is an individual activity, as well as a collective process, so we encouraged our professors to generously share their own perspectives on these various and often complex issues. We also wanted the opportunity for our students to see that professors could have varying views on a number of these topics. What we were surprised to find, in the course of planning the colloquies and in their execution, was the very high amount of continuity and similarity that emerged in the course of our thinking through these topics out loud with our peers and our students. At McMaster Divinity College, we believe that we have not only an excellent research faculty but an excellent teaching faculty—they are one and the same faculty. All indications are that this is true, from the individual responses of students to various examples of mentoring that occur, to the results that our students demonstrate as they enter their various Christian vocations. The papers and discussions at the colloquy confirm that their excellence in teaching is not an accident, but the result of intentional thought and reflection by our faculty, who work hard to make the classroom experience a rewarding one for our students.

In the first essay, Stanley Porter draws upon over twenty-five years of teaching experience at a range of educational institutions (besides being President of McMaster Divinity College) and recounts some of his own unique educational experiences. He sets the groundwork for thinking about teaching by discussing the importance of developing a philosophy of education. He breaks this topic down into a number of different components, all of them at the end of the day focusing upon the importance of the teacher for the educational experience. However, having said that, this does not mean that there are not genuine differences in opinion regarding this educational experience. There are. Porter first discusses a number of different philosophical approaches to education, each of which has had significance at various times and in various ways within the educational environment, and then he discusses various ways that teachers position themselves in relation to their students. There are multiple ways that teachers fashion themselves in front of their students, and such positioning reflects their view, attitude, or, indeed, philosophy of education. Porter argues that every teacher has a philosophy of education, including that of teaching, but that the best ones have explicitly thought through what that philosophy is.

In the next set of three papers, we turn to some of the nuts and bolts of teaching, although these are offered within the context of further reflection on the vocation of being a theological educator. Michael Knowles, our professor of preaching, discusses teaching and course objectives. He notes that there has been significant debate, even within theological institutions, regarding the task of theological education. Using the McMaster Divinity College rubric of "knowing," "being," and "doing," Knowles outlines the cognitive, formative, and practical goals that a teacher might create for a course. These can be a helpful means not only of devising a course syllabus but of thinking through larger issues of how we relate to our theological, cultural, personal, and vocational contexts. They also may help teachers think through the various ways that students learn and how the requirements for a course can address the varied learning styles of our students. Knowles also relates these to actual assignments and their particular objectives within the larger classroom and pedagogical environment.

Mark Boda, who has taught at both undergraduate and graduate level institutions, addresses somewhat similar issues, but focuses more particularly upon student learning styles, the life experiences of students, and particular learning outcomes for courses. Boda attempts to show how students' learning styles and their life experiences are integral to who they are as students, and how this should be taken into account in a conscious way by teachers. This involves formulating clear objectives for courses, correlating objectives with assignments, and then designing assignments that allow students to engage with the material in ways that enable them to fulfill these objectives. Boda also includes a section on one of the most difficult areas of teaching—grading. Grading is often a dreaded aspect of teaching, but even if it is not welcomed by all it can be much more useful if teachers have a clear idea of what grading is and is not, what it does and does not do.

Continuing along a similar line, but with more focus upon the course syllabus, Cynthia Westfall, one of our professors of New Testament, discusses the various goals and types of syllabi. She emphasizes that there is not a single syllabus for a given course that will work in every environment. There are various factors that must be taken into consideration. These include the level of instruction (undergraduate, graduate, seminary), the configuration of the course itself (daily, weekly, etc.), and the particularities of the institution and its students. She then goes through and discusses the various individual components of a syllabus, based upon the template that we use at McMaster Divinity College. One of the requirements that we have for our PhD students is that they develop three syllabi during the time of their doctoral studies with us. We have found that this is an excellent exercise, and can even make the difference between employment or not. When our students graduate, they have already thought through what it means to construct the outlines of a course, and are ready to hit the ground running when the occasion arises.

To this point in the book, we have already discussed a number of important topics, including an overall philosophy of education and philosophy of teaching, various elements of the overall learning environment including course goals, student learning styles, assignments, grading, and syllabi. We now turn to three papers on particular issues in theological education. The first, by Lee Beach, an experienced pastor and professor who also directs our Ministry Formation program, addresses the issue of shaping a lesson to create the best classroom learning experience. Beach endorses the validity of experiential learning, but also notes that such learning does not happen by accident. It requires preparation, an overall main idea to be accomplished, and objectives in order to realize this main idea, creating an environment in which such learning can take place, assessing knowledge and learning, and recognition of the potential helpful role of discussion in such learning. Throughout his essay, Beach provides a number of useful classroom tips, especially on how to handle classroom discussion. There are any number of ways that such discussions can go well or not so well, depending upon how the teacher handles the topics and student reactions.

The next two essays are about as practically focused as can be imagined in a book such as this. In these two essays, we draw upon experienced biblical language teachers to discuss major issues that confront the teacher of Greek or Hebrew. Though these chapters may have more direct application for seminary teachers, they also contain a number of useful ideas that teachers at other levels and of other subjects can apply in their own ways to their own pedagogical situations. Many new seminary teachers think that they will inevitably get "stuck" teaching the languages, because they lack seniority. Both of these essays make clear that the teaching of biblical languages can provide a great opportunity to overcome anxiety on both the teacher's and the students' part! Lois Dow, who has taught Greek for over thirty years in a variety of cultural contexts, draws upon her wide range of experience to give practical insights into teaching Greek. She notes that the teaching of Greek has an added benefit for the teacher—firming up knowledge of the language that can only be gained by being called upon to teach it. I think that this is probably true of virtually any subject—we truly internalize it once we have to explain it to others and guide them in their learning. Dow emphasizes that the teacher of Greek needs to think through what it means to teach Greek before the course starts, rather than after. In order to do this, the prospective language teacher must consider what approach to use, the right textbook for this purpose, creation of the right classroom environment, providing helps for the students, the ways to go about marking, and finding a way for students to keep their Greek alive, whether it is from week to week, semester to semester, or even year to year.

Paul Evans, who has taught Hebrew at a number of different institutions in his teaching career, offers similar instructive advice regarding the teaching of Hebrew. He reiterates the importance of thinking through in advance what the teacher wishes to accomplish in the classroom. He also notes that it is usually not sufficient simply to teach through a textbook or expect a textbook to do all of the work of generating and retaining student interest. As a result, Evans suggests a number of ways for the teacher to enhance the classroom experience. These can include games, songs, and other elements of a supportive environment. Two themes that Evans includes, as does Dow, are related to motivation of students and the importance of finding the right textbook. Evans presents a number of ways that teachers of Hebrew—and, I would add, of other subjects—can think of engaging their students, including reinforcing the reasons for their studying the subject. He also notes that textbooks vary significantly, and some are better or worse, especially depending upon the goals of the individual teacher and the institution. Even then, there are often other things that the teacher can do to encourage students in their love of Hebrew (or any subject!).

The next two essays address transitional issues regarding the purpose and career of the teacher. In the first of these two essays, Wendy Porter, who teaches in the area of theological reflection as well as music and worship, outlines a means by which theological educators can bring theological reflection into the classroom. We all know that the default of education—and this is true of theological education as much as it is of other areas of education—is cognitive knowledge. Cognitive knowledge is of course important, but it is not the only kind of knowledge and the gaining of it is not the only goal of theological education—even in highly cognitive areas. Theological reflection is a constructive means to bring our Christian faith to bear on our experiences in productive and deep ways. It addresses the part of the human that can be overlooked as we develop our minds, in particular our hearts. Theological reflection, even in seminary classrooms, does not occur by accident, but must be intentional, as we bring Scripture, Christian tradition, culture, experience, and reason to bear on what it is that God is doing in our lives and what he is trying to teach us through our experiences. Porter not only lays out ways to do theological reflection in the classroom, but provides a compelling case for its necessity if we ourselves are going to be truly theological educators and our classrooms are going to be places of spiritual and theological growth and maturity.

Steve Studebaker, our professor of systematic and historical theology, addresses the transition of the student from the doctoral program itself, where one is a student and on the receiving end of the educational process, to that of the classroom as teacher, where one is on the giving end of that process. Studebaker reflects back on his own experience, making the transition from a doctoral student to his first teaching position at an undergraduate Christian liberal arts institution. As a result, he passes on words of wisdom that were gained in this difficult period of transition. He learned that a new teacher needs to embrace the classroom environment and develop it, rather than expecting it to be like (and treating it like) the graduate school seminar. This simple realization can make all the difference, not only for the teacher but for the students who may well find this particular classroom experience life-transforming. Studebaker also believes that a new teacher, rather than lamenting the huge teaching load of a first appointment, can utilize this environment as a means of developing his or her research. Not only does the professor continue to develop as an academic, but I think that students greatly appreciate the opportunity (whether they realize it overtly or not) to work with a professor who continues to learn. Finally, for many if not most of those reading this book, teaching will mean teaching within a confessional context. This has its own challenges and rewards, which need to be taken into account both in the classroom and outside of it.

The final two essays turn to the larger life of the teacher, that is, the teacher within a Christian context not only in the classroom but within the wider sphere of vocational life. In the first of these essays, Gord Heath, professor of Christian history and an experienced teacher, turns the tables or—to use his metaphor—turns the professor upside down. Rather than the kinds of accomplishments and achievements that are valued in a secular work environment, Heath reminds us all of the values of Christian theological education and the kinds of values that are demanded of its teachers. These are not the values of getting to the top at all costs and at the expense of others, but the values reflected by the great Teacher himself, Jesus Christ, who taught from the position of a servant. There are many temptations that teachers are susceptible to. This may come as a surprise to some, but they are real nonetheless. There are few things quite so ego-satisfying as the unbridled adulation of students, including (especially?) graduate students, as they praise their teachers. Pride can become one of the great dangers even of theological educators. Heath recognizes these temptations and recommends that we be aware of our potential failings and look to others in the past who have had to struggle similarly with such temptations. Besides Jesus himself, we can turn to those such as the Church Fathers and other greats of the church.

In the final essay, our academic dean, Phil Zylla, a former pastor and now professor, reflects upon his own experience as a theological educator and his own pilgrimage to where he is today as a teacher of others. In fact, being a pilgrim is the dominant metaphor that he uses to encompass his approach. In order to do this, returning to several themes mentioned elsewhere in this volume, Zylla points out that we need to be intentional in our own spiritual and theological integration. This involves deep reflection upon the vocation and practice of theological education within a larger view of the world. This also means creating a safe and hospitable place for our students to engage with us in their own theological reflection and integration. Hospitality means not merely being welcoming, but offering constructive guidance and even critique where necessary, having a voice and using it to express our own self-critical reflection—but without taking ourselves too seriously. In other words, we should also keep a sense of humor as we examine ourselves in light of what God is doing in our lives to shape us into the teachers that we need to become.

This set of essays covers a wide range of topics. Some of the topics or ideas are treated in various ways by several of the contributors. This helps us to realize that there are common themes that unite the theological educator's vocation. Some of the topics are more focused and specialized, and related to particular areas of the theological teacher's activities. These themes also need to be taken seriously, because they too are part of the intertwined character of what it means to become a theological educator.

Our students responded incredibly positively to these colloquies, and participation in a teaching colloquy is now a regular and required part of our PhD program. We did not add this requirement simply to create another burden or a further box to check in a list of requirements. We have added it because we believe that the life of a theological educator is too important to leave to chance or accident. No doubt many good teachers have emerged without having exposure to similar colloquies, but we know—all too often from our own experiences—that there are many pitfalls that can be avoided, and, more than that, that there is a wealth of important experience that those who have gone before us have gained and from which we can all benefit.

1

Developing a Philosophy of Education

Stanley E. Porter

THE IMPORTANCE OF A PHILOSOPHY OF EDUCATION

Everyone involved in the field of education has a philosophy of education—even if they don't know what it is or have not been called upon to articulate it. For some, this philosophy is derived from the best and worst examples of pedagogy that they have witnessed. For others, it is based upon a prescribed culture of the institution in which they function. In the ideal case, this philosophy of education will be the result of critical reflection upon the educational task and the individual scholar-teacher's perspective on the best means for accomplishing it. Those who graduate from formal educational programs are required to think critically about their philosophy of education as part of what it means to become a qualified teacher. However, those in higher education are often not the productive beneficiaries of advanced educational training—or any formal educational training at all—so it is imperative that somewhere along the way as they are being initiated into pedagogical technique they also reflect critically on the development of a suitable philosophy of education. This is important because, as I said at the outset, everyone has a philosophy of education, whether they realize it or not, and they will end up functioning as educators out of this philosophy, whether or not it is critically well-formed.

My own formal exploration of a philosophy of education began when I was an undergraduate and I had the opportunity, as part of a summer abroad course, to explore various European educational models.[1] The examination of these models—through reading institutional literature, talking with students and others within these educational systems, and comparing what I found with my knowledge of the North American educational system—enabled me to appreciate that education functions within various philosophical systems, and that the practices of education are, in many ways, reflective of fundamental though often implicit views of education and its related pedagogy. In this paper, I wish to examine some of the major philosophies of education, the various roles of the teacher within this set of philosophical frameworks, and some of the problems related to adult learning, as I am addressing these comments to those who are thinking about, and perhaps training to be, educators of adults in post-secondary institutions, whether these be colleges and universities, seminaries, or graduate schools. My approach is not to be an overt advocate for one position over another, although my biases will no doubt emerge in the course of the presentation, but I wish to outline some of the options that one might weigh in determining one's own philosophy of education.

INSTITUTIONAL OR PROGRAM-BASED EDUCATIONAL PHILOSOPHY

A tension exists within education between institutional and program-based educational philosophies and personal philosophies. One frequently sees the results of these conflicts. They take the form of people trying to reconcile how a particular program—which may reflect a particular philosophy—is to relate to the institutional educational approach and philosophy. There are two directions in which such tensions pull the institution and the program. Either the program must buckle under to the philosophy of the institution, or it runs the risk of being overwhelmed by the institution

1. Let me give more autobiographical information. I have become a student of education, almost inevitably. I am the son of two teachers. I am a graduate of a futuristic high school (see below), and studied at both secular and Christian higher-educational institutions. I have taught at all levels from first grade through PhD, and virtually all areas in between, including elementary, secondary, undergraduate, seminary, and graduate school. I have held full-time appointments at both secular and Christian educational institutions, in three countries and on two continents, and have been an administrator at both secular and Christian institutions, one in the UK and the other in North America. I have been teaching for over twenty-five years, and have been an administrator for over seventeen years.

itself. Otherwise, an institution runs the risk of having no cohesive educational philosophy, but being merely a composite of varied philosophies according to programs. The modern university often suffers from such a dilemma. The modern university was founded on the principle of it being a place where universal knowledge was held, developed, and promulgated. However, the university of today—with its various areas of specialization, budgetary constraints, and student demand—often sacrifices universal knowledge for specialized knowledge. The same kind of tension is found between individual educational philosophies and those of the program or institution. These tensions are perhaps less readily obvious, as it is possible for faculty members to subsume their individual wants or desires (perhaps because they do not have a well-developed educational philosophy?) so long as the program or institution allows them to continue to do the kind of teaching and research that they desire. However, this can hardly be healthy for either the individual or the institution, as it also pulls the two sides in potentially opposing directions. The ideal situation—though I am realistic enough to know that such an ideal is often not achieved—is one where the faculty members have robust educational philosophies that, while perhaps not synonymous with the institutional program, are at least compatible with and complementary to the educational philosophy of the program and larger institution. The only way to hope to achieve such a robust and healthy relationship is through knowledge of the various types of philosophy that have been held through the years. I will deal with several of the more common recent, modern educational philosophies. There are currently six that are worth brief examination.[2]

Classical Education and Its Continuation in Perennialism

Classical education has its roots in classicism itself, that is, in the learning attributed to the Greeks and Romans.[3] Greek education, and its continuation and development by the Romans, despite the later impression that we have, especially in its more recent manifestation as the "Great Books" approach, was practical in design and intent. There are three major features to note about the classical educational system, before we turn to its continuation in the perennialist approach. The first is that

---

2. The following are my interpretations of the very helpful discussion found in Knight, *Philosophy and Education*, esp. 91–130.

3. For a history of the development of education, including Christian education, see Reed and Prevost, *History of Christian Education*.

the goal of education was that those who benefited from it would be able to lead the good life of a productive citizen. Therefore, besides the basic literacy and numeracy skills that were thought important for those who wished to transact business in such a world, the emphasis in advanced education was upon learning the art of oratory. Rhetorical skills were essential to being able to perform as a good citizen, by being able to represent and defend oneself in the gatherings of citizens. The second feature is that the education was elitist. For the most part, the only ones who were able to participate in the educational system were those who were financially and societally positioned to be able to afford education—or those such as slaves who would benefit their masters by learning how to write and calculate. The educational system was based around two major schools. The first was the grammar school, and the second was the rhetorical school. Those who went to grammar school learned basic literacy or numeracy either before entering or in the first couple of years. What was later codified in medieval times as the trivium and the quadrivium formed the basis of this bipartite educational structure. Classical education was based upon a fixed body of knowledge that was enshrined in the curriculum, and the teacher's role was to ensure that the student mastered this body of material, so as to create an educated citizenry. Hence the student would be exposed to grammar, logic, arithmetic, geometry, cosmology, and music, with rhetoric as the climax of the educational system, so as to learn and then be prepared to use and pass on the tradition and be a productive citizen. The third feature of the Greco-Roman educational system, as already noted, was that it was based upon imitation of the great examples of the past. Therefore, Homer, the venerated poet, was the most widely used author, followed by the great playwrights, such as Euripides, as students learned by imitation of the great authors of the past. They preformed a variety of learning exercises so that they could learn to create literary works that imitated what they found in the best examples of the classical authors.[4]

The classical educational approach is continued in what has been called perennialism.[5] Perennialism emerged in the twentieth century as a response to educational developments that were thought to compromise classical education. The classical approach had fallen on hard times with

---

4. For recent discussion of the ancient educational system, see Porter and Pitts, "Paul's Bible," 11–21.

5. See Knight, *Philosophy and Education*, 103–5. Works that capture the perennialist approach are Bloom, *Closing of the American Mind*, and Hirsch, *Cultural Literacy*.

the Enlightenment and the rise of industrialism. These movements led to a democratization of society, with the rise of an affluent middle class that was concerned with disseminating education more widely. In the meantime, classical education had lost its practical dimension and had come to be seen as opposed to applied education, with an emphasis upon theoretical and, almost by definition, non-applied knowledge, which modern educational thought rejected. Perennialists attempted to shift the emphasis back to an essentialist approach that focused education upon the enduring truths and great works of the past. One of the more obvious perennialist manifestations was the "Great Books" approach, which believed that there was a relatively fixed corpus of material that constituted the canon of necessary works for one to read and appreciate to be considered well educated. Whereas only a few post-secondary institutions accepted these works as the sole basis of the curriculum, the influence of the "Great Books" approach on many fields of study has been significant, as it has helped to establish and regulate the canon of works included in the curriculum. Whereas the practical goal of the Greeks and Romans was lost in the exaltation of the canon of the great writers and thinkers, the goal of developing well-informed and well-read citizens—that is, those who were well-educated in the major thoughts and ideas that stood as the basis of Western society—was strongly maintained in the perennialist approach. Knight describes six principles of perennialism, which I adapt here: (1) the inherently rational nature of the human is emphasized, so that the unique characteristic of the human as a rational being is the basis for emphasis upon the rational faculty; (2) human nature has been constant through the ages, with the implications that modern humanity can learn from humanity of any age, including the ancients, and that education should be consistent and have a common basis for all those being educated; (3) since human nature is a constant, human knowledge is also a constant, and this common body of knowledge provides the basis of what is taught to all being educated; (4) the common, constant, and enduring body of knowledge is the basis of all education, rather than the student or the teacher or any other variable factor; (5) this common body of knowledge is captured and enduringly enshrined in the greatest works created by the great rational minds of the past, and is just as relevant today as it was in the past, and provides the content of education; and (6) such a classically based education provides the best foundation for leading a productive life, rather than the classroom itself being a mirror of life.[6] Perennialism continues to have a large influence. This is seen in many recent debates over the nature of the canon of works to be read in higher education, with sides being taken by those who wish to maintain a fixed canon against those who wish to open up the canon. The fact that the canon is being discussed attests to the importance of perennialism as a viable philosophy of education.

Progressivism/Humanism

In some ways, I should have begun with progressivism or humanism as the first modern philosophy of education, because it was this approach that reacted against classical education and led to the backlash with perennialism. As noted above, the Enlightenment and then the industrial revolution led to a widespread democratization of society, as wealth was more evenly distributed across a wider scope. With this change in societal structural patterns and economic distribution came a rethinking of education itself. Progressivism was the educational philosophical result of this change in societal structure.[7]

Progressivism in education followed along with a number of other intellectual changes in modern society brought about by the rise of modernism. These include the influence of pragmatism, in which there was a call for education to be of practical worth to the individual and especially to society; the influence of modern psychological theories, in which the reality of the inner psychological life of the individual was embraced and explored; and primitivism, which elevated the role of the child and child-like impulses as essential to the educational process. Whereas classical education, at least as it was manifested in the late nineteenth and early twentieth centuries, was oriented toward restricted access, emphasis upon the role of the teacher, and the place of memorization and accumulation of knowledge, progressivism rejected all of these major premises—although it is unfair to say that all progressivists held to the same set of pedagogical presuppositions.

Knight has detailed six principles that characterize progressivism, and which I expand upon: (1) the child or, in the case of post-secondary education, the student, is the basis and reason for education, rather than any fixed body of knowledge; (2) the student takes an active role in education, rather than simply passively receiving a body of knowledge; (3)

---

6. Knight, *Philosophy and Education*, 106–9.
7. See ibid., 92–94. The classic progressive work is Dewey, *School and Society*.

the teacher, rather than being the authority figure who guides learning, is a facilitator of learning for the student, by exposing students to various educational opportunities and resources; (4) the educational institution is meant to be a reflection of the composition of society as a whole, rather than being an elitist institution reserved for the few; (5) the educational methods should focus upon solving problems and thinking critically and interactively with material, rather than the student simply being given bodies of information or material; and (6) the educational environment, again reflective of society, is to be democratic and collegial, with students encouraged to develop as learners, rather than being restricted in their educational pursuits.[8]

The influence of progressivism in education has been immense and continues to be widely recognized. Although the movement itself reached its peak in the 1950s, it is still found in humanistic educational developments since that time.[9] These humanistic developments, influenced by more recent philosophical thought such as existentialism and its place in psychology, included a greater emphasis upon the values of progressivism, especially in the place of the student within the educational process. As a result, the educational environment was encouraged to be supportive rather than competitive, collaborative rather than competitive, individualistic rather than group-oriented, and creative rather than rote and mnemonic. The 1960s educational environment is reflective of the principles of humanism, but the principles continue to be widely embraced with their emphasis upon the creative and developmental within education. This has resulted in various forms of non-traditional educational practice, including various types of open or non-structured learning environments, where the traditional classroom, curriculum, and schedule are replaced by self-motivated and individualized instruction.

Essentialism

Like perennialism, essentialism was also a backlash against progressivism and its subsequent humanism, with their emphasis upon the student and their creative and developmental potential.[10] Unlike perennialism, how-

---

8. Knight, *Philosophy and Education*, 94–98.

9. See ibid., 98–102. Work that reflects the humanist approach is Holt, *Freedom and Beyond*.

10. See Knight, *Philosophy and Education*, 109–12. Work that reflects the essentialist approach is Damon, *Greater Expectations*.

ever, essentialism rejected the elitist leanings of some perennialists and argued for an educational philosophy founded upon essential and basic knowledge. Essentialism has had a significant influence upon education, especially at the lower levels of instruction, as a counter to progressivism and humanism. Movements that refer to emphasis upon the 3 Rs (reading, writing, and arithmetic), "back to basics," and the more recent "no child left behind" effort have essentialist leanings.

The essentialist movement in the United States benefited immensely from the mid-twentieth-century space race with the Soviet Union, when, with the launch of Sputnik in 1957, it appeared that the West was about to be surpassed by the East. The result was an emphasis upon basic subject matter, especially the sciences and mathematics. Standardized testing of students is, to a large extent, a result of the essentialist movement, as it was determined that there was an essential minimum amount of knowledge that every student should demonstrate, whether it is at the elementary, secondary, or post-secondary level.

Knight articulates three basic principles of the essentialist movement, which I adapt here: (1) basic or essential knowledge stands at the heart of the educational enterprise and forms the basis of the curriculum, hence the emphasis upon such basic subjects as reading, writing, and arithmetic at the lower grades, with other subjects such as science, mathematics, history, English literature and language, and other languages emphasized at higher grades, and with minimization of study of non-basic or non-essential subjects; (2) the disciplined classroom under the guidance of a strong teacher is required in order to ensure that students acquire this basic knowledge, because education itself requires hard work and diligence, rather than it being a time for creative exploration of one's inner urges and inclinations; and (3) the final authority in the classroom is not the student or the student's needs, but the educated and competent teacher, who stands as an authority figure to guide the students in their acquisition of basic knowledge.[11] Essentialism continues to have an impact upon the educational scene, especially at the lower levels of education, although its implications for higher levels are also readily to be seen.

---

11. Knight, *Philosophy and Education*, 112–14.

Reconstructionism

Reconstructionism was also a reaction to the status quo in educational philosophy.[12] However, reconstructionism was less a movement that directly rebelled against classical education, and more one that reacted to the social issues of the times. The 1930s were a time of deep economic despair, which led to widespread social, political, and societal unease, and it was out of this milieu that educational reconstructionism was born. It shared some of the concerns of progressivism, but was much more of a pragmatic response to the conditions of the times. Reconstructionism, in keeping with the political tone of the era, called for what amounted to a rebellion against the contemporary educational norms. Rather than education being the reflector of society and the perpetuator of society's norms and standards, including its accumulated educational knowledge, reconstructionists called for educationalists to assert themselves and remake education as a progressive and liberating social force to reconstruct the social, political, and economic scene along collectivist lines that would eliminate the current social ills.

Knight has described five principles of reconstructionism, which I adapt here: (1) reconstructionism takes an apocalyptic view of society, and argues that society as we know it cannot endure without a radical reconfiguration, especially in its educational institutions, so as to address all of the global problems with which we are faced; (2) the solution to such problems is much larger than education itself, but education is to take a role in the reconfiguring of the global social order so that these horrendous problems of injustice and inequity can be addressed on the level that they deserve; (3) education is to play a major role in this transformation, hence its label reconstructionism, as it is an agent for influencing the social, political, and economic norms of the day; (4) reconstructionism is to function within a framework of democracy, in which democratic principles permeate the classroom so that each individual is empowered, both teachers and students; and (5) these empowered teachers should exercise their constructive role in reshaping society through the classroom so that positive social change is the result, based upon especially the use of the social sciences.[13]

---

12. See ibid., 115–16. Work that reflects the reconstructionist approach is Counts, *Dare the School*.

13. Knight, *Philosophy and Education*, 116–19. I am the product of a "futuristic" high school that used what was called "flexible scheduling." Each morning each student received a computer-generated schedule of courses for the day, reflecting the previously submitted course configuration requirements of the individual teachers and our own individual course selection for the term. In my three years in the high school, and

Reconstructionism continued to be influential in certain circles in the second half of the twentieth century, in light of the post-war tensions of the West and East, with advocates for the social engineering role to be played by education. It has also been manifested in futurism, the view promoted by those who believe that education, rather than looking to the past, serves its best purpose when it helps prepare people for the future by enabling them to envision and create it.[14]

Behaviorism

Behaviorism, within and outside education, is the product of the rise of naturalistic thought, another of the products of the Enlightenment.[15] Enlightenment thought and the rise of modern science shifted the epistemological perspective from one that entertained the role of the divine into one in which solely natural causes are responsible for the world in which humans live. Behaviorism takes this perspective even further by its assertion that not only is the world metaphysically naturalistic but human beings are simply part of this natural world and subject to its laws like any other phenomena.

Three philosophical origins have been traced in educational behaviorism. The first is philosophical realism, in which humankind is seen to be a part of nature and to respond to its laws; the second is positivism, with its emphasis upon the "positive," as opposed to metaphysical, facts of the measurable and observable world; and materialism, which contends that reality is merely and only material in nature. Such an environment would not necessarily seem to be well suited to providing the basis of an educational philosophy—and it certainly does not for one constructed on classical or human-oriented grounds. Instead, behaviorism stresses the conditioned nature of human existence, and the role that education plays in this conditioning.

Knight outlines four behaviorist principles, which I adapt here: (1) rather than the human being unique or distinct because of any particular characteristics, the human is simply an animal, though perhaps a more

---

within any given year, I never had the same schedule twice to my knowledge. I think that this was one of the greatest adventures in education imaginable, and am saddened that it eventually failed (after I graduated) because of personal considerations.

14. See Knight, *Philosophy and Education*, 119–21. Work that reflects the futurist approach is Toffler, *Future Shock*.

15. See Knight, *Philosophy and Education*, 121–23. Work that reflects the behaviorist approach is Skinner, *Beyond Freedom and Dignity*.

highly developed one, but nevertheless subject to the same principles of animal behavior and conditioning; (2) evolution and conditioning influence how humans, like all animals, respond, and education, as a tool of behavioral engineering, can play a significant role in the conditioning process; (3) the teacher's role in a behaviorist educational environment is to provide an environment in which effective behavior modification can occur, through the use of positive reinforcement, rather than the kinds of negative stimuli that have been provided in other educational models; and (4) in light of its philosophical background, behaviorism emphasizes a certain type of efficiency, similar to that of any natural organism, with the result that there is an emphasis in behaviorist circles on accountability in education as the results are tested against an optimized standard of precision and objectivity.[16]

The results of behaviorism, especially in the emphasis upon quantifiable results (assessment, the bugaboo of recent educational theory), are still present, perhaps most insidiously in the view of humanity and its manipulation that it promotes.

Educational Anarchism and Its Relatives

The final educational philosophy I will describe is in some ways a category that subsumes a number of different movements and trends. I have, after Knight, called it educational anarchism,[17] but it also entails a variety of alternative educational philosophies that have directly rebelled against more formalized educational agendas, including movements as diverse as ones that embrace training of pastors within the environment of the local church rather than within the seminary and that embrace the postmodernist and post-structuralist epistemological critique.[18] What unifies them is their rejection of the validity and normativity of the development of formalized education, and their embracing of a de-formalization and disestablishment of educational institutions, including in extreme cases such notions as objectivity and truth.

Educational institutions themselves, according to anarchists, are seen to be the major source of the problem, because they promote values that are not to be equated with education itself or hold to questionable

16. Knight, *Philosophy and Education*, 123–26.
17. See ibid., 126–27. Work that reflects educational anarchism is Illich, *Deschooling Society*.
18. See Peters and Wain, "Postmodernism/Post-Structuralism."

notions of knowledge and their epistemological foundations. Those who argue against the institutions of education itself believe that the tendency to formalization—whether it is in terms of grades as indicators of learning, granting of diplomas as measures of achievement, repetition with learning, or subject mastery with creativity—has had a detrimental effect on education itself. What is purportedly needed is an individualized enterprise that allows students to create their own educational system of choice of how and what it is that they study, that is, a relativized educational experience depending on personal interests.

The post-modern and post-structuralist critique leads to a similar result but more specifically concerning the nature of knowledge itself. The post-structural and post-modern critique has been that both structuralism with its a-historical (synchronic) emphasis upon structures of knowledge and modernism with its claim to foundational knowledge have come to an effective end, so that education itself must realize that knowledge is socially and culturally conditioned and embedded and that the very notion of foundational truths is subject to question.

The implications for education are significant for establishing the basis of a curriculum, but more importantly for justifying the educational program itself. The ongoing discussion itself of post-modernism and post-structuralism has indicated, however, that, rather than rejecting modernism and structuralism and their constructs, these movements are in many ways continuing developments of the modernist and structuralist agenda, but with a more chastened assessment of their epistemological certainties.

Much more could be said about these—and other—movements within the philosophy of education. A number of factors are constants in the discussion of educational philosophy. These include: (1) the student, (2) the nature of the curriculum, (3) the nature of the educational task, and (4) the teacher. Even the behaviorists and educational anarchists, despite their widely divergent views, recognize the role of the teacher as one of significance in the educational task. Without minimizing the role and place of the other factors, clearly the one that emerges as the most important for all of the various educational philosophies is the role of the teacher. Therefore, I believe that it is pertinent to discuss the varied role of the teacher, as a major contributing factor in developing a mature and articulate philosophy of education.

THE ESSENTIAL ROLE OF THE TEACHER—
AND THE NEED FOR A TEACHING PHILOSOPHY

As Jaime Escalante (1930–2010) says in a video posted on YouTube, "every time you talk about school—teacher. The teacher is the critical point." Escalante ought to know. He is the real-life mathematics teacher who is depicted in the 1988 film, *Stand and Deliver*, of a high school math teacher who transforms a group of students that other teachers had given up on into a stellar group of calculus over-achievers. The movie is an account of what in fact was an even more stellar and enduring true story of Escalante's development of a mathematics program at Garfield High School in California over the course of over fifteen years, taking students with low levels of achievement through a thriving mathematics program that propelled them to the forefront of educational accomplishment—in large numbers. There are three concise points that Escalante emphasizes in his video that make clear the essential role of the teacher. The first is that "you have to like to teach." He emphasizes the hard work that he put into his teaching. The second is that "sometimes you win, sometimes you lose." Every teacher faces the prospect of sometimes spectacular success, but also sometimes colossal failure within the classroom. The third is "don't quit." The importance of the teacher is too great simply to give up. Escalante's career certainly reflected these principles, as he struggled against institutional and cultural constraints on the achievements of his students and his own efforts. Finally, he states: "Each of us remembers the great teacher, the one who touches our life, the one who gives us encouragement, who presses us to do the best." He concludes: "That's why many times I did say, and I am going to repeat, I am proud to be a teacher."

The role of the teacher is essential in any educational philosophy. However, the question still remains—what kind of teacher? There have been many types of teaching styles suggested and developed over the years. I briefly describe a number of those here, as an incentive to think of the role of the teacher in developing an educational philosophy.

Teacher as Authority Figure—"Address me as Your Excellency"

The teacher as authority figure is a long-standing tradition in Western education. The word for "lecture" in the tradition-bound German educational system is *Vorlesung*, which roughly translated means "read before." That is what traditional German teaching was based upon—the professor entering the lecture hall at precisely the right time to begin the class session, walking to the podium and opening his lecture book, and reading out the day's lecture, beginning exactly where he had left off the previous session. At the conclusion of the hour, the professor closed the book and turned and walked out of the room, to the enthusiastic knocking on their desks of the students—the knocking indicating their approval of the lecture by the great one who had deigned to disseminate such nuggets of truth to lowly mortals. There is no wonder that some have joked that the closest a human can get to being god on earth is to be a German university professor—who at one time controlled not only who studied but what they studied, especially for advanced degrees, where thesis topics were doled out by the professor according to his own research interests. Much has changed in the educational system, including the German educational system, since the 1970s to mitigate such an approach to education. Nevertheless, the model of teacher as authority figure has continued to remain an important one, especially in higher education.

There is no doubt still a place within most educational philosophies for the teacher as an authority figure, especially those philosophies that are classically oriented and knowledge-based, because they promote the teacher as the one who controls and regulates the learning process and the dissemination of knowledge. Most models of education are still knowledge driven, and so the role of the teacher as one with educational authority still plays a vital part. However, most educational models do not rely entirely or even predominantly on such a figure to control and regulate all of the educational mechanism. The danger of such a model is that it is too conservative, very controlling, and potentially stifling to advancing non-traditional knowledge, because all of the means of educational advancement rest in the hands of the authority figure.

Teacher as Font of Knowledge—"For my seventeenth point..."

Related to the role of the teacher as authority figure is that of teacher as font of knowledge, that is, the recognized figure who has comprehensive and inclusive knowledge of the subject. A friend of mine told me once that he studied with a well-known Nobel Prize winner during his university studies—except that he never saw the great scientist. The scientist never once came to the class, which was taught by a series of graduate students. But the Nobel winner had such power and prestige and his knowledge was so highly sought as to allow him to continue his research while others did the teaching—and my friend could "brag" about how he had studied with the great man he never saw. It is not only students or former students who respect teachers with knowledge. While I was in graduate school, I conferred once with one of my professors. During the course of our discussion, we came upon a question that we did not know the answer to. My professor said, "We'll ask professor so-and-so. If he doesn't know the answer, it is not worth knowing." Clearly, here was a professor who was seen to be the font of knowledge. It is usually not too hard for a teacher to convince a group of undergraduates that he or she has extensive knowledge of the subject, and it can even be done by teachers of graduate students—though I wouldn't want to count on this ability day in and day out. It is much harder to convince fellow teachers that one has overwhelming knowledge of a discipline. However, there are some who can do just that. One of the biggest items of discussion in debates over educational philosophy is not so much the importance of the teacher but the role that the teacher is to play. There has been a recent trend to minimize the teacher as authority figure and even to lessen the teacher as repository of knowledge, as a swing has been effected in education from teacher as source to teacher as facilitator. In the more recent models, teachers have been looked to as those who can prompt and inspire students to facilitate their own learning. The question, however, is the basis on which such prompting takes place. A worthwhile goal for a teacher is to encourage students to ask their own questions and thereby to make their learning their own, but there must be a basis for such probing to take place. This is where the knowledgeable teacher comes into play, as one who knows enough of the discipline, and thereby the key questions, to know the directions to prod the students and the types of questions that are worth asking.

Teacher as Technophile—"Uh oh, he's unplugged"

The third example I give, the teacher as technophile, may seem like a recent development with the advent of ever-more sophisticated and complex technological innovations. However, there have always been those teachers who avail themselves of the latest technological opportunities and devices. At one time it was the overhead projector, then it was the video player, and now it is the smart technology that allows for interactive communication with the Web, students near and students afar, as well as the teacher, all within the course of a single teaching session. A colleague recently produced a virtual journey using the satellite photographs available through Google Earth, so that those of us going on an educational trip could "see" where we were going to be traveling before we ever took off from the airport on one continent to travel to another. Such innovations have certainly increased the accessibility of education, providing an entirely new definition of what used to be called "distance" education by providing the means for the educational classroom to be extended to wherever there are suitable internet connections. More immediately, these technological advances have enabled teachers to provide much more variegated presentations and dissemination of material, by accessing sources that are better transmitted electronically than through photocopies or other means.

The teacher as technophile will probably increase in importance in the classroom of the future, especially as more and more institutions develop their in-house electronic resources, such as smart classrooms, and as more institutions venture out into the realm of electronically mediated learning by means of online courses, whether they are conducted in synchronous or a-synchronous formats. The question becomes the basis of such technophilia. The teacher who is devoted to technology no doubt needs to be one who has mastered the technological requirements. I anticipate that teachers of the next and subsequent generations—those who did not have to learn how to incorporate computers into their day to day academic and other pursuits, but who had them available from their earliest daily endeavors—will have much less challenge in finding and utilizing such technology. Nevertheless, there is the question of where their resources originate. Does the teacher who is a technophile develop such materials him- or herself, or is such a teacher dependent upon the resources developed by others? There is a place within the sphere of the technophile to appreciate that there is dependency upon others for generation of such resources, even if one is a deft hand at putting such material into electronically presented format.

Teacher as Entertainer—"Now for my next trick,
I'll pull an apothegm..."

The teacher as entertainer in some ways has come to encompass any number of different types of teaching styles. The fundamentally consistent characteristic of such teachers is that they are able to entertain students in the classroom, regardless of the subject matter. Some of these teachers continue to be entertaining with the simplest of props—such as just their own abilities and a chalk board—while others have adapted to the modern electronic environment and are able to utilize the latest technology for entertainment purposes. The teacher as entertainer has certainly grown in significance with the rise of assessment within higher education. It is standard procedure at most educational institutions to survey students at the end of every course, in order to evaluate the general satisfaction of students with the content of the course and the quality of the teacher, or even to post such ratings online (with ratings of whether the professor is "hot" or not, qualities vital to the educational experience). There were no doubt pressures to create a friendly educational environment before such assessment-tools became standard fare; however, the entertainment challenges have increased when the point of comparison is the kind of entertainment that is readily available on television, in the movies, and on video. The MTV generation, with its quick cuts, shortened attention span, and craving of the new and brazen, has contributed to an increased desire for the teacher as entertainer.

Educational philosophies have probably confused teacher substance with teacher entertainment type in many instances. Teachers who have been associated with substantive content and material have probably paid less attention to creative presentation than they should have, to the point where the content-based approach has in some instances fallen on hard times, not because of the material itself but because of the nature of its presentation. In that sense, there is a place for the teacher as entertainer, who can show that substantive material can be presented in new and challenging ways that meet educational objectives while retaining student interest. However, there is also the temptation to become an entertainer at the expense of substance and content—if for no other reason than it requires hard work on both ends to be both substantive in content and entertaining in presentation. The teacher as entertainer needs to ensure that the medium does not solely become the message (to use the language of Marshall McLuhan), but that the message has integrity in its own right as it is presented in new and relevant media.

Teacher as Best Bud—"Oh boy, another fieldtrip!"

When I was in elementary school, I had what I considered to be a great teacher. He was a man first of all, which struck all of us boys as something different from the usual female teachers. He was also a sports fanatic, which we considered something beyond our wildest dreams, as he liked us to get out and play football and baseball, because he too liked playing football and baseball. As it happened, he was also a very conscientious teacher, who never crossed the line of letting his enthusiasm for sports trump his better instincts as a teacher. (I know, because several of us once took an extra physical education period, thinking that he would approve—only to be confined to the class when the actual physical education period was taken.) This is a balance that not all teachers who seek to be popular with their students are able to negotiate. Of course, at the post-secondary educational level, we are not talking about sports and P.E. However, there are similar types of challenges that one confronts. There are many subjects that simply are not as appealing as others, and demand that the teacher address the learning environment in ways that will mitigate the pain associated with the subject. We all know that there are particular types of courses and subject matter that fall into this category, whether they are . . . well, they are better left unstated. There is also the simple human desire to be liked, including by one's students, with whom one forms a certain amount of rapport over the course of a term or more of study together. The solution for many is to relate to the students as a friend and confidante, as one who is a fellow traveler on the educational journey.

As I stated above, sometimes educational content and the way that it is presented has had a more detrimental effect than anything else on the view of the teacher within various educational models, so it is understandable that some teachers have decided that the best way to present themselves and to develop students' love for the subject is to come alongside them as their friends and supporters. This is entirely understandable, especially in contexts where rapport is essential to the nature of the discipline. The danger of such an approach is that it may compromise a necessary objectivity on the part of the teacher, so that it becomes increasingly difficult for the teacher to perform the necessary tasks of an educator when the student is too close a friend. Such tasks include grading, critiquing work, giving advice in various academic and non-academic areas, and general mentoring. The teacher as friend must also be the teacher who retains the proper boundaries so that the friendship as an edifying educational experience for the student, as well as the teacher, is maintained.

Teacher as Coach or Mentor—"It's all in the technique"

We live in an age when there are all sorts of coaches who are doing all sorts of coaching that is not traditional-sports related. We have personal trainers for our fitness and general athleticism. We have business coaches to help us in our work in the marketplace. We have spiritual counselors who help us to find the right spiritual space for our communing with God. We have a variety of people who act as our mentors. Why not have educational coaches as well? These teachers as coaches or mentors are those that view the educational task as one of facilitation and implementation. In other words, rather than seeing themselves as authority figures or communicators of knowledge, these teachers see themselves as those who come alongside to facilitate the teaching agenda with each student. In the same way that a coach might encourage his or her athletes to better performance, the teacher as coach creates the optimal teaching environment, finds the proper strategy with each class or even student, and determines the specific media to use to create the learning experience. The result is a team effort, with the teacher as the coach and the students as the individual players, who are mastering what is required for them to excel in their particular environment. There is the recognition of both the individual and the group dynamic to education—individual in that various students need particularized approaches to the subject matter, and collective as the students bond together to form a team that is mastering the particular subject.

The teacher as mentor has a long and useful history in the educational arena, as demonstrated in several of the philosophies of education discussed above. Those models that have moved away from the teacher as repository of knowledge have often shifted the emphasis to the teacher as some type of facilitator of knowledge-gaining. In other words, they have changed the model from the teacher as authority figure or keeper of knowledge to one of coach, who is responsible for developing the academic as opposed to athletic abilities of their students. Such teachers certainly have a place in modern education. However, one of the tensions with such a view of the teacher is the relationship between technique and substance. Education certainly involves the mastery of technique, including the technique for developing self-knowledge among students. But it requires more, such as the mastery of a body of knowledge that increases the ability of the student to apply the technique and manipulate the data so as to create new and developed knowledge.

Teacher as Cult Figure—"I love these graduate seminars!"

One of my former students once passed on a cartoon to me that I used to keep on my wall. A teacher was talking to a colleague, as the teacher entered his classroom. In the classroom there were a number of students kneeling down facing the teacher, bowing in homage to him. The one teacher turns to the other and says, "I love these graduate seminars!" There is no doubt that graduate teachers are knowledgeable and often powerful figures, who should and do command suitable respect from their students. There are no doubt others who trade on this ethos—and command what amounts to adulation and near veneration, to the point of almost being cult figures. Of course, a certain amount of respect is probably not a bad thing in and of itself, if it is handled and treated in the right way. Students probably learn better when they have respect for their teacher, who also has a certain amount of respect for him- or herself. Students can be motivated to do more work and perhaps take greater intellectual risks if they believe that they are part of a cause that is greater than simply another term paper in another graduate course on the way to another dissertation. There is the story told, however, of a teacher at a prestigious institution who was giving a paper at a conference. This same institution employed another teacher who had a larger than life profile. After the paper and during the question time, a person in the audience asked a question regarding the appearance of a particular phenomenon. The teacher answered, "Well professor larger-than-life says that that does not occur." That was the answer to the question and the resolution of the issue—the larger than life professor said that such does not occur and that ended the discussion. At that point, I think we must say that teacher as cult figure has passed from healthy and fruitful respect to inhibitory veneration.

The role of the teacher as cult figure must be closely watched, especially in our cultish or superstar hungry age. There is, I believe, an unhealthy climate within our wider society to create heroes, who are blown up to disproportionate heights. A friend told me the story of the first time he was giving a paper at a scholarly conference. He was a last minute substitute for another scholar who had to cancel for unavoidable reasons, and so my friend was unknown in the conference venue. He got to the room early for his paper, and was sitting in a place where he could hear the comments of other scholars as they entered the room. Several noted the replacement speaker, but didn't know who he was, but they did notice that a person they had heard of was giving a paper down the hall, and so they went to the other paper—even if it was on a completely different topic than the one they were anticipating being given in the room by the unknown scholar. Thus the educational world is itself not immune from such pressures of undue adulation. There is often a reason why a particular teacher commands respect and even adulation from others; however, that should never be a substitute for substance, and for others assessing the teacher honestly and objectively to recognize strengths and weaknesses.

Teacher as Environmentalist—"Manipulating the atmospheric lights"

By environmentalist, I do not mean a teacher who is concerned with whether the institution is "green" or who regularly recycles paper, but, paraphrasing the words of Nathaniel Hawthorne, one who is concerned to manipulate the educational lights. As the various educational philosophies above so clearly relate, the teacher has a significant role to play in creating the educational environment, whether that is an environment that is knowledge based or authority based or entertainment oriented or whatever. In any case, most of the philosophies—even those that reject the traditional classroom environment—recognize the crucial role that the teacher plays in creating and maintaining an environment in which the educational process can transpire, however that task is conceived. This means that the teacher as environmentalist must pay attention to a number of different and shifting educational and pedagogical variables, such as the role of knowledge within the classroom, the attitude of the teacher toward the subject matter and towards the students, the level and type of involvement and support that the teacher utilizes in relating to the students, the creation of the means by which educational achievement is implemented and gauged, and the sets of objectives and results that the teacher expects. These are all part of the educational environment or atmosphere that the teacher must observe, pay attention to, and control for successful educational achievement.

The teacher as environmentalist is probably the most complex pedagogical model of all of those that have been presented so far, because it requires the most from the teacher. The teacher in this model is at the center of the educational endeavor, with responsibility for all of the various factors that go into such a complex mix. The teacher, while not necessarily directly responsible for the dissemination of all information, is ultimately charged with the task of ensuring that such suitable information is available to students.[19] Similarly, the teacher is responsible for providing the right means by which learning is to take place, whether this involves traditional or technologically enhanced means. Finally, the teacher as environmen-

---

19. In some educational contexts, the teacher will be responsible for integrating their subject matter with the Christian perspective or worldview. See Downey and Porter, eds., *Christian Worldview*.

talist is tasked with providing the right supportive atmosphere that allows students to be able to avail themselves of the information and resources so as to fulfill the educational agenda. There is probably no single teacher who is able to handle all of these educational assignments equally well, so it requires that the teacher find the right combination of means to ensure that the educational philosophy is implemented by enhancing those areas of weakness while emphasizing those of strength.

Teacher as Colleague or Collaborator—"Let's work together on this"

The final approach I will mention is the teacher as colleague or collaborator. As might be expected (not only because of its placement last but because of my previous comments), this is the approach that I strongly favor for virtually any type of post-secondary educational environment (and even, conceivably, in some secondary ones as well). One could treat the roles of colleague and collaborator as separate approaches, but they have enough in common to be presented together. The collaborative model is already widely used in the natural sciences, where teachers and students have been gathering in laboratories to work on common problems for some time. The arts and humanities, however, have been very slow to use this cooperative approach. The sciences have long had a collaborative ethos, in which professors essentially treat their students as junior colleagues, while they remain as students. These junior colleagues are heavily involved in research projects and perform laboratory experiments under the direction of the senior colleague, the professor. Various studies, and my own efforts, have shown that students can be productively involved in research even at the undergraduate level, and certainly at the graduate level. At the most basic level, such collaborative involvement can serve to capture the interest of students in a particular area of study. Such collaborative work of course benefits students directly, not only helping to build a resume that may help them go on to further research or study, but also creating a more deeply developed excitement about and involvement in the area of study, to the point of making them better students than they would have been without collaborative research opportunities. The collaborative model, though it may well involve more direct effort of the professor, such as personal meetings and laboratory time, also directly benefits the professor in numerous ways. More than simply the production of more scholarly papers is involved in the collaborative model, as professors model their profession to their students and invite them into opportunities that would be otherwise very difficult to imagine.

The teacher as colleague or collaborator is perhaps the most potentially threatening to the teacher, especially one coming out of one of the traditional authority-as-knowledge based approaches to education—of which there are many that still endure. Such collaborative situations, however, need not be threatening, but can be seen as providing opportunities for teachers to form close and instructive professional relationships with their students. The interaction of students and teacher can lead to the kind of innovative and creative thinking that can result in new intellectual discoveries. These can be created not only because the students are new to a discipline (as Thomas Kuhn so wisely observes),[20] but because the dynamic intellectual atmosphere of several minds challenging and encouraging each other can spark new insights.

There is no single model of teaching, either throughout history, according to discipline or subject matter, or even within any given educational institution. There certainly is not one current model or one approach to teaching for the future. Every teacher must evaluate his or her own strengths, characteristics, propensities, and educational environment, and make judgments on the best approach or approaches within their operative educational philosophy. There are certain approaches that work better and worse within various educational philosophies, but, as we have seen from the discussion in this section and the previous one, there is the common factor that the teacher is a vital part of any educational philosophy. Thus serious consideration of the role of the teacher is a necessary requisite of a successful implementation of such a philosophy.

ADULT LEARNERS

In the above discussion, we have examined a number of different educational philosophies, and some of the various approaches to teaching that are and can be used within such philosophies. At this point, I wish to address the issue of teaching adult learners. The teacher within a postsecondary educational environment must incorporate from the outset a specific view of adult learners within his or her philosophy of education. This is necessary to do justice to some of the particular issues related to adult students that distinguish them from issues faced by younger learners. The issue of adult learners spans quite a wide range, from traditional younger adults who are recent graduates of high school and proceeding to undergraduate study at university or college, to slightly older adults who,

---

20. See Kuhn, *Structure of Scientific Revolutions*, 90 n. 15.

having graduated, are engaging in further study at seminary or graduate school, to older adults of a wide range of ages, who are re-entering education after being in some other career. These older adults might range from their young thirties to their sixties and beyond. The comments below cannot hope to address all of the issues regarding adult learners, but are designed to raise some pertinent questions that teachers must take into account in formulating their philosophy of education.[21]

Cultural and Social Shifts

One of the major factors to recognize in adult learning is the recent—and one dares to say, increasing—shifts within the culture and society. It has always been true that there have been cultural and social shifts that are more or less gladly welcomed by the populace, but in recent times it seems as if the pace of change has increased. This has consequences, especially for adult learners, who may have learned to negotiate life in a particular way, only to have the foundations of that approach shaken by significant changes. In his treatment of obstacles to adult learning, especially of Christians, John Hull offers seven consequences of modernism that he believes intrude in the educational process. They are: (1) bureaucracy, (2) technical rationality, (3) individualism, (4) futurity, (5) liberation, (6) plurality, and (7) knowledge.[22] In all of these areas, Hull notes, there are pressures that make adult learning difficult. Even though he particularly addresses those involved as Christians in Christian education, his observations are worth noting. Bureaucratization results in a regimentation to life that attempts to conform people to particular patterns, especially ones that separate them from childhood. Thus, adult learners, especially those returning to study after a period of time, are faced with uncertainty as they defy their imposed characterization. Technical rationality, which has come to dominate modern society, moves against the kind of theoretical and even numenal atmosphere one finds in an educational institution. Individualism is one of the most difficult and potentially pernicious factors, because it opposes the notion of an educational community (and especially a theological community), and accentuates educational competition, even in environments where

---

21. I have found Hull, *What Prevents*, very useful for my thinking in these areas.

22. Ibid., 3–39. Some may question whether the modernist paradigm is still pertinent, but the consequences he notes seem to be relevant whether one wishes to cast the assessment in terms of modernism or post-modernism.

collegiality should be emphasized. Futurity emphasizes the tension between the orientation of modern society and the nature of education as a retrospective and perhaps even conservative discipline, with its emphasis upon the accumulated knowledge of the past. Liberation is opposed by the reality, especially found in a theological context, that one cannot simply by will easily escape one's past. Plurality seems to indicate relativity, rather than a healthy recognition of variety. Finally, knowledge poses its own difficulties as it introduces new ideas and concepts that provide challenges to established ways of thinking. Thus, there are a number of challenges of the contemporary social and cultural context that pose potential difficulties for adult learners—especially those who have become more well-situated within the contemporary paradigm, and for whom exposure to the stimulating challenge of the educational atmosphere might cause stress on their established ways of thinking and acting.

Social Positioning

The next challenge is the social positioning of the adult learner. I don't think that it is too much to admit that every person has a social position. These social positions come into being because of various factors, such as family of origin, nationality, socio-economic status, and even education. Many of these factors are outside the control of a given individual, at least initially, but they are variable in many instances on the basis of introduction of any number of new factors, such as a change of job, or a relocation of place, or a change in situation brought about by education. In any case, by the time one reaches adulthood, this social positioning is fairly well established. In other words, a person usually understands their particular social position in relation to major markers within society, including position, place of abode, and the like. Education, however, presents a particular opportunity and challenge for the adult. On the one hand, education represents not an end but a means to effect a change in social position, but on the other hand, it also represents a change in social position as one transfers from parental dependence or the independence of the working world. The position of being a student represents a constructive step to change and even enhance one's social position, but one must do so by taking a backward step to return to the position of being a student. Student status is, when compared to that of most other social positions, seen to be a subordinate status, when one is not as fully responsible for one's own life, but called upon to fulfill the obligations of others. This period of transition represents a major issue for adult learners, especially those who re-enter the educational sphere after a number of years away. The difficulty, in this instance, is not so much the return to education, but what it represents regarding social positioning. This is even true of those who continue into post-secondary education directly from high school, rather than directly entering the work force. This change in social positioning, even if only temporary, can pose problems of self-perception, independence, identity, and even economics and social stability for the adult learner.

Need to be Right[23]

One of the major issues for adult learners is caused by the shift from their position as adults, with all of the attendant responsibilities and encumbrances (and these often involve such important factors as a spouse and family, parental obligations, extended family responsibilities, employment issues, and the like), to that of a student. Within the sphere of responsible adult life, people often develop firm sets of beliefs. These beliefs are almost like a dam against the flood of the changing external world. As a result, adult students, as they enter or re-enter post-secondary education, are often confronted with what Hull describes as cognitive dissonance between the need for certainty in the world in which they live and the uncertainty of higher education itself, with its inherent instability and the destabilizing force of the educational process. Hull notes three types of cognitive dissonance that adult learners seem most frequently to confront: (1) the first is dissonance that occurs within their own particular set of beliefs, as the students are exposed to a variety of ideas that reveal internal inconsistencies within their systems of belief; (2) the second is dissonance between their own system of belief and other systems of belief with which they come into contact and perhaps even close contact through the courses that they take or the people that they meet; and (3) the third is dissonance that occurs when their important and even fundamental beliefs are seen to be, or at least appear to them to be, underdeveloped, perhaps questionable, or even outright wrong.[24] When the need to be right in everyday life confronts the reality that other beliefs or even entire belief systems may be superior, the consequences can be traumatic for the adult learner.

---

23. This heading is taken from one of the chapter titles in ibid., 89–146.
24. Ibid., 97.

Pain of Learning, or Re-Learning[25]

As a result of all that has been said above, it is not surprising that for the adult learner there can be pain attached to learning or re-learning. All of the factors above contribute to this situation. The person may find that he or she is confronted with a variety of new social and cultural forces, that their social position is, if not threatened, at least adversely affected, and that their firm structures against the ebb and flow of life have been challenged. They are being challenged by the educational process itself, in which they are exposed to new ideas, different ways of examining life, and competing presuppositions and conclusions—any or all of which may have an inherent appeal because of their origins as part of the educational process. The results can be varied. Some adult learners may reject outright such challenges to their belief systems without actually examining them. Others may cautiously explore the new ideas and systems with an idea to constructively examining their own beliefs and ideally improving upon them. Still others may wholeheartedly and enthusiastically welcome and embrace many if not most new ideas that they encounter, without necessarily thinking through all of the internal and external consequences of adopting such beliefs. However, most adult learners find it somewhat difficult to be forced by the educational process to scrutinize their firmly held beliefs, and to engage in the learning of new ideas that pose a challenge to their positions. Part of the challenge of learning is that one must learn new ideas, which also implies that one must un-learn or re-learn certain ideas. This may be the most challenging part of the learning process, when one comes to the position of admitting that some beliefs that one held were perhaps not fully formed or only partially held or even outright wrong, and then replacing them by learning new ideas that mark an improvement on the old. There is not only the task of learning and replacing old with new ideas, but the consequences of such learning and re-learning. This may mean that one jeopardizes one's previous status by admitting to and even embracing new and challenging ideas, or at least one may be forced to explain these new developments in thought. In any case, this poses a challenge to adult learners, especially those who have had a longer course of life or life-experiences that have helped to establish firmly held beliefs and ideas.

These are some of the particular challenges of adult learning that must be taken into account in developing a philosophy of education. There are no doubt many more considerations that may be encountered in

25. See ibid., 89–146.

the process of working in such an educational environment. Nevertheless, these challenges lay out some of the opportunities for a teacher of adults.

CONCLUSION: TEACHING, NOT TRAINING

In conclusion, I wish to refer to an important article by the philosopher Gilbert Ryle. In this article, Ryle, a well-known philosopher though not a theorist or philosopher of education, addresses the situation of the differences between teaching and training. He notes that he has no particular "teaching tricks or pedagogic maxims to impart" to his audience.[26] Instead, he says, he wishes to try to sort out the difference between a number of different notions, in particular the difference between teaching and training. He notes that even when the most ordinary child is called upon to do something like learning to read, she or he does it by sounding out words and putting them together into meaningful sentences. This the child does by him- or herself, without the parent or teacher being able to do it for the child, so that the child ends up able to create and use language that is wholly created by him- or herself. In other words, rather than the child being trained, the child learns to read by teaching him- or herself. Thus the basis of the entire educational system—as opposed simply to the higher educational ranks—is based not upon training but upon one teaching oneself. Ryle extends this further by saying that the concept of one teaching oneself goes intimately together with the idea of one thinking for oneself.[27] This ability to teach oneself and think for oneself is what distinguishes education from merely training.

Ryle is right that the basis of the educational system is not particular "tricks" or even methods, as useful as these may be, but the notion of encouraging and developing a concept that is at the heart of human experience and the educational endeavor: teaching oneself and hence thinking for oneself. There are various opinions on how such a position is to be attained, as attested by the discussion above on the various philosophies of education. As one thinks through these various educational philosophies, one needs to decide which ones encourage and develop the concept of training and which ones mandate that one teach oneself and hence learn to think for oneself. The teacher, as we have seen, has a crucial position in such an educational matrix, and can choose to address this pedagogical situation through any number of different and non-competitive means. In

---

26. Ryle, "Teaching and Training," 105.
27. Ibid., 105–6.

the final analysis, the most important consideration is that one develop a suitable philosophy of education that allows both teacher and student to continue to learn, teach, and think in ways that advance knowledge and the dignity of the human educational enterprise.

BIBLIOGRAPHY

Bloom, Allan. *The Closing of the American Mind*. New York: Simon & Schuster, 1987.
Counts, George S. *Dare the School Build a New Social Order?* New York: Day, 1932.
Damon, William. *Greater Expectations: Overcoming the Culture of Indulgence in America's Homes and Schools*. New York: Simon & Schuster, 1996.
Dewey, John. *The School and Society*. Rev. ed. Chicago: University of Chicago Press, 1915.
Downey, Deane E. D., and Stanley E. Porter, eds. *Christian Worldview and the Academic Disciplines: Crossing the Academy*. McMaster Divinity College Press. Eugene, OR: Wipf & Stock, 2009.
Hirsch, E. D., Jr. *Cultural Literacy: What Every American Needs to Know*. New York: Houghton Mifflin, 1987.
Holt, John. *Freedom and Beyond*. New York: Dell, 1972.
Hull, John M. *What Prevents Christian Adults from Learning?* 2nd ed. Philadelphia: Trinity Press International, 1991.
Illich, Ivan. *Deschooling Society*. New York: Harper & Row, 1970.
Knight, George R. *Philosophy and Education: An Introduction in Christian Perspective*. 2nd ed. Berrien Springs, MI: Andrews University Press, 1989.
Kuhn, Thomas. *The Structure of Scientific Revolutions*. 2nd ed. Chicago: University of Chicago Press, 1970.
Peters, Michael, and Kenneth Wain. "Postmodernism/Post-structuralism." In *The Blackwell Guide to the Philosophy of Education*, edited by Nigel Blake, Paul Smeyers, Richard Smith, and Paul Standish, 57–72. Oxford: Blackwell, 2003.
Porter, Stanley E., and Andrew W. Pitts. "Paul's Bible, His Education and His Access to the Scriptures of Israel." *Journal of Greco-Roman Christianity and Judaism* 5 (2008) 9–41.
Reed, James E., and Ronnie Prevost. *A History of Christian Education*. Nashville: Broadman & Holman, 1993.
Ryle, Gilbert. "Teaching and Training." In *The Concept of Education*, edited by R. S. Peters, 105–19. London: Routledge & Kegan Paul, 1967.
Skinner, B. F. *Beyond Freedom and Dignity*. New York: Vintage, 1971.
Toffler, Alvin. *Future Shock*. New York: Random House, 1970.

2

Pedagogy and Course Objectives

Michael P. Knowles

Perhaps the most difficult of many transitions required of a recently-graduated, newly-hired seminary professor involves plotting an unfamiliar and sometimes lengthy route from the lonely life of doctoral research and scholarship toward the richly-variegated and potentially chaotic world of classroom instruction. It takes time for new teachers to descend from the rarified altitudes of specialist research to the more oxygenated climate of general theological education: the newest faculty appointee typically has a difficult time appreciating why students who are preparing for congregational ministry should not be more enamored of fourteenth-century French mysticism or the latest developments in discourse analysis. First time instructors are notorious for grading according to standards that are well beyond the reach of their students. The expectations that each has of the other, and even their respective understandings of the nature and purpose of theological education, are sometimes worlds apart.

Much earlier in my own career, I worked with a church growth consultant who helped congregations in their own process of transition from introspection and stagnation to growth and a more outward-oriented focus. He proposed that the process of change invariably began with two basic questions: first, "Why are we doing *what* we are doing?" and second, "Why are we doing it the *way* we are doing it?" In his own search for answers to those questions, David Kelsey of Yale University Divinity

School published a study in 1993 called *Between Athens and Berlin: The Theological Education Debate*. The book was intended primarily as a summary of then-current debate over the question, "What's *theological* about theological education?" Kelsey observed a fundamental divide between two models of theological education, which he labeled "Athens" and "Berlin," respectively. "Athens," he wrote, serves as shorthand "for a type of schooling for which paideia is the heart of education. In Greek *paideia* meant a process of 'culturing' the soul, schooling as 'character formation.'"[1] The goal of paideia is the development of the whole human identity, something that comes about in response to the learner's encounter with ultimate Goodness. Accordingly, paideia in Christian usage refers to the nurture of the whole person in the image and knowledge of God, under the influence and direction of the Holy Spirit: "If Christianity is seen as a paideia, as it has been in its most ancient traditions, then [Christian theological education] is simply a theological education whose goal is knowledge of God and, correlatively, forming persons' souls to be holy."[2] By contrast, "Berlin" (so named after the faculty of theology included in the University of Berlin at its founding in 1810) represents a model of theological education that consists of "orderly, disciplined critical research on the one hand, and 'professional' education for ministry on the other."[3] The essential skill that this form of theological education develops is a capacity for critical inquiry, without deference to prior truth claims. Corresponding to the study of "philosophical theology" and "historical theology" that this approach implies is the study of "practical theology," that set of practical skills whose purpose is to serve the well-being of society as a whole. Whereas, in theological education, the "Athens" model begins with divine revelation, and aims at a deep, inner transformation of the student in terms of self-knowledge and knowledge of God, "According to the 'Berlin' model, theological education is a movement from data to theory to application of theory to practice."[4]

Each of these models has important implications for the kind of faculty and educators—as well as students—they require. According to the "Athens" model,

---

1. Kelsey, *Between Athens and Berlin*, 6 (italicization conventions here and throughout are original).
2. Ibid., 11.
3. Ibid., 12.
4. Ibid., 22.

Teachers themselves are also seeking personally to appropriate wisdom about God and about themselves in relation to God. At most, the teacher "teaches" only indirectly by providing a context in which the learner may come to that combined self-knowledge and God-knowledge that *is* a "personal appropriation" of revealed wisdom. Central to this context are those texts and practices, such as Scripture and the practice of the Christian life, whose study is believed to lead to understanding God.[5]

On the "Berlin" model, by contrast, "The teacher does not exist *for* the student, as is the case in paideia. Instead, the teacher is basically a researcher who needs the student to help achieve the goal of research in a cooperative enterprise."[6]

The importance of this distinction for newly-minted theological educators lies in the fact that the aims, goals, and methods of doctoral research are those of Berlin, whereas those of most (if not all) seminaries and theological colleges in which most graduates will teach their first courses are those of Athens. After all, congregations do not need gifted research assistants: they require pastors. Thus, whereas doctoral programs are primarily intended to form scholars, seminary students seek to be formed primarily as disciples, spiritual mentors, pastoral care-givers, missionaries, church planters, and congregational leaders. The key aptitudes required for successful completion of a research-based dissertation—clarity of focus, rigor of method, careful reasoning, independent initiative, and innovative expression—are not the skills that make for a good pastor, counselor, or team leader. Above all, there is nothing especially godly or godlike in the ability to write a thesis, and neither logical precision nor rhetorical virtuosity will transform one's students, or their respective congregations, into the image of Christ. To some extent, indeed, the *more* successful one is at doctoral research and writing, the *less* successful one is liable to be in shaping the congregational leaders of tomorrow. So, for example, most doctoral students survive by learning to work in relative isolation over long periods of time, all the while reluctant to divulge details of their research for fear of having it misappropriated by others.[7] Accordingly, it never occurs to

---

5. Ibid., 20.

6. Ibid., 23.

7. There is, however, a famous exception to this rule, remarkable precisely by virtue of its rarity (at least in the field of theology): beginning in the late 1940's, Frank Moore Cross and David Noel Freedman collaborated to produce not one but two doctoral dissertations in Semitic Languages and Literature at Johns Hopkins University in Baltimore.

them when they take up classroom responsibilities that providing opportunity for dialogue, shared problem-solving, and group projects will demonstrate the challenges and benefits of collaborative learning—a mode of education uniquely suited to congregational ministry.

DEVELOPING COURSE OBJECTIVES

New faculty typically craft their first courses in one of two ways: either the institution assigns a pre-existing (usually introductory) course on a particular topic, or the instructor builds a course outline on the basis of research conducted for comprehensives and/or the dissertation. In the first case, course goals may already be in place. In the case of the latter, whatever goals or interests impelled the course of research are likely to carry over into the classroom—whether or not they fit the needs of the learners. In either situation, a review of intended outcomes is called for. What difference will this course make in the lives of the students? What will have changed between week one and week thirteen or twenty-six of the course? Why *these* changes in particular? Above all, how will the course seek to achieve the envisaged results?

One helpful way of organizing educational outcomes at both the course and program levels centers around a threefold focus on "Knowing," "Being," and "Doing," elements which together constitute the foundation of the Athens model. From this perspective, course design addresses three significant areas of envisaged change:

a. *Cognitive* parameters: the conceptual dimensions of a coherent Christian worldview, together with the more specific features of particular areas of understanding.

b. *Formative* characteristics: character formation; self-understanding; spiritual formation; sense of self and spiritual identity as a Christian disciple or minister.

c. *Practical/Operational* skills: facility in ministerial practices or competencies, as appropriate to a specific field of application.

Accordingly, planning educational outcomes for a specific course involves the instructor asking how as a result of their classroom participation, independent research, and completion of course assignments, students will think and understand differently; act differently; perceive differently; understand themselves, their past and their future differently; undertake ministry and engage their world differently. Especially when one's students are preparing for congregational leadership, emphasizing the multi-dimensional nature of education acknowledges that simply imparting facts or methodologies will not form leaders whom people will want to follow.

Of course, similar considerations obtain for the instructor, who comes to the task of teaching with his or her own goals and interests. Identifying one's own expectations and reasons for having embarked on a teaching career is an important first step, not only in seeking to fulfill them, but also in distinguishing personal goals from those that serve the interests of one's students. A useful exercise for a teacher is to write down two lists entitled "Three goals for myself in every course I teach," and "Three goals for my students in every course I teach."

For students and faculty in institutions accredited by the Association of Theological Schools in the United States and Canada, standards for the Master of Divinity program specify four areas of pedagogical engagement:[8]

a. *Religious Heritage*: Scripture; church and denominational history; biblical, historical, doctrinal, and pastoral theologies, and their integration within a Christian worldview;

b. *Cultural Context*: the social structures and diverse cultural settings within which local, national, multi- or international ministry is conducted;

c. *Personal and Spiritual Formation*: the nurture and development of "personal faith, emotional maturity, moral integrity, and public witness" as aspects of personal identity in relation to the roles of pastor, teacher, or congregational leader.

d. *Capacity for Ministerial and Public Leadership*: instruction and practice of leadership principles appropriate both to congregational development and to the exercise of Christian ministry outside a church context.[9]

In keeping with these standards, the "Knowing, Being, Doing" paradigm can be expanded to include goals in each of the four areas, as represented by the following "Curricular Grid for Theological Education."

---

8. See *Association of Theological Schools Bulletin* 49 (2010), 110–11; online at http://www.ats.edu/Accrediting/Documents/2010DegreeProgramStandards.pdf.

9. Foster, Dahill, Golemon, and Tolentino (*Educating Clergy*, xi–xii and *passim*) formulate similar categories for theological education: pedagogies of interpretation ("the disciplined analysis of sacred texts"), formation ("the formation of . . . pastoral identities, dispositions, and values"), contextualization (understanding "the complex social, political, persona, and congregational conditions that surround [clergy]"), and performance ("the skills of preacher, counselor, liturgist, and leader").

	Knowing (Cognitive Concepts)	Being (Normative Identity)	Doing (Practical Skills)
Religious Heritage			
Cultural Context			
Personal and Spiritual Formation			
Ministerial and Public Leadership			

Curricular Grid for Theological Education

Program goals vary somewhat for other ATS-accredited degrees, and the "Curricular Grid" can be adapted accordingly. Even if they are not all stated explicitly on a course outline, each of these areas needs to be taken into consideration at the planning stage. Not only does clarifying educational goals help the instructor to select appropriate instructional material and methods of evaluation, it provides a standard by which instructors and students alike can assess the effectiveness of the course, with a view to future improvement.

For any given course, seeking to identify goals in all twelve sections of the "Curricular Grid for Theological Education" will immediately clarify the strengths and weaknesses of the proposed plan.

TEACHING AND LEARNING: CONNECTING OBJECTIVES WITH INSTRUCTION AND ASSESSMENT

Once the instructor has decided what a particular course intends to accomplish (and why), a more difficult question quickly follows: how will the various elements of the course actually achieve these goals in the lives of students? The answer has to do with the way different people learn, and the fact that different people learn in quite different ways. For instance, a few hours reviewing research on almost any topic will demonstrate the truth of the popular distinction between "lumpers" and "splitters," captured in the witticism attributed to American actor and humorist Robert Benchley (1889–1945): "There are two kinds of people in the world, those who believe there are two kinds of people in the world and those who don't." The one approach to research identifies similarities or infers connections between apparently disparate pieces of evidence, while the opposite tendency is to subdivide coherent sets into smaller sub-divisions by making ever finer distinctions than those previously envisaged. The latter is an atomistic or analytic concern, an attempt to delineate details with increasing subtlety and precision; the former is a synthetic, holistic, or systematizing concern that relates part to whole, and whole to greater whole, searching for the "big picture" on a larger and larger scale. The challenge for a course instructor consists of being able to accommodate both perspectives—and many others—in classroom pedagogy.

Some students process information inductively, analyzing evidence so as to formulate an explanatory theory; others argue deductively, analyzing evidence from the perspective of a prior theory or interpretive framework; still others proceed by abduction, reasoning "backwards" from effects to antecedent causes. Learning style theorists have proposed (and critiqued!) any number of more complex schemes to account for the different ways in which we process information: among the more enduring and popular have been the Kolb *Learning Style Inventory* (LSI) and the Myers-Briggs Type Indicator (MBTI). This is not the place to explore these models or the distinctions between them: here it is sufficient to observe that any first-time teacher will be wise to recognize that only a small proportion of their students is likely to share his or her own preferences with regard to information processing and learning style.

Another way of categorizing differences in learning style functions by analogy to the human body, distinguishing between styles of information processing via ears, eyes, and hands respectively:

Ears	Oral/aural learners	"tell me" (word wealthy)
Eyes	Visual/spatial learners	"show me" (image rich)
Hands	Tactile learners	"let me try" (nuts and bolts)

So, for example, students in the first group might prefer to start an essay by composing a detailed, logical outline; the second group might prefer not to write an essay at all, although a series of diagrams with connecting loops and arrows will help them get going; members of the third group are more like to jump in at the deep end, revising as they go, all the while wondering what difference another essay will make and wishing they could get started on "real" ministry. At least in the humanities (including theology), doctoral students frequently belong in the first of these categories, and assign course work that conforms to their own style of learning. They may not even realize that a majority of the students arrayed before them would likely prefer to process the course material in some entirely different manner. Yet incorporating all three approaches creates a much richer, multi-dimensional learning experience for all concerned. It is entirely possible (for some students, even preferable) to learn about biblical archaeology by reading all six volumes of *Excavations at Jericho* by Kathleen Kenyon, its first excavator.[10] But other students would be more inspired by reading a biography of this pioneering archaeologist, building a scale model of Tell es-Sultan (the mound built up by the ancient city and its inhabitants), or exchanging emails with (perhaps even volunteering to work for) an archaeologist currently at work in the Jordan Valley. If nothing else, an instructor reading lecture notes for two hours without benefit of PowerPoint, video clips, class discussion, or opportunity to respond will win few converts among students from an independent-minded and media literate generation.

Scholars trained in the classic mold sometimes object that it is not their job to "entertain" students. But rather than dismissing multi-dimensional pedagogy out of hand, it seems wiser to acknowledge that genuine differences—from simple to profound—distinguish styles and modes of information processing. Consider, as an experiment, the ways in which different people prepare for a trip. When they consider going on a trip, different travelers might

a. Read a book about their destination
b. Check out internet reviews
c. Talk to friends who have already visited
d. Look it up on a map
e. Buy the ticket and arrange accommodation once they arrive
f. Contact consular authorities to request government-approved tourism information
g. Think more about who their companions will be than where they will be going
h. Leave the planning to someone else

---

10. *Excavations at Jericho* has five volumes, but volume 5 is in two parts, so there are six books in the set.

Similarly, when they bring home a new computer, different users would prefer to

a. Read the operating manual from cover to cover
b. Disassemble the hardware to see how it all fits together
c. Boot it up and play with the operating system until they get things figured out
d. Apply principles learned from previous computer experience
e. Invite a friend to show them how it works (while catching up with recent news)
f. Leave it in the box until they're in a better mood!

Given that instructors also have their own learning styles, and craft teaching modules or course assignments that correspond to these preferences, it is important that they accommodate a comprehensive range of different approaches. This is especially important if one's students are from a variety of ethnic backgrounds, because different cultures frequently value different ways of teaching and learning. In my own case, I almost never assign written examinations, not only because I am not very good at them (and forever absolved myself of writing exams once I had completed my doctoral comprehensives), but also for the much better pedagogical reason that (even in the case of language learning) most examinations are simply exercises in short-term memory. Yet compelling as such reasons seem to me, this tends to disadvantage students whose pedagogy has been shaped by cultures that value tradition, and honor those who repeat the wisdom of respected elders and ancestors.

Broadly speaking, the subject of theology seems especially suited to holistic learning, for the simple reason that it involves the whole of human identity in relation to the reality of God. Even so, many of those who set the tone of contemporary scholarship maintain the modernist illusion that research and teaching can be carried out in a manner independent of personal convictions or engagements. When a biblical scholar such as Walter Moberly or Ulrich Luz proposes that prayer and meditation—being drawn directly into the world of which the text speaks—is essential for true understanding, it seems like a radical proposal.[11] Similarly, assigning a prayer journal as a course requirement might be greeted with scepticism, if not suspicion, in more than a few

---

11. See Moberly, "How May We Speak of God," 201–2; Luz, *Matthew in History*, 32.

North American seminaries. Yet notwithstanding such risks, theology requires a full panoply of instructional approaches if it is to foster the kind of formation and transformation of human persons that is envisaged by the "Athens" school.

By the same token, methods of assessment—which are essentially exercises in pedagogical appropriation—need to be equally broad. Students themselves have strong preferences about the best way to earn a good grade. Given their choice, they might select one or more (but certainly not all) of the following, confident that this was a task at which they could excel:

a. Reviewing a book
b. Interviewing practitioners
c. Leading a study group
d. Offering a class presentation
e. Composing a liturgy
f. Convening a panel discussion
g. Writing an essay or examination
h. Coordinating a field trip
i. Forming a ministry team
j. Constructing a working model

The traditional standards of an essay, a book review, and a final examination are really only appropriate to a narrow range of subjects and a limited number of adult learners. By contrast, a course in Christology, for example, could encourage the study of paintings, sculpture, woodcarvings, or iconography from representative historical periods. A Psalms course might invite students to compose similarly-themed poems of their own, or to compose a musical setting for a canonical psalm as part of a multi-media class presentation. Students in an ethics course could be required to volunteer a certain number of hours at an urban shelter or rescue mission. And a class on the history of preaching could include the option of performing a sermon—in costume!—from an earlier era. Simplest of all would be to coordinate course requirements with student field education responsibilities. The possibilities for creative engagement are almost limitless. This is not to disparage traditional methods of instruction and evaluation, so much as to suggest that creativity is called for because congregational ministry will largely imitate the classroom experiences (whether good or bad, dull or imaginative, inspired or mundane) that have shaped its leaders. Nor is it to suggest variety for its own sake: the point is for teaching methods and course assignments alike to be coordinated with intended pedagogical outcomes.

Pursued in the school of "Athens," seminary education poses much the same questions as does congregational ministry itself: what does true godliness or Christ-likeness consist of? What does spiritual leadership consist of, and how does transformation take place? In what way does each component of a pedagogical process contribute to change? What role does each participant play? Following Paul's explanation of spiritual pedagogy in 2 Cor 3:18 and 4:5–6, it helps to think of theological education as an exercise in gradual illumination, whereby the light that the instructor seeks to cast on a particular aspect of theological reflection is refracted into a range of different presentation styles, then mirrored in a variety of different learning exercises in such a way as to reflect "enlightenment" and transformation in the lives of all involved. Theological education entails a series of exercises—of cognition, volition, and practice—by which we learn to approximate and appropriate Christ's re-creation of us, one step at a time. Indeed (again following Paul's explanation), a scripturally grounded vision of theological education proceeds on the assumption that holistic learning is a matter not simply of human initiative or endeavor, but also of cooperation with and participation in the work of God's Spirit. In this sense, then, seminary professors do well to understand the properly theological aspects of their task as much as its pedagogical dimensions.

PREACHING: A PEDAGOGICAL ILLUSTRATION

By way of illustration, the following example considers strategies for teaching an introductory preaching class. To begin with, this view of preaching builds on an action/reflection or "reflective practice" model of theological education. This model, often employed to discern the theological dimensions and dynamics at play in a pastoral encounter, envisages a process whereby successive stages (consisting of informed reflection on a particular experience; critical analysis in light of a prior conceptual framework; new interpretation or insight; followed by correction, coordination, and integration vis-à-vis previous understanding; all leading to further action and engagement) together constitute an ongoing cycle of holistic, integrative learning.[12]

---

12. The action/reflection model is based on the pioneering work of Donald Schön in *Educating the Reflective Practitioner*. For various models of application within

Accordingly, the action/reflection model provides a framework for understanding preaching itself. Christian preaching at its best will acknowledge, engage, and address a full range of learning styles: it will reflect on experience, correlate new spiritual insight within a Christian worldview, and offer a way forward in discipleship and ministry. Because Christian pilgrimage itself involves experience and exploration, intellect and imagination, intuition and application, so good preaching will offer listeners multiple access points and a range of opportunities for response. Although no one sermon can hope to inspire each and every hearer, preachers do well to "complete the circle" each time they speak, suggesting ways for their audience to move from reflection to analysis to integration, action, and further reflection on experience. Perhaps it is more realistic to acknowledge that different circumstances and needs call for different styles of preaching, which correspond in turn to the respective emphasis of these different approaches to learning: situational preaching responds to a particular moment or occasion in the lives of the hearers; an exegetical sermon emphasizes analytic reflection on sacred texts and their testimony to God; evangelistic or paranetic preaching urges its hearers to respond with specific forms of concrete action. And so on, for each of the different rhetorical approaches at the preacher's disposal.

Viewed in this manner, the various elements and approaches to preaching outlined above correspond to different components of the church's larger theological project. Scripture, after all, testifies authoritatively to the human experience of God; church history offers a cumulative record of how God's people, informed by Scripture, have encountered and responded to God in turn; the integration of exegesis and experience is reflected systematically in the formation of theological creeds and a Christian worldview; and the theological interpretation of human experience gives rise, ideally, to ethical action and social justice initiatives. The church's mission and engagement with the rest of humanity thereupon becomes the object of further reflection and an occasion for yet deeper theological insight.

Depicted in linear terms, these correspondences line up more or less as follows. Admittedly, the parallels are far from exact in each case, yet they

---

theological education, see, e.g., "'Theology-in-Action': Praxis," in Graham, Walton, and Ward, *Theological Reflection: Methods*, 170–99; Kinast, *What Are They Saying about Theological Reflection?*; Patton, "Action and Interpretation," in *From Ministry to Theology*, 79–110; Payne, "Field Education and Theological Reflection"; Whitehead and Whitehead, *Method in Ministry*.

are nonetheless sufficient to suggest, at each level, an integrated vision of Christian pedagogy that applies not only to the activity of preaching, but also, as we will see, to the manner in which preaching itself may be taught:

Conceptual Category	Learning Preference	Theological Discipline	Preaching Style
Experience →	Participating →	History →	Situational
Reflection →	Analyzing →	Biblical Exegesis →	Expository
Insight →	Systematizing →	Theology →	Doctrinal
Integration →	Applying →	Ethics →	Paranetic
Action →	Engaging →	Mission →	Evangelistic

Alternatively, given that these are components of a learning *cycle*, it would perhaps be more appropriate to depict the various elements of these related processes as a series of concentric circles, in simplified form as follows:

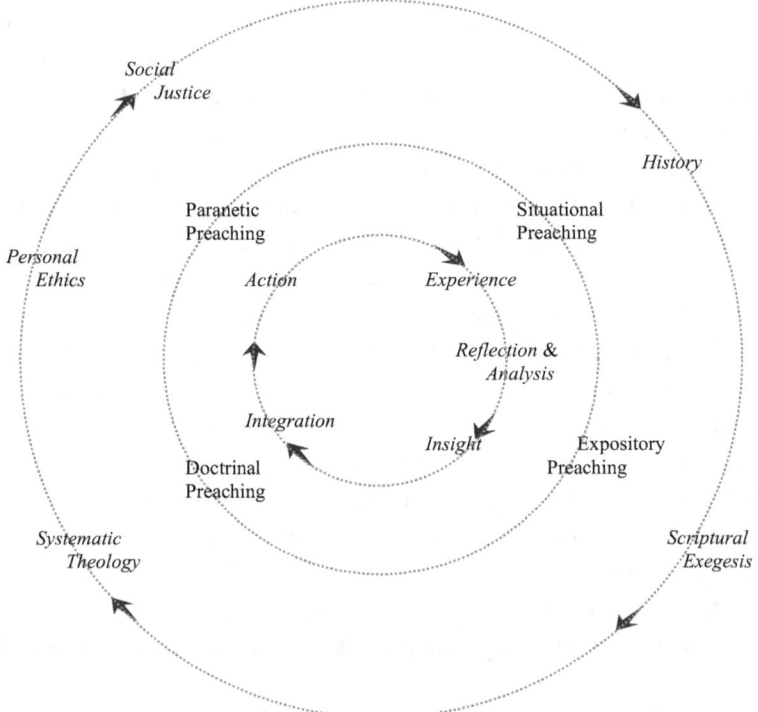

Again, these illustrations are not meant to be exhaustive: their purpose is simply to indicate the way in which a holistic approach to Christian preaching is able to engage, on the one hand, a full range of learning styles and, on the other, all the various dimensions of the church's theological enterprise and the resources these provide.

This holistic orientation underlies the formulation of pedagogical goals for an introductory preaching course, with the latter organized more specifically around the categories of "Knowing," "Being," and "Doing" (see above). Corresponding to cognitive or conceptual objectives might be lectures and assigned readings that describe the components and purpose of preaching. Written assignments in this area could include an analysis of published sermons that exemplify different styles or approaches to preaching, or an exercise that requires students to reflect on their own preferred strategies for biblical exegesis and sermon composition. Both of the latter assignments have the added benefit of helping to clarify the student's own preaching style, which is an important dimension of Formative/Affective learning. No less importantly, giving all course participants responsibility for evaluating one another's sermons forms the class into a learning community, providing an exercise in mutual accountability and shared pedagogy. More concretely, it formalizes the fact—even to the point of forcing recognition—that preachers are assessed and "graded" by their hearers every time they enter the pulpit. And (because of the range of learning styles present in any group of adults), making students answerable to one another actualizes the importance of addressing all dimensions of the action/reflection model. In a praxis-oriented subject such as preaching, operational skills can be taught and evaluated in relatively straightforward fashion, by having students speak both formally and informally, whether extemporaneously or with prior preparation, before an audience of peers. Finally, the various components and dimensions of the entire learning process are all subject to ongoing revision, insofar as student participants complete anonymous course evaluations at the end of the semester.

Here is how the course objectives for a preaching course might appear:

> *Cognitive/Conceptual:* (knowing)
>
> - To introduce basic hermeneutical issues that apply to the process of moving from biblical and social exegesis to proclamation.
> - To examine and evaluate the component elements of preaching and their respective contributions to effective communication.
> - To explore appropriate methods and content for preaching, and their impact on style and presentation.
>
> *Formative/Affective:* (being)
>
> - To provide students the opportunity for reflection on spiritual and ministerial identity in relation to Christian proclamation.
> - To help students identify their preferred style or styles of preaching, and gain confidence in public presentation.
>
> *Practical/Operational:* (doing)
>
> - To examine representative models of preaching, both contemporary and historical, in relation to students' own ministries of preaching.
> - To provide students with practice in the composition and delivery of sermons, together with opportunities for comprehensive peer evaluation.

To summarize, the foregoing description links pedagogy, course goals, teaching strategies, and methods of assessment by integrating them within a vision of holistic learning based on the action/reflection model of theological education.[13] It proposes that instruction and evaluation alike involve processes that are variously cognitive, verbal, operational, and communal, and that much the same conditions apply in the congregation as in the classroom. Just as seminary education aims at a holistic transformation of ministerial or congregational leaders, so Christian

---

13. The worksheet for planning course objectives at the conclusion of the article offers a template for applying a similar analysis to other theological education courses.

preaching seeks to form "disciples"—followers of Christ and learners in the broadest sense of the word.

REMEMBERING GRACE

Beyond questions of pedagogy, however complex, lies a final dimension of greater import. The fact that *theological* education is in view implies that God is also deeply involved in the process of teaching, learning, and transformation. It follows, then, that the human participants—teachers and students alike—are accountable for their involvement not only to one another, but also to God. The implications of this assertion are no less profound, if possibly unexpected. For at the heart of properly Christian pedagogy lies an acknowledgment that, in Jesus of Nazareth, God does not simply require humanity to respond in some particular manner, but actually enables transformation to take place. In this sense, then, pedagogy and course objectives are not simply linked together as complementary aspects of a human endeavor, but are both shaped in turn by the operational character of grace. Theological education that seeks to nurture the whole human person in the image and knowledge of God ultimately relies on the God of whom it speaks in order to achieve this goal. Stated simply, theological education in all its dimensions seeks the transformation of teachers and learners alike, acknowledges its own limitations in this regard, and remains open to the reality of grace.

COURSE OBJECTIVE WORKSHEET

Course: _____

Semester/Year: _____

Instructor: _____

	Pedagogical Goals:	Instructional Strategies:	Evaluative Instruments:
Knowing *Cognitive*			
Being *Formative*			
Doing *Operational*			

Religious Heritage; Cultural Context; Personal/spiritual Formation; Ministerial/Public Leadership

BIBLIOGRAPHY

Association of Theological Schools Bulletin 49 (2010).

Foster, Charles R., Lisa E. Dahill, Lawrence A. Golemon, and Barbara Wang Tolentino. *Educating Clergy: Teaching Practices and Pastoral Imagination*. Stanford: Carnegie Foundation for the Advancement of Teaching; San Francisco: Jossey-Bass, 2006.

Graham, Elaine, Heather Walton, and Frances Ward. *Theological Reflection: Methods*. London: SCM, 2005.

Kelsey, David H. *Between Athens and Berlin: The Theological Education Debate*. Grand Rapids: Eerdmans, 1993.

Kenyon, Kathleen M., et al. *Excavations at Jericho*. 5 vols. London: British School of Archaeology in Jerusalem, 1960–1983.

Kinast, Robert L. *What Are They Saying about Theological Reflection?* WATSA. New York: Paulist, 2000.

Luz, Ulrich. *Matthew in History: Interpretation, Influence, and Effects*. Minneapolis: Augsburg Fortress, 1994.

Moberly, R. W. L. "How May We Speak of God? A Reconsideration of the Nature of Biblical Theology." *Tyndale Bulletin* 53.2 (2002) 177–202.

Patton, John. *From Ministry to Theology: Pastoral Action Reflection*. Nashville: Abingdon, 1990.

Payne, Don. "Field Education and Theological Reflection in an Evangelical Tradition." In *Preparing for Ministry: A Practical Guide to Theological Field Education*, edited by George M. Hillman, 55–71. Grand Rapids: Kregel, 2008.

Schön, Donald A. *Educating the Reflective Practitioner: Toward a New Design for Teaching and Learning in the Professions*. San Francisco: Jossey-Bass, 1987.

Whitehead, James D., and Evelyn Eaton Whitehead. *Method in Ministry: Theological Reflection and Christian Ministry*. Rev. ed. Kansas City: Sheed & Ward, 1995.

3

Designing and Evaluating Learning Experiences for Courses

Mark J. Boda

One of the advantages that I had as a young professor was that I was married to someone who had just completed a research masters degree in education at a major university. Although I had adequate skills in communication from having served in two pastorates and had grown up in the home of an educator, I had little expertise in creating courses within an academic environment. My wife helped me to reflect more deeply on the learning experiences that I would be creating for my students, not only in the classroom environment, but also in the assignments they would complete outside classroom time. I began to think outside the dominant model that I had experienced and began to reflect on the variety of means that would prompt discovery in an accountable environment.

The dynamic of a course is that it provides an environment for intentional and measurable learning. Humans are always in the process of learning, but a course is one means through which students can attain particular competencies (whether cognitive, affective, or pragmatic). If a course is an environment for intentional and measurable learning, then it is important for professors to reflect on their specific intentions for their students' learning experiences and connect those intentions to specific measures that will assist students to attain those intentions. Many professors in the rush of the first years of teaching rely on the forms of courses that they took in their own formative years of education. They do not take the time for deep reflection on the original intentions of those courses let alone the original contexts in which they were experienced, which may not match the context in which the professor now sets out to create courses. Even this assumes that those formative courses were shaped in intentional ways, rather than relying themselves on earlier pedagogical traditions. It is important then for professors to take the time to reflect on their learning intentions for any given course in light of the context in which the course is experienced and connect these intentions to measurable outcomes that are relevant to the present context of learning.

This essay focuses on the learning experiences that professors design for their students in any given course. Based on my own experience of teaching in the academy for the past two decades, I want to present three elements that I think are key to excellent learning experiences for students: the learning styles of the students, the life experiences of the students, and the learning outcomes of the course. Following this, I will look at strategies for evaluating learning experiences.

DESIGNING LEARNING EXPERIENCES

Linking Learning Experiences to the Learning Style of the Students

One of my sons came home from school during his seventh grade and informed me that he had a major assignment to complete on Joan of Arc and needed to get to work on it since it was due after the weekend. Foolishly I did not ask him some more pointed questions as to the nature of the assignment but left him to focus on the assignment as much as possible that weekend. I could hear him rummaging around the recycling bins in our basement, looking for materials for what soon became an epic recreation of the castle of Rouen in which Joan of Arc was imprisoned as she awaited trial. This activity went on for Saturday and a good portion of Sunday afternoon and as we neared the evening I thought I would just ask him whether there was any written component to this assignment. He turned to me as he glued the last pieces of recycling for the keep at the center of the castle and informed me that the assignment was not to create the castle but only to write a two-page essay on Joan of Arc. At this point I suddenly became concerned as I steered him to an encyclopedia for some information and to a computer to write an essay. As I reflected on this experience, I realized what became increasingly obvious about my son, that is, that he is a visual and tactile learner. Although he is good at writing, it was interesting that his first impulse was to observe the scene key to his project and to do something with his body, to create something as part of the learning experience, even when it was not required at all. This was a helpful discovery as a father cum professor, because it made me realize that there were many learners like my son in my courses.

It is important for a teacher to begin reflection on the learning experiences of a course with the student in mind. When stated this way it seems very obvious, but I know from my own experience as a teacher that I have often approached courses from my own perspective, with my own learning interests and styles in mind rather than those of my students. In the end, the learning environment is not about me and my needs for learning but rather about my students and their learning.

Much research has been done on the variety of learning styles found among students.[1] Probably Flemings's VARK model is the most easily accessible with its four basic types: Visual learners, Auditory learners, Reading/writing learners, and Kinesthetic/tactile learners.[2] Visual learners are those who learn through images, auditory learners through sound, reading/writing learners through the written page, and kinesthetic/tactile learners through movement, touch, and action. A more advanced learning style model is that of Sean Whitely in his Memletic approach.[3] He divides the learning styles according to the avenues of learning, echoing Flemings's Visual, Aural, Reading/writing (Whitely: Verbal), Kinesthetic/tactile (Whitely: Physical), and adding Logical (mathematical) for those who prefer using logic, reasoning, and systems. In addition, however, Whitely tracks the preferred context of learning: Social (interpersonal), those who prefer to learn in groups or with other people, or Solitary (intrapersonal), those who prefer to work alone and use self-study.[4]

No person can be identified solely within a single category, and most people learn through all of these avenues. But I have discovered that individuals within my classroom often have dominant learning styles and that includes me as the teacher designing learning experiences for my courses.

---

1. See a fine review in Hawk and Shah, "Using Learning Style Instruments."

2. Fleming, *Teaching and Learning Styles*; Fleming and Mills, "Not Another Inventory"; Fleming, and Baume, "Learning Styles Again"; Dunn and Dunn, *Teaching Students*; Dunn, Dunn, and Price, *Learning Style Inventory*.

3. Whiteley, *Memletics*.

4. See also the earlier work of Grasha and Reichmann (described in Grasha, *Teaching with Style*), who divide learning styles in terms of: avoidant, participative; competitive, collaborative; dependent, independent. These are largely related to social categories.

Awareness of even these simplistic models sensitized me as a professor to the variety of students within my classes as well as the variety of ways learning outcomes could be achieved through the learning experiences of my courses. For me, this began with reflection on the ways the learning experience that I created within the weekly class time engaged the variety of learning styles. Using different learning styles not only helped me to engage a broader group of students by appealing to dominant learning styles, but it also helped students develop minority learning styles.

Most important for the purpose of this chapter is reflection on the learning experiences that I created outside the weekly class time, that is, those experiences that are often called assignments. Often, our approach to assignments can become limited to our own dominant model of learning, and for those who have spent five years in a doctoral program this often means Reading/writing and Logical learning styles within an Intrapersonal social environment (that is, the style of the typical professor). For me, this meant that I needed to cultivate a greater awareness and sensitivity to the visual, aural, kinesthetic/tactile learning styles, and interpersonal social environment for learning. This was especially important for me as I taught within a ministry-formation context in which the development of the visual, aural, kinesthetic/tactile, and social dimensions of learning are extremely helpful for the practice of ministry. This does not mean that the other styles and modes of learning are abandoned, as they are essential for deep reflection on and practice of ministry. To venture in new directions like this, however, demands careful development of new modes of learning and appropriate tools for evaluation of the results. You will need to gauge the openness of the broader academic environment; you will need to discover the dominant modes within your faculty and carefully introduce new modes with the support of your administration and colleagues. At times, you may need to draw in the expertise of others for evaluation of the learning results, but such a collegial exercise showcases an important value for your students who need to learn collaborative skills for their future vocation.

My own course on Psalms has given me an opportunity to link learning experiences to the learning styles of my students. In that course, all students are required to do a common assignment in which they follow a process that I have developed for interpreting a psalm, which forces them to engage the psalm within its original Israelite context and then show how the psalm relates to their own contemporary social and religious context. The results of this work are presented in a research-paper format with engagement with secondary literature. However, I have sought to enhance what appears to be a learning experience that engages the traditional reading/writing, logical, and intrapersonal learning styles by placing students in groups of two, where they are able to interact over a draft form of their interpretation with another and with a more advanced doctoral student, receiving feedback and providing space for interpersonal and aural dimensions of learning.

While all students interpret a psalm using a common approach, the second major assignment in the course is chosen by each student from an extensive list of learning experiences related to the Psalms. These range from development of artistic expressions related to the Psalms, to ministry tools using the Psalms, to research papers (see Appendix A: Psalms Syllabus). The results of these various learning experiences are then shared at the end of the semester in a class that takes place in our chapel, providing an opportunity for interpersonal, aural, and visual learning.

The possibilities are endless, but it does entail openness to experiment with new approaches and to revise in light of results. It also may mean more work and development of new ways of evaluating the results of an assignment, even by drawing in colleagues to help evaluate assignments. But I have found the results rewarding as students have engaged the learning process in much deeper ways, passionately pursuing projects that utilize their favored learning style and help them to see the content of the class in different contexts.

Linking Learning Experiences to the Realities of Life

The college I attended for my doctoral degree, Trinity Hall, is the fourth oldest college at Cambridge University. It began in the wake of the great medieval plagues in England, established by the Bishop of Norwich to replenish his cadre of canon lawyers. The inner court of the college is surrounded by doorways opening into a spiral stone staircase with various rooms found at various points up the staircase. Young men (really boys) would be sent to the college and placed under the care of a don, who would typically live in college at the bottom of the staircase with his young charges living in the rooms above him. These boys were taken off the great manors of the land to be trained for law in the church. Being set apart from their homes and the surrounding culture was part of the college experience, as the boys were trained intellectually to serve within church and court. The earliest college at Cambridge, Peterhouse, interestingly lacks the front wall that would create the quad style that typifies colleges in Cambridge,

Oxford, and around the world today. It is often noted that the front side of the quad was added to protect these young scholars from the townspeople who lived around the college. The colleges did not enjoy favored status in these college towns as the royal house enforced price controls on local businesses to save costs for training their courtiers. When these young scholars would venture out in the evenings or weekends and get in trouble through inappropriate behavior (drinking, etc.), this could easily enrage the local townspeople and lead to riots against the colleges. To this day, in the evening my College closes tight its large medieval wooden gate at the front of the college and forces all foot traffic through the porter's lodge. In earlier times, this was to enhance the security of the college from upset townspeople seeking revenge on drunken scholars. What this tradition reveals is that the ivory tower of academia has never been a reality. One could take young boys off their manors and out of their cities in order to train them in new ways of thinking, believing, and acting, but all the thinking, believing, and acting of their upbringing enters with them into that ivory tower. The academy has never produced a hermetically sealed learning environment. Rather than denying the connection to life, it is more constructive to embrace the inevitability of this connection and create learning experiences that enhance it.

Learning experiences that connect with the realities of life are helpful for engaging students in the learning process. Although learning for learning's sake is a certain ideal with the academic world, most humans are much more motivated when they can see the impact of their learning on their everyday living. In light of this, I think it is important as professors that we look for ways our course material intersects with the realities of life. This intersection need not be only at the later stage of "application" of course content, but also in the early stages of learning as students approach the content of the course in class time, or in the middle stages of learning as students are reflecting on concepts gained from the course.

Such connection to life experience is a key feature of the broader learning environment within the seminary at which I teach. The medical school situated next door to my seminary forms its medical students by placing them in teams working on patients. At the core of our seminary ministry formation program is a ministry reflection seminar in weekly gatherings that bring students alongside a faculty member and a practitioner to reflect on a specific incident within the students' ministry experience (ten hours each week) in a theologically responsible way. I have seen the power of these groups to facilitate deeper reflection on Bible and theology with the learning experience prompted by the realities of life, rather than the realities of life being at the end of the process.

While this is important for the learning experiences that are created during weekly class time, it is essential for the assignments that the students accomplish out of class. Such assignments will have an impact on the class learning experience as I hope the following examples will show. In a hermeneutics course that I taught for several years, I wanted students to grasp the importance and impact of hermeneutics on the lives of people, especially the hermeneutic of a leader. In the first month of the semester, students were required to attend the main service of a particular church at which the main leader of the church was preaching. They were to listen carefully to the speaker to discern from his or her words and methods the speaker's practical hermeneutic: his or her approach to Scripture, method for studying, applying, and presenting the Scriptures, theology of Scripture, etc. After listening for the month, they were to ask the leader for an appointment, hopefully taking the leader out for a coffee, at which they were to ask pointed questions to discern the leader's philosophical hermeneutic, that is, what the person thinks their hermeneutic is. I did this early in the semester to help students see how hermeneutics plays out in reality and to show them the impact it has on an entire community of people.

Assignments also can have a practical outcome. In the Psalms class I described above, nearly all the assignments have a connection with real life. Even those who wrote research papers on a certain theme were asked to share their results with the class at the final worship class. The various assignments each forced the students to connect the content of the course with a practical outcome, whether that was a series of songs, artworks, scribal creations, dances, church services reflecting the full breadth of expression found in the Hebrew Psalter, or a manual for using the psalms to care for various physical and psychological needs. The genius of these assignments lay in their ability to force the students to reflect on the content of the course by applying it and then in each case providing an opportunity to practically use (test) this applied truth in a real life situation.

Another simple example is one that I have used in my Wisdom courses. Old Testament wisdom literature contains themes that connect well with people's lives, whether that is the practical instructions found in Proverbs or the topics of suffering, meaning, mystery, and sexuality found in Job, Ecclesiastes, and Song of Songs. Early in the course, students are asked to go to a large bookstore in the area and find a secular book that intersects with the theme of one of the four main wisdom books:

for Proverbs, a modern work on living successfully; for Song of Songs, a modern work on sexuality; for Ecclesiastes, a modern work on philosophy; for Job, a modern work in narrative and/or poetry on suffering and religion. The students are asked to read and reflect on the Old Testament wisdom book and the secular modern wisdom book and identify points of similarity and dissimilarity between the two works. For the Old Testament wisdom book, they are to draw from material in class, textbooks, and their own broader study of the book. At some point during the time, we cover that Old Testament book in class, and I have them share what they have been reading. I have found that this assignment helps students to see the enduring nature of the themes that we are covering in class and that are found in these ancient books.

These examples highlight ways that we as professors can facilitate connections between the content of the course and real life situations. Another way to facilitate such connections is to reflect on ways that the course can encourage the social dimension of learning, since for many people that is where vocation will be experienced. Already, I have talked about incorporating the social dimension into class assignments with the opportunity in my Psalms course for students to interact with another student as well as a tutor over the first draft of their interpretation of a psalm. At times, this social dimension can be encouraged through group assignments as students tackle a project together, a task that is a regular component of nearly all vocations. With group projects, however, it is important that we as professors provide direction for the groups, specific processes for tackling projects and clear expectations for outcomes. I always provide a mark for the group project but then ask students to evaluate one another as to each group member's quality and quantity of work on the project, detailing specific roles and tasks that each member accomplished. The final mark of each student may not be identical to the mark for the group project, based on these evaluations. The internet also provides an opportunity for facilitating the social dimension of the course, and, in light of the power of digital social networking today, this is an important skill for students to develop. In my courses, I have used what I call "Virtual Lectures" that allow me to bring in an expert in a particular field from outside my institution to first provide some perspective on an issue for my students via the internet and then to spend some time interacting with my students through a chat (synchronous) or blog (asynchronous) environment. Such internet venues can also be used for reflecting on the experience in class, continuing to discuss a topic introduced in class, working on class projects, and peer exchange and review of assignments.

As we design courses we should ask how the course will facilitate engagement with life, whether that is in the development of skills, practical reflection, or social engagement.

Linking Learning Experiences to the Learning Outcomes and Objectives of the Course

When I was a young teen, I had the wonderful opportunity to go camping in the backwoods of Saskatchewan with a group of young teen boys and an adult leader. One early summer weekend, after preparing for weeks for the hike and gathering the food and materials necessary for a safe and enjoyable experience, we set out as a group along a firebreak. Our leader had his detailed topographical map in hand and a compass for direction, and we began our trek. By late afternoon with the sun beginning to set, however, we were in a state of confusion, and our leader clearly had a look of concern. The problem was that the map pictured a body of water near the spot where we were standing, but there was no water in sight. So our leader calmly gathered us together at the centre of this large field with high grass. He instructed us to spread out from the centre of the field where he would stay and remain in our sight. We began to move, trying to catch a glimpse of the body of water pictured on the map. Suddenly, I stumbled over a hard object on the ground. Crying out to my leader, I announced that I had found a round piece of metal attached to a metal stake in the ground. On the face of the metal piece was the drawing of a crosshair and in each quadrant of the crosshair were numbers, with the top two numbers one number apart (e.g., 25, 26) and the bottom two numbers one number apart (e.g., 35, 36). Upon his arrival a smile came across my leader's face as he realized that I had stumbled upon the answer to our dilemma. The stake had been driven there at the turn of the last century as government officials surveyed the province of Saskatchewan, dividing it into square mile quadrants and at the intersection between the quadrants driving a stake to mark the spot. This stake then identified for us precisely where we were on the topographical map: at the intersection of (e.g.,) 25, 26, 35, 36 quadrants. While we were very close to where we thought we were on the map, what was formerly a bog had dried up.

As professors, we create syllabi that often serve as the only map for our courses and a good syllabus can go a long way towards serving this function. What our students need, however, are clear stakes that orient them to where they are in this map and how this relates to the vision for growth laid out by the syllabus.

I suggest that we as professors need to reflect on the significance of the various components of our courses in a systematic way, an exercise that forces us to link all the learning experiences in the course to the various outcomes and objectives of the course. Doing this exercise for some of my courses forced me to reflect on the function of all of the elements in my courses and to design ways to integrate these various elements, whether they were in or out of class time. In terms of assignments out of class time, I found it helpful to students to show the cohesion between the various components of the course, orienting them to how each element functions within the broader framework of the course learning experience.

A tool I have used for such reflection is found in Appendix B below and in this case lays out the relationship of the course to the broader curriculum, identifies the key course learning outcomes, and then tracks the relationship of the various learning experiences (textbooks, class sessions, and assignments) to the learning outcomes/objectives (and the textbooks to class sessions and assignments). This helps me evaluate the entire learning experience of the course and ensure that I have a breadth of learning objectives and then have designed specific learning experiences that are designed intentionally to facilitate these various outcomes and objectives. This helps me in designing my syllabus as well as in communicating the vision for the course and its various components. This exercise forces me to justify everything in the course experience by its connection to the guiding values expressed through the learning outcomes. This has helped me be more intentional in teaching and facilitating learning, and I believe it has helped my students see the purpose behind the various classes and assignments, offering an integrative experience with purpose.

In our seminary/graduate school, we have adopted an institution-wide set of outcomes related to the cognitive, affective, and pragmatic dimensions of learning, what we call in accessible terms: knowing, being, and doing. The cognitive (knowing) dimension involves the acquisition of knowledge areas; the affective (being) dimension involves reflection on and experience of one's personal, vocational, and spiritual identity; the pragmatic (doing) dimension involves the acquisition of specific skills. This multiple dimensional approach to teaching and learning was one that I adopted early in my teaching career. As I began teaching, I found that my goals were nearly all expressed in cognitive terms (knowing), not surprising since this is a key outcome of most doctoral programs. However, as I reflected on my courses, I soon discovered that although I did not always express non-cognitive outcomes or goals for my courses, I was designing learning experiences that targeted other outcomes but had not expressed this in my course outcomes explicitly. I began incorporating being and doing outcomes and goals in my courses so that I could be more intentional in what I was trying to accomplish. This forced me to reflect more deeply on these outcomes and ways I could facilitate them more effectively in the course experience. The affective or "being" dimension of learning is important no matter what type of program one is teaching in and can be facilitated through learning experiences like journaling, group interaction, devotional introductions, prayer, as well as various projects or written assignments. The pragmatic (doing) dimension of learning can be facilitated through nearly all assignments as students need to learn specific methods for working with knowledge as well as learning specific skills for practices related to the course content. The key in all of this is finding and developing a breadth of learning experiences that will address these various dimensions of learning and assist students to deepen their learning.

In a recent course I taught on the theology of sin and its remedy in the Old Testament, I required that students reflect at the outset of the semester on their theology of sin and its remedy within their own personal theological tradition. This helped them to bring to the foreground their own identity as a learner in this particular course and helped them assess their own cognitive framework from the standpoint of personal identity within a tradition. As they were involved in the various learning experiences throughout the semester, whether in class or out of class, whether individually or communally, they could reference this initial reflection and ask how the knowledge encountered connected with their present theological identity. This initial exercise was matched with a concluding reflection at the end of the semester for which they were required to reflect on how their theology of sin and its remedy had been challenged and how they had revised their theology as a result of their reflection in this course. This was a measurable way for me to facilitate the "being" dimension of learning for these students.

Conclusion

Hopefully the discussion above has whetted your appetite for new approaches to learning experiences in courses. The key in all of this is for professors to think intentionally and creatively about the various learning experiences, connecting them to the learning style of the students, the realities of life, and the learning outcomes of the course.

EVALUATING LEARNING EXPERIENCES

Designing learning experiences is a key initial step to a successful course, but most learning experiences will need to be evaluated and so I want to provide some guidance on how to grade assignments.

It may come as a surprise to many that my lowest grade during my masters degree was in Old Testament Introduction. Interestingly, this did not reflect my passion for this subject at the time but rather a lack of understanding of one of the learning experiences in that course. It was my first semester in my seminary degree, and I had prepared extensively for my midterm exam in Old Testament Introduction, poring over the professor's notes, memorizing his thoughts in order to answer any question on the exam. What I did not realize was that this professor based his midterm exam mostly on the reading that was required in the course to that point. Unlike my undergraduate professors who seemed to place greater value on what was covered in class, possibly to keep us motivated to listen to their words, this professor used the midterm exam to ensure elements of the course outside class time received attention from the students. I don't remember him saying this in class or emphasizing this in the syllabus, but I soon discovered that all exams at this institution were placed on hold at the library for access by the students. Past exams clearly focused on the reading over the lectures. Whether this was good pedagogy is not our focus at the moment. Rather, I realized how important it was to learn all I could about the various learning experiences in my courses before undertaking them. This experience would mark my own courses and syllabi as I devised them as a professor, reminding me to carefully describe my expectations and provide some insight into how the learning experiences would be evaluated.

I also remember receiving a lower grade on a paper in another one of my Old Testament classes. I was so disappointed that I arranged a meeting with the esteemed professor for some insight into the mark that I had received with the hope that he would see the error of his ways and increase the mark. Alas, he carefully explained that my paper lacked "integrity," a descriptor that devastated me until I realized that what he meant was that it lacked cohesion and clear flow. The mark remained, but through his careful and firm evaluation I learned an important lesson about my writing that would shape my future work.

As professors, we often underestimate the impact of evaluating learning experiences on our students and we often spend little time reflecting on the process of evaluation. We often forget about the emotional character of grading, at least until a student is in our office either weeping in frustration or screaming in anger. I have found that the more time I spend reflecting on why and how I evaluate students' assignments and communicating clearly the evaluation I give to my students, the less problems I encounter with students over grading. I also have realized that as professors we all bring our own perspectives and past experiences to the grading process. To grade appropriately means that one needs to be secure within oneself and clear as to the purposes and processes of evaluation. Once the first grades have been given to students in a course, the character of the class shifts, partly because people connect grades with their own self worth, but also because it reminds the students that the course involves accountability and they are now accountable to you as their guide in the learning process. Giving honest and fair evaluation is important to the learning process. It helps students to gauge their learning progress, providing insight into how they are succeeding and areas in which they can improve. To give a low grade when the student has performed well is to risk discouragement and frustration, but also to give a high grade when one is not deserved is to promote deceit and inappropriate self-perception. In a consumer approach to education, students do not pay for high grades, but they do pay for honest and accurate evaluation. In the following section, we will look briefly at three key foundational issues related to grading: the various uses of grades, the various types of grading, and the various standards of grading,[5] before providing some personal reflections on best practices.

Various Uses of Grades

The emotional nature of grading highlights the fact that grades are not merely a record of the past, nor just a progress report on the present, but an important determiner of the future. As we professors give a student a grade we need to realize that this grade will have an impact on the future of the student since it is used by various parties to gain insight into certain

---

5. These are based on the superb chapter "The A B C's of Assigning Grades," in McKeachie, *Teaching Tips*, 110–21.

decisions related not only to the student, but also to the professor, the department, even the school. Grades are used by students to help them discern whether they will focus on a particular field of study or pursue a specific vocation. Grades can motivate students to work harder in present or future courses or prompt them to avoid similar courses with the same content or professor in the future. At times, students use grades to evaluate the kind of person they are. Not only students, but also professors use grades to determine a student's level of "motivation, skills, knowledge, and ability."[6] This will influence the professor's counsel to the student, either encouraging or discouraging the student's pursuit of certain courses. At times, grades will influence the professor's perception of the student, whether he or she is a good student with the appropriate work habits and cognitive maturity. Professors also use grades to assess their success in teaching. When students across the class do poorly, the professor should take this to heart by reflecting on ways the learning experience could be enhanced. While administrators (deans, program directors, and counselors) use grades to determine whether a student is operating at an appropriate level for their program or is worthy of honors (dean's list) or funding, they also use grades to reflect on the quality of their academic program and especially the quality of their professors. Administrators are concerned about grades being too high, sometimes highlighting a problem in the evaluation instruments used by professors, or too low, sometimes highlighting a problem in pedagogy. Individuals and organizations outside of the particular academic environment also use grades in their decision making. Employers may look at the grades of a student in a particular area of study to determine whether the student is qualified to work in their firm. Although grades are not as important as a degree in an area, when there is competition between multiple candidates, grades may play into the final decision.

Grades are thus an important dimension of the learning experience and for this reason reflection on evaluation is important as we design learning experiences for our students.

Various Types of Grading

Throughout my 25 years of education as a student, I encountered a variety of approaches to grading learning experiences in my courses. The three most common were qualitative, contract-based, and competency-based

6. Ibid., 111.

types of grading. The most common by far was the qualitative type of grading, the one that assigns a letter or percentage grade to a piece of work produced for the professor. This is by far the most common form of grading, both for the grades assigned to a student for a course within academic programs and for grades assigned to a student for assignments within particular courses. For contract-based grading, "students and instructors develop a written contract about what the student will do to achieve given grade levels."[7] For competency-based grading, "the student is graded on a pass-fail basis for achieving 'mastery' or 'competence' in terms of carefully specified objectives."[8] Professors who use this model may allow for multiple attempts at submission of material until the assignment reaches the level of competency envisioned. There are, of course, strengths and weaknesses in each of these types of grading. Qualitative grading provides a clear sense of the level of one's work but may not reward students for the quantity of work undertaken for a particular assignment nor allow for revision of material to improve one's abilities. Contract grading provides clear standards for the attainment of grades and places responsibility for the final grade entirely in the hands of the students. However, contract grading may not offer a student a clear sense of the quality of the work with its focus on quantitative evaluation. Competency-based grading is basically what is used in most thesis writing, as the student presents and revises material until it is ready for defense. This approach provides an opportunity for students to learn from their mistakes and test solutions through revision. However, it also places considerable time demands on the professor who must read the material multiple times, and also does not differentiate between the student who is able to produce excellent material on the first try and those who must revise multiple times.

These various types of grading are neither good nor bad in and of themselves but, rather, are best suited to different types of learning experiences. Certain types will be stronger for particular learning experiences, and the weakness of any of them can be minimized by various strategies. For instance, contract grading can be used to define a particular quantity of work to be accomplished by the student, but this can be combined with an element of evaluation that assesses the quality of the work. If contract grading is used for reading in a course, the student can be required to provide some form of written or oral reflection that allows for qualitative

---

7. Ibid., 113.
8. Ibid., 114.

assessment. Courses often use a combination of these types of grading, using, for instance, contract-based grading for reading, competency-based grading for a skill gained and documented, as well as qualitative grading for a written paper. Reflection on the types of grading may prompt you as a professor to develop new learning experiences as well as to design new evaluation tools for assessing learning.

Various Standards for Grading

When assigning grades, one has to have some standard against which to judge the individual performance of a student. This standard may be an abstract mean (i.e., the ideal student in the professor's estimation), contemporary student peers (i.e., other students who are presently in the same class facing the same demands), or the individual learner (i.e., the student's own individual standard and thus progress during the course). Most grading is based on the ideal student according to the professor's estimation—a student that is constructed from years of experience with students and with the content, skills, and values of the course. In the early years of teaching, professors are often forced to reflect on the performance of contemporary student peers when assigning grades. Although the dreaded "curve" is rarely used today, marking in light of other students is helpful when evaluating students. Gauging the individual progress of a student is difficult but can be helpful for at least part of students' grades, especially when the students set out quantifiable goals for themselves at the outset of the course and are given an opportunity to quantify completion through specific evidence.

Best Practices

I have come to the conclusion that grading is an important pastoral exercise in the academic world. It involves speaking the truth in love, offering an honest evaluation, but doing so in a way that motivates further growth and passion. Here are some best practices for speaking the truth in love.

First, professors should lay out clear expectations for assignments in their syllabi and tell the students how they will mark the assignments. The students should not be continually guessing as to what the professor is looking for in a particular assignment. Exemplar samples of past assignments are also helpful, since some students need to see practically what professors are talking about in abstract terms. Second, professors should provide feedback to their students. We are certainly beyond the age when professors would give out a letter grade to their students without comments. As I said earlier, students are not paying for A grades, but they are paying for feedback from a seasoned professional.

Third, professors need to provide clear comments on their students' projects. Students should be able to read a professor's comments, and, for some of us (me, for instance), that may mean shifting to digital commenting, using, for instance, commenting features in Adobe PDF files or Microsoft Word DOC files. I shifted early in my teaching career from commenting in red, which to me signified death (blood), to green, which to me signified growth. This relates to an important fourth element of best practices: professors should provide a balance in their commenting between strengths and weaknesses, opportunities and threats. The first scale (strengths, weaknesses) looks to the present work and how well it reflects the quality and quantity the professor expected. Weaknesses should not be avoided, but strengths should be highlighted so the student has a sense of what he or she has accomplished. The second scale (opportunities, threats) looks to the future, offering your thoughts on the potential of the present work. Highlight those elements in the paper that you see as deserving of further development, offering a way forward for the student's growth. But also note those elements in the paper that you fear will hamper the student's growth or potential dangers if a trajectory established in a student's writing is continued.

The fifth best practice is often related to written work but also has potential for other types of assignments, including oral presentations and projects. Provide feedback not only on the content of the assignment, but also on the presentation of the assignment and its argumentation. The content of the assignment refers to the level of engagement with the key issues related to the topic of the paper and the crucial secondary literature. The presentation of the assignment refers to the adherence of the paper to proper spelling, syntax, and punctuation as well as the faithfulness of the paper to the institutional style guide for bibliography as well as layout. Argumentation refers to the level of engaging rhetoric in the paper, which entails a proper introduction of the topic, conclusion to the paper, and appropriate flow throughout the paper. In my institution, we have developed a helpful rubric for evaluating research papers that takes these three areas into account (see Appendix C).

As mentioned above, my present institution requires the development of three fundamental learning outcome areas for each course: knowing, being, and doing. Designing opportunities for experiencing growth in all three areas is important when creating and revising courses, but these three areas should also be taken into account when evaluating students' work. We can spur growth and correct performance by offering comments in relation to knowing, being, and doing. Students need to know where they have missed some aspect of knowledge related to the topic, which would be helpful for thoroughness but also for sparking further growth. Professors can also provide feedback on the method the student has employed for the paper or sermon. Students, however, also need to be given some feedback that will spur their "being," motivating them to deepen their relationship with God or to reflect on their own self, encouraging further growth, or identifying ways this assignment may relate to their own vocational path.

CONCLUSION

Designing and evaluating learning experiences is essential to the task of teaching and learning in the academy and my hope is that my reflections above have sparked some new ideas and forced deeper reflection on past experiences in order to shape future learning. The key in all this is to reflect on what will provide the best opportunity for the greatest number of students to grow in a particular area. As a professor, you have been given an incredible privilege to capture the imagination of a new generation of learners, but with this comes the awesome responsibility to guide these learners along carefully designed paths that lead to new discoveries.

APPENDIX A: PSALMS SYLLABUS

OT 3SA3/6SA6 (final)
McMaster Divinity College
Dr. Mark J. Boda
Professor of Old Testament
Winter Semester 2010
Thursday, 8:30–10:20 a.m.

Contact

Office phone: xxx-xxxx
Email: xxx@xxx
Faculty Webpage: http://xxx
Course Webpage: http://xxx

Description

An exegetical study of the Old Testament Psalter with attention given to historical setting, literary form, rhetorical meaning, canonical context, and theological teaching. Students will be exposed to the breadth of hermeneutical approaches to the psalms while honing their skills at the interpretation of Hebrew poetry.

Purposes

Knowing: That the students have a firm and thorough intellectual grasp of the content, literary form, historical context, and theological teaching of the book of Psalms in its historical, canonical, and contemporary contexts.

Being: That the students gain an appreciation for the book of Psalms, its expression of theology, and its significance for contemporary worship and teaching. That the students encounter the triune God showcased in the psalms and experience a deepening in their relationship with this God.

Doing: That the students acquire competency in interpreting psalms maintaining a balance between ancient context and contemporary significance.

Textbooks

Brueggemann, W. *The Psalms and the Life of Faith*, edited by Patrick D. Miller. Minneapolis: Fortress, 1995. ISBN #0800627334

Futato, Mark. *Interpreting the Psalms: An Exegetical Handbook*. Grand Rapids: Kregel, 2007. ISBN #9780825427657

Broyles, Craig C. *Psalms*. NIBCOT 11. Peabody, MA: Hendrickson, 1999. ISBN #1565632206

Schaefer, Konrad. *Psalms*. Berit Olam. Collegeville, MN: Liturgical, 2001. ISBN #0814650619

    All required textbooks for this class and others at the Divinity College are available from the College bookstore.

Course Internet Resource Site

A course internet resource site has been developed for those in this course this semester. (username and password will be made available in class). This site will host materials related to the course.

Program

Classroom Experiences

We will spend considerable time together on Thursday mornings. This time will be used to orient you to the psalms in their original context both in the historical context of Israel as well as in the literary context of the Psalter. These times together will lay the foundation for your independent learning experiences below.

January			25	Class
7	Orientation	**March**		
14	Class		4	Class
21	Class		11	Class
28	Class		18	Class
February			25	Class
4	Class	**April**		
11	Class		1	Class
18	No Class: Reading Week		8	Class: Worship

Independent and Collaborative Learning Experiences

Outside the classroom sessions, learning experiences have been designed in order to integrate and apply the content learned.

Overview: Besides your participation in our class experiences there are basically two learning experiences that you will complete for this course.

> **Interpreting the Psalms**
> In this learning experience you will take one psalm and interpret it. You will be given a detailed guide explaining how to interpret a psalm. Then you will take one psalm and interpret following the guide. Through email you will receive input from your classmates on your interpretation and then you will do more work on your passage, consulting secondary literature and revising your work, and ultimately produce a research paper.
>
> **Integrating the Psalms**
> In this learning experience the psalms will become paradigms in form and theology for contemporary expression. You will choose only ONE of many possible learning experiences (one that fits your interest and learning style).

Interpreting the Psalms

Goal: The goal of these learning experiences is to use the principles for interpreting Hebrew Psalms to interpret a psalm.

A. Phase One: Initial Interpretation

1. Begin by reading the guide for interpreting psalms that will be made available in class with an example from Psalm 11.

2. Read Futato (2007) on interpreting the Psalms as a reference to fill out the interpretive steps covered in the guide above.

3. Take one psalm (approved by professor) you have not studied in depth before and practice the steps for interpretation on this psalm. After reading the psalm in 3 translations (or translating the psalm yourself, if you have taken Hebrew, which is not expected for this course), practice interpretation on the psalm without reference to secondary literature (that is, commentaries, etc.). As you encounter things in the psalm that you do not understand or cannot resolve without reference to secondary literature, write down a question that you will be able to follow up later. Understandably this is an initial draft of your work, so do not be afraid if you have not resolved issues yet. Try to encounter the text for yourself using the steps I have given you and Futato's guidance as well.

4. This will be exchanged by email with your partner from class and the professor to discuss and evaluate.

Due Date: 20 January @ 11:59 pm.
Value: 5%
Medium: send in digital format (.pdf) to one other student and professor via email

B. Phase Two: Peer Review

Take another student's initial interpretation and write up a basic review for them. Provide evaluation that both affirms areas of strength (25%) and areas for improvement (75%) in the initial draft that has been posted. Email this review to this student and the professor.

Due Date: 27 January @ 11:59 pm.
Value: 5%
Medium: send in digital format (.pdf) to one other student and professor via email

C. Phase Three: Research Paper

After receiving feedback on Phase One, you will return to this passage and consult a minimum of 10 secondary sources beyond the textbooks for the class (especially you should use commentaries). These secondary sources must include both books and articles, must reflect recent research (after 1950, and best after 1980), and must be elongated treatments of your biblical text, period, or book. This requirement does not include ancient sources used (Josephus, Qumran) or Bibles, Versions, Study Bibles, Bible Dictionaries (or other reference works). Internet resources are usually **not** acceptable and must be approved by the professor (unless through the ATLA resources at McMaster). Go through this material and revise your initial raw research. Finally, drawing from this depth of research you have done on this psalm, create a minimum 10 page research paper that reflects your research and follows the outline below (the percentages are the amount of your paper that should be devoted to each point):

Cover page (note how much of Futato 2007 you have read)
Introduction (2.5%)
1. Basic theme and overall flow of the Psalm (10%)
2. How rhetoric (imagery and structure) set within history and culture point to the basic theme (50%). Allow the structure of the passage to structure your discussion, which is an integrated piece.
3. How this relates to the theology and structure of the Psalter (10%)
4. How this relates to the rest of the canon (15%)
5. Application (10%)
Conclusion (2.5%)

Value: 40%
Due Date: 10 February @ 11:59 p.m.
Medium: send in digital format (.pdf preferred) to professor via email

INTEGRATING THE PSALMS

Goal: The goal of these learning experiences is to display the impact of our study of Hebrew worship in the Psalter on contemporary worship and faith.

A. Phase One: The *first step* in this learning experience (no matter which one you choose) involves  participating in the class learning experiences on the cycle of worship, reading Brueggemann (1995), and reading the entire Psalter (before reading the Psalter make sure you have read the guide for the Phase Two track you choose, you may have something you need to note as you read through these psalms). On the cover page of your assignment please note how much of Brueggemann (1995) and the Psalter you have read.

B. Phase Two: The *second step* in this learning experience is to choose ONE of the learning experiences within ONE of the tracks below (if you have another creative idea please feel free to suggest it):

1. Shepherding Track

a. Psalms for the Sick and Dying: Create a resource tool for ministering to the sick and dying through the psalms. This tool should give you the ability to access different psalms for different stages in the sick-dying-funeral mode as well as to know how to use them in these different settings. You will need to investigate the psychological aspects of these stages in order to know how to shape your resource tool. You will visit one person who is sick or dying and in the course of your visit(s) use the tool. A one-page description of this experience should accompany the resource tool. Begin by studying the different stages of the sick-dying-funeral popularized by Kübler-Ross (*On Death and Dying* [New York: MacMillan, 1969]; there are 5 stages, see Mills library for resources). As you read through the Psalms from beginning to end (1–150) look for Psalms that would be helpful to use during each stage. Do focused study on one psalm for each of the five stages so that you have a firm grasp of its meaning and significance and how it relates to the particular stage. Write this up in a resource tool that presents both the psychological aspects and biblical content with integrity (each stage should take 3–5 pages). Then visit someone at least once (but hopefully more than once) and write up your reflections on that experience. You will share your experience at the end of the semester.

b. Psalms for the Anorexic: Do the same as above but for the conditions of anorexia nervosa and bulimia nervosa. The following materials would be helpful:

> Costin, Carolyn. *The Eating Disorder Sourcebook: A Comprehensive Guide to the Causes, Treatments and Prevention of Eating Disorders.* Toronto: N.T.C., 1999.
> Crabb, Larry. *Connections: A Radical New Vision.* Nashville: Word, 1997.
> Crook, Marion. *Looking Good.* Toronto: NC Press, 1992.
> Treasure, Janet. *Anorexia Nervosa: A Survival Guide for Families, Friends and Sufferers.* London: Psychology Press, 1997.

2. Worship Arts Track

a. Asaph recommissioned: Write three psalms with accompanying music portraying the cycle of worship (Orientation, Disorientation, New/Reorientation) as well as the richness of theology in the Hebrew Psalter. These must be newly created this semester by you and will be shared with the class at the worship finale. Accompanying each piece of written music and lyrics will be a two page summary of the underlying thought and flow of the piece. Suggestions should be offered as to how and where each piece could be used in the context of a local worshipping community. You will share some of your work with the class near the end of the semester.

b. Bezalel and Oholiab recommissioned: Produce three separate pieces of visual art that explore and express the cycle of worship (Orientation, Disorientation, New/Reorientation) as well as the richness of theology in the Hebrew Psalter. These must be newly created this semester by you. Accompanying each piece will be a two page artist's statement summarizing the underlying thought and emotion of the piece. Suggestions should be offered as to how and where each piece could be used in the context of the worship of the local church. You will share some of your work with the class near the end of the semester.

c. David recommissioned: Create three separate expressions of dance that explore and express the cycle of worship (Orientation, Disorientation, New/Reorientation) as well as the richness of theology in the Hebrew Psalter. These must be newly created this semester by you. Accompanying each piece will be a two page artist's statement summarizing the underlying thought and emotion of the dance. Suggestions should be offered as to how and where each dance could be used in the context of the worship of the local church. You will share some of your work with the class near the end of the semester.

d. Divine drama recommissioned: Create three separate 5-10 minute dramatic presentations (complete with script, lighting/sound/staging instructions) that explore and express the cycle of worship (Orientation, Disorientation, New/Reorientation) as well as the richness of theology in the Hebrew Psalter. These must be newly created this semester by you. Accompanying each presentation will be a two page artist's statement summarizing the underlying thought and emotion of the presentation. Suggestions should be offered as to how and where each piece could be used in the context of the worship of the local church. You will share some of your work with the class near the end of the semester.

e. Ezra recommissioned: Taking your lead from the medieval scribal artistic tradition, reproduce three psalms from the basic types in the cycle of worship (Orientation, Disorientation, New/Reorientation). These must be newly created this semester by you. Accompanying each piece will be a two page artist's statement summarizing the underlying thought and emotion of the piece. Suggestions should be offered as to how and where each piece could be used in the context of the worship of the local church. You will share some of your work with the class near the end of the semester.

3. Worship Leadership Track

a. Levitical Liturgy: plan six church services that incorporate various types of psalms. Each service must be unique, integrated, and creative. You should include worship elements as well as texts, sermon themes/passages. At the top of each service plan you must introduce us to the theological vision you have for that service and any appropriate time of the year or in the life of the church it would be used. After each element in the service you must include a short explanation of what is expected in this element. You will share some of your work with the class near the end of the semester.

b. Levitical Scripture Reading: Design three half-hour Scripture Reading experiences based on compositions within the book of Psalms. These must reflect the breadth of expression represented in the cycle of worship (Orientation, Disorientation, New/Reorientation) as well as the richness of theology in the Hebrew Psalter. These must be newly created this semester by you. Accompanying each piece will be a two page summary of the underlying thought and flow of the piece. Suggestions should be offered as to how and where each piece could be used in the context of the worship of the local church. You will share some of your work with the class near the end of the semester.

4. Research Track

If you are heading towards a research degree (thesis) you are encouraged to write a second research paper on a topic related to the reading in Brueggemann. This paper has the same requirements as the previous assignments on Interpreting the Psalms and should engage a depth of scholarship on a topic agreed with the professor.

C. Phase Three: The *third step* in this learning experience is to share your project with the rest of the class at our closing worship class.

Value for Project: 40%
Due Date: 31 March @ 11:59 p.m.
Medium: send in digital format (.pdf preferred) to professor via email; for visual materials send photographs or video (or link to online access, e.g., www.youtube.com).

Value for Presentation: 10%
Due Date: 8 April

Format and Evaluation

So I can properly evaluate your work the following style guide is to be used for papers in this class.

- **Medium for Submission:** All material in this class is to be submitted in digital format to me via email. Please use .pdf format and ensure that what you send is what you want me to read. If you need a program for creating .pdfs go to http://primopdf.com for a free .pdf maker.

- **Layout:** All material that is submitted should be double spaced with 1 inch margins utilizing a readable font (10–12 pts). It must have a title page, footnoting where appropriate, and bibliography, all of which are not included in the length required. It should be written in excellent modern literary English with proper grammar, spelling, punctuation, and rhetoric (including an introduction, conclusion and logical flow of argument). If it helps, an outline may accompany the paper, but this is not included in the length of the paper. Secondary and Primary sources should be used, cited, and footnoted appropriately and the paper should follow the "McMaster Divinity College Style Guidelines for Essays and Theses" available at the College and course website.

- **Gender Inclusive Language:** McMaster Divinity College uses inclusive language for human beings in worship services, student written materials, and all of its publications. In reference to biblical texts, the integrity of the original expressions and the names of God should be respected. The NRSV and TNIV are examples of the use of inclusive language for human beings. It is expected that inclusive language will be used in chapel services and all MDC assignments.

- **Citations**: You must cite the source of your material very carefully using a consistent system, not only when quoting from a section, but also when drawing from it as resource. Quotations should be kept to a minimum as I favor integration of secondary literature (footnoted).

- **Statement on Academic Honesty**: Academic dishonesty is a serious offence that may take any number of forms, including plagiarism, the submission of work that is not one's own or for which previous credit has been obtained, and/or unauthorized collaboration with other students. Academic dishonesty can result in severe consequences, e.g., failure of the assignment, failure of the course, a notation on one's academic transcript, and/or suspension or expulsion from the College. Students are responsible for understanding what constitutes academic dishonesty. If you are a Divinity College student please refer to the Divinity College Statement on Academic Honesty at http://www.mcmasterdivinity.ca/programs/rules-regulations.

So I can properly evaluate your work and help you grow in your biblical and writing skills the following evaluation guide should be kept in mind as you write:
- **Presentation**: Is the spelling correct? Does the grammar/syntax reflect proper English? Is the paper laid out properly?
- **Argumentation**: Is there a good introduction and conclusion? Does the argument flow with ample support? Is the question answered?
- **Content**: Are all the points considered? Is there proper documentation of sources used?

Accountability

A core value in my classes is the nurturing of a "learning community." Such a community fosters growth within the individuals who enter into its life. Growth occurs through the positive affirmation and teaching of principles, through personal engagement and study, but also through accountability within this community.

Accountability means first of all that you will commit yourself to this class throughout the semester. Your attendance is required, expected, and celebrated at every scheduled session. From time to time you may find that you are late for class. Late arrivals, hereafter called "tardies," are unacceptable and will lead to a negative disposition in the professor and your classmates. Such "tardies," however, can be redeemed at the rate of Timbits (mini-donuts) for the entire class at the session following the second tardy as well as a coffee for the professor. Details can be obtained from the professor.

Accountability also means handing in assignments on time. I do not give extensions on assignments except in the most dire of circumstances, which include serious sickness and family crises. An excuse (referred to as the "Cyberexcuse") based upon computer problems is not legitimate and will not be accepted (even if it is on a McMaster machine, if you need a "typewriter," I have one in my office). Unless you have a legitimate reason for the learning community (that is, Psalms class) to extend the due date of an assignment please do not ask. When I deal with an individual on such matters I treat that student as a member of the larger community called Psalms class. It is unfair to offer privileges to some members of that community that are not available to others. Late material will be docked at the rate of 2% for each day (including weekends) it is late. All assignments in this class must be handed in by the final day of classes in this semester or the student will receive a failing grade.

Accountability is not only for you, but also for me as a member of this learning community. Class material will be presented with creativity and excellence. Assignments will be marked with appropriate comments within a reasonable period after they are submitted. I am not only available, but welcome and enjoy connections with each of you outside of class time. Please see my office hours on my office door or make an appointment with me whenever you would like.

Disclaimer: This syllabus is for information only and remains the property of the professor. This syllabus is prepared with the best information available, but the professor reserves the right to change the content and format of the course.

© M. J. Boda, 2009

APPENDIX B: TOOL TO CONNECT LEARNING OUTCOMES WITH COURSE ELEMENTS[9]

Course Number:	OT3SA3
Course Name:	Old Testament Psalms
Course Term and Format:	Winter Semester 2010, Resident course
Course Description:	An exegetical study of the Old Testament Psalter with attention given to historical setting, literary form, rhetorical meaning, canonical context, and theological teaching. Students will be exposed to the breadth of hermeneutical approaches to the psalms while honing their skills for the interpretation of Hebrew poetry.
Relationship to Curriculum:	Old Testament Elective within Ministry Studies degree/diploma programs.

Course Learning Outcomes:	1. Knowing: That the students have a firm and thorough intellectual grasp of
	  a. content of the book of Psalms
	  b. literary form of the book of Psalms
	  c. historical context of the book of Psalms
	  d. theological teaching of the book of Psalms
	  e. in its historical context
	  f. in its canonical context
	  g. in its contemporary context
	2. Being: That the students gain an appreciation for the book of Psalms
	  a. its expression of theology
	  b. its significance for contemporary worship
	  c. its significance for teaching
	  d. That the students encounter the triune God showcased in the psalms and experience a deepening in their relationship with this God.
	3. Doing: That the students acquire competency in interpreting psalms maintaining a balance between
	  a. ancient context
	  b. contemporary significance.

Book/Resource	Relationship to Learning Experiences in Class	Relationship to Learning Experiences outside Class	Learning Objective
Brueggemann, W. (P. D. Miller, ed.). *The Psalms and the Life of Faith*. Minneapolis: Fortress, 1995. ISBN #0800627334	Minor	Major for Learning Experience II	Major: 1d, 1f, 1g, 2
Futato, Mark. *Interpreting the Psalms: An Exegetical Handbook*. Grand Rapids, MI: Kregel Publications, 2007. ISBN #9780825427657	Minor	Major for Learning Experience I	Major: 3 Minor: 1
Broyles, Craig C. *Psalms*. New International Biblical Commentary Old Testament series 11. Peabody, MA: Hendrickson, 1999. ISBN #1565632206	Minor	Major for Learning Experience I and II	Major: 1
Schaefer, Konrad. *Psalms*. Berit Olam. Collegeville, Minn.: Liturgical Press, 2001. ISBN #0814650619	Minor	Major Learning Experience I and II	Major: 1

(Required Resources)

9. I was first awakened to this form of reflection on my courses through a tool used at Tozer Seminary at Simpson University (Redding, CA), where I once taught a summer course. I have revised the original form for my own purposes. With thanks to Sam Gantt, Director of Educational Technology, and Robb Redman, Dean, both at Tozer Seminary at that time.

Recommended Resources:	Miller, P. D. *Interpreting the Psalms*. Philadelphia: Fortress Press, 1986. ISBN 0800618963	Minor	Major for Learning Experience I	Major: 3
	Petersen, David L. and Kent Harold Richards. *Interpreting Hebrew Poetry*. Guides to Biblical Scholarship. Minneapolis, MN: Fortress, 1992.	Minor	Major for Learning Experience I	Major: 3
	Ryken, L., J. C. Wilhoit, and T. Longman, eds. *Dictionary of Biblical Imagery*. Downers Grove: IVPress, 1997.	Minor	Major for Learning Experience I	Major: 3
	Bullock, C. Hassell. *Encountering the book of Psalms: A literary and theological introduction*. Encountering biblical studies. Grand Rapids, Mich.: Baker Academic, 2001.	Minor	Minor for Learning Experience I and II	Major: 3
	Johnston, Philip, and David G. Firth. *Interpreting the Psalms: Issues and approaches*. Downers Grove, Ill./Leicester, England: InterVarsity Press/Apollos, 2005.	Minor	Minor for Learning experience I and II	Major: 1, Minor 3
	Kraus, Hans-Joachin. *Theology of the Psalms*. Translated by Keith R. Crim. Continental Commentaries. Minneapolis: Augsburg 1986.	Minor	Minor for Learning Experience I and II	Major: 1, 3
	McCann, J. Clinton, and Nancy Rowland McCann. *A Theological Introduction to the Book of Psalms: The Psalms as Torah*. Nashville, TN: Abingdon, 1993.	Minor	Minor for Learning Experience I and II	Major: 1, 3
	Allen, Leslie C. *Psalms 101-150*. WBC 21. Waco: Word Books, 1983.	Minor	Major for Learning Experience I and II	Major: 1
	Craigie, Peter C. *Psalms 1-50*. WBC 19. Waco, Tex.: Word Books, 1983.	Minor	Major for Learning Experience I and II	Major: 1
	Eaton, J. H. *The Psalms: A historical and spiritual commentary with an introduction and new translation*. London; New York: Continuum, 2005.	Minor	Major for Learning Experience I and II	Major: 1
	Goldingay, John. *Psalms*. 3 vols. Baker commentary on the Old Testament wisdom and Psalms. Grand Rapids, MI: Baker Academic, 2006.	Minor	Major for Learning Experience I and II	Major: 1
	Wilson, Gerald H. *Psalms (1-72)*. NIVAC. Grand Rapids: Zondervan, 2002.	Minor	Major for Learning Experience I and II	Major: 1

Learning Activities:

	Learning Experiences in Class	
Theme		Learning Outcome
Opening Devotional of Psalms of Ascent each week		Major: 2, minor: 1, 3
Week #1: Orientation to Course		Major: 2
Week #2: Psalms in Biblical community and theology		Major in these classroom experiences is to facilitate acquisition of 1, but through passionate presentation, adequate discussion, and small group work to see 2 and 3 facilitated.
Week #3: Orientation Psalms		
Week #4: Orientation Psalms		
Week #5: Disorientation Psalms: Stage 1		
Week #6: Disorientation Psalms: Stage 1		
Week #7: Disorientation Psalms: Stage 1		
Week #8: Disorientation Psalms: Stage 2		
Week #9: Disorientation Psalms: Stage 2		
Week #10: Reorientation Psalms		
Week #11: Special Lecture		
Week #12: Psalms as Theological Witness		Major: 1f, g
Week #13: Worship Class		Major: 2

Learning Experiences outside of Class		
Activity	Particulars/Value	Learning Outcome
I. Interpreting the psalms	Goal: *The goal of these learning experiences is to use the principles for interpreting Hebrew Psalms to interpret a psalm.*	
A. Phase One: Initial Interpretation 1. Begin by reading the guide for interpreting psalms which will be made available in class with an example from Psalm 11. 2. Read Futato (2007) on interpreting the Psalms as a reference to fill out the interpretive steps covered in the guide above. 3. Take one psalm (approved by professor) you have not studied in depth before and practice the steps for interpretation on this psalm. After reading the psalm in 3 translations (or translating the psalm yourself, if you have taken Hebrew, which is not expected for this course), practice interpretation on the psalm without reference to secondary literature (that is, commentaries, etc.). As you encounter things in the psalm that you do not understand or cannot resolve without reference to secondary literature, write down a question that you will be able to follow up later. Understandably this is an initial draft of your work, so do not be afraid if you have not resolved issues yet. Try to encounter the text for yourself using the steps I have given you and Futato's guidance as well. 4. This will be exchanged by email with your partner from class and the professor to discuss and evaluate.	Due Date: 20 January @ 11:59 pm. Value: 5% Medium: send in digital format (.pdf) to one other student and professor via email	Major: 3 Minor: 1, 2
B. Phase Two: Peer Review Take another student's initial interpretation and write up a basic review for them. Provide evaluation that both affirms areas of strength (25%) and areas for improvement (75%) in the initial draft which has been posted. Email this review to this student and the professor.	Due Date: 27 January @ 11:59 pm. Value: 5% Medium: send in digital format (.pdf) to one other student and professor via email	
C. Phase Three: Research Paper After receiving feedback on Phase One, you will return to this passage and consult a minimum of 10 secondary sources beyond the textbooks for the class (especially you should use commentaries). These secondary sources must include both books and articles, must reflect recent research (after 1950, and best after 1980), and must be elongated treatments of your biblical text, period, or book. This requirement does not include ancient sources used (Josephus, Qumran) or Bibles, Versions, Study Bibles, Bible Dictionaries (or other reference works). Internet resources are usually not acceptable and must be approved by the professor (unless through the ATLA resources at McMaster). Go through this material and revise your initial raw research. Finally, drawing from this depth of research you have done on this psalm, create a minimum 10 page research paper which reflects your research and follows the outline below (the percentages are the amount of your paper which should be devoted to each point): Cover page (note how much of Futato 2007 you have read) Introduction (2.5%) 1. Basic theme and overall flow of the Psalm (10%)	Value: 40% Due Date: 10 February @ 11:59 p.m. Medium: send in digital format (.pdf preferred) to professor via email	

2. How rhetoric (imagery and structure) set within history and culture point to the basic theme (50%). Allow the structure of the passage to structure your discussion which is an integrated piece. 3. How this relates to the theology and structure of the Psalter (10%) 4. How this relates to the rest of the canon (15%) 5. Application (10%) Conclusion (2.5%)		
II. Integrating the psalms		
	Goal: The goal of these learning experiences is to display the impact of our study of Hebrew worship in the Psalter on contemporary worship and faith.	

A. Phase One: The *first step* in this learning experience (no matter which one you choose) involves participating in the class learning experiences on the cycle of worship, reading Brueggemann (1995) and reading the entire Psalter (before reading the Psalter make sure you have read the guide for the Phase Two track you choose, you may have something you need to note as you read through these psalms). On the cover page of your assignment please note how much of Brueggemann (1995) and the Psalter you have read.
B. Phase Two: The *second step* in this learning experience is to choose ONE of the learning experiences within ONE of the tracks below (if you have another creative idea please feel free to suggest it):
  1. Shepherding Track
  2. Worship Arts Track
  3. Worship Leadership Track
  4. Research Track
	Value for Project: 40%
	Due Date: 31 March @ 11:59 p.m.
	Medium: send in digital format (.pdf preferred) to professor via email, for visual materials send photographs or video (or link to online access, e.g., www.youtube.com).
		Major: 3
		Minor: 1, 2

C. Phase Three: The *third step* in this learning experience is to share your project with the rest of the class at our closing worship class.	Value for Presentation: 10% Due Date: 8 April	

APPENDIX C: GRADING RUBRIC: CRITERIA FOR GRADING OF WRITTEN ASSIGNMENTS

Grade Range	Content	Argument	Presentation
90–100 A+ 85–89 A 80–84 A-	Mastery of subject matter; creativity and individualized integration of insights and their relationships; exceeds required elements	Clear, logical structure; with comprehensive introduction, persuasive argumentation, and innovative conclusions	Detailed adherence to relevant style for formatting of text, notes, and bibliography; no errors of grammar or syntax; elegant presentation
77–79 B+ 73–76 B 70–72 B-	Above-average grasp of principles and concepts, and their inter-relationship; completion of all required elements	Coherent structure and consistent argumentation; well-stated introduction and conclusion	General adherence to relevant style and format; few errors of grammar or syntax
67–69 C+ 63–66 C 60–62 C-	Adequate understanding of theoretical foundations; minimal completion of required elements	Rudimentary structure; minimal introductory and concluding statements	Significant errors of grammar, syntax, or style
57–59 D+ 53–56 D 50–52 D-	Low level of comprehension; required elements incomplete or missing	Lack of coherence or structure in argumentation; no introduction or conclusion	Abundant grammatical, syntactical, and stylistic errors
0–49 F	Inability to grasp basic concepts; required elements missing	Incomprehensible or illogical structure and argumentation	Failure to follow stylistic guidelines; incomprehensible syntax
Comments			

Students may be graded and given comments in each category (Content, Argument, Presentation) with a formula for calculating an overall grade for the assignment.

BIBLIOGRAPHY

Dunn, R., and K. Dunn. *Teaching Students through Their Individual Learning Styles: A Practical Approach.* Reston, VA: Reston, 1978.

Dunn, R., K. Dunn, and G. E. Price. *Learning Style Inventory.* Lawrence, KS: Price Systems, 1984.

Fleming, Neil D. *Teaching and Learning Styles: VARK Strategies.* Christchurch, New Zealand: Neil D. Fleming, 2001.

Fleming, Neil D., and C. Mills. "Not Another Inventory, Rather a Catalyst for Reflection." *To Improve the Academy* 11 (1992) 137.

Fleming, Neil D., and D. Baume. "Learning Styles Again: VARKing up the Right Tree!" *Educational Developments, SEDA Ltd* 7.4 (November 2006) 4–7. Online: http://www.vark-learn.com/documents/Educational%20Developments.pdf.

Grasha, Anthony. *Teaching with Style.* Pittsburg, PA: Alliance, 1996.

Hawk, Thomas F., and Amit J. Shah. "Using Learning Style Instruments to Enhance Student Learning." *Decision Sciences Journal of Innovative Education* 5.1 (2007) 1–19.

McKeachie, Wilbert J. *Teaching Tips: A Guidebook for the Beginning College Teacher.* 8th edn. Lexington, MA: Heath, 1986.

Whiteley, Sean. *Memletics: Accelerated Learning Manual* (Summary Version). Melbourne: Advanogy.com, 2003.

4

Developing a Syllabus

Cynthia Long Westfall

INTRODUCTION

Every graduate student who aspires to be a professor should recognize the importance of developing syllabi in the various areas of their field as they take courses and prepare for their career. It is helpful for a PhD candidate to create a repertoire of syllabi in order to be in a position to take advantage of opportunities to teach as they arise. As in preaching, you want to be prepared to teach "in season and out of season" or when it is convenient and when it isn't convenient (2 Tim 4:2). You may have an opportunity to apply to teach a course as an adjunct or be a candidate for a position that comes open unexpectedly right when a major paper is due. Ultimately, the applicant who submits a good syllabus will most likely be the one who gets the job. I know of a case where there was an opening for a PhD student to teach an elective for a professional graduate course. Three students were interested, but only one was able to submit a syllabus by the deadline for application. That student got the job, the experience, and the CV advantage from having taught a graduate course before that student was even ABD (all but dissertation).

The preparation of a syllabus involves a complex process. It includes a variety of potential formats, different types of courses, and various formal features including the header, the course description, course objectives, various types of requirements including the types of assignments, textbooks, classroom policies, the course schedule, and possibly a bibliography. If you put the effort into designing your syllabus well, you will have planned your course and will have the basic structure in place to have a successful semester and a good experience upon which you can build your career.

FORMATTING A SYLLABUS

There are innumerable styles for formatting a syllabus. Therefore, it is helpful to collect various types of syllabi that you find useful and attractive. There are three primary sources where you might find syllabi for your collection: syllabi from courses that you have taken in your undergraduate and graduate study, syllabi that you may find online from a variety of schools, and syllabi from the academic institutions at which you want to teach.[1] Maintain a file of e-copies of the syllabi so that you can easily generate variations on basic designs, and you can get ideas for features and graphics to improve your design.

When you apply to teach a course, the most important source for the format of a specific syllabus is the school that is offering the course. In a sense, you are determining how to package your syllabus to show that the school will be pleased with you and the course that you want to teach. Furthermore, each school has a mission and a curriculum that the courses should reflect—exegete the school's mission and other descriptions of the school to understand what is distinctive about the school and essential to the approach and content of the courses offered. Collect a representative sample of the school's syllabi (they may be available online), and attempt to obtain course syllabi from past years or syllabi from similar courses—the academic dean may be able to supply you with syllabi that are good models for that school. If there is a consistency in the styles of the syllabi or of the department in which you plan to teach, then a good syllabus will probably need to reflect the culture of that school in appearance. Eventually, you might have a signature syllabus that you are comfortable with, but it is always advisable to be aware of the formats and the culture at a new school, and be ready to adopt the school logo.

---

1. An online gateway for resources on developing syllabi can be found at http://coe.nau.edu/part_time_fr/SYLLABUS_DEVELOPMENT.htm. You may find examples of syllabi for McMaster Divinity College online at www.mcmasterdivinity.ca/programs/course-syllabi. See also SBL Educational Resources for examples of syllabi in biblical studies: http://www.sbl-site.org/educational/Syllabii.aspx.

DEVELOPING DIFFERENT TYPES OF COURSES

When we think of developing a syllabus, it may be that we assume we should design traditional courses that meet once, twice, or three times a week stretched over a term or semester in the Fall or Winter. An outline for a traditional course still requires planning and adjustment, because the topics that you want to offer may be different in number, depending on how many times you will meet as a class during the semester or term.

However, you may have more success in finding your first teaching job if you design some syllabi for non-traditional types of courses. For various reasons, many colleges, seminaries, and graduate programs are offering modular courses and online courses, and they are often looking for adjunct faculty to teach those courses. Modular courses are more intense than those in the traditional system, and are often offered as summer courses, but they are also offered during semester breaks, consecutive weekends, or as the default course system. A college course may be offered, for example, from 9 a.m. to 4 p.m. twice a week for four weeks. Because of their intensive nature, modular courses tend to require a variety of teaching methods besides the tradition lecture method. Few teachers wish to lecture from 9 a.m. to 4 p.m., and it is not advisable from the standpoint of an optimal learning experience. A modular course requires careful integration and alternation of different teaching methodologies that could have the added advantage of appealing to an increased number of learning styles.

Young and relatively inexperienced PhD students may have the advantage in designing syllabi for online courses. Online courses are the cutting edge of pedagogy at the university and graduate level. Younger teachers may be able to develop and market their computer literacy, a quality that may be lacking in the more experienced professors who have tenure or a great deal of teaching experience.[2] Online courses feature a number of different approaches to learning and require the greatest adaption of material from traditional or modular courses. It would be beneficial to gain experience and expertise in utilizing software that manages e-learning, such as Blackboard, as well as free course management systems that are on the web.

---

2. Online expertise may also enrich conventional courses in a variety of ways. For example, see the following article from *The Chronicle* on creating a syllabus with a spreadsheet and Calendar App: http://chronicle.com/blogPost/Create-Your-Syllabus-With-a/24416/?sid=wc&utm_source=wc&utm_medium=en.

FORMAL FEATURES IN A SYLLABUS

The outline of your syllabus will include some typical formal features. Again, the best approach in the beginning of your career is to consult the typical outline in the syllabi at your institution for the contents and the order. However, most syllabi will contain the following characteristic features:

1. Header
2. Course description
3. Course objectives
4. Course requirements
5. Required textbooks
6. Classroom policies
7. Course schedule
8. Bibliography

The order of the features may vary and some of the features may be optional. However, there is a logic to this order that may assist you in your first day of class when you introduce your students to your course.

Syllabus Header

Formal features that will be useful in your header will be found in the samples of the syllabi from a given school. Besides gleaning the format and suitable graphics (such as the school logo) from a school's syllabi, the school catalogue is an important resource for your syllabus for designing a header, and also for other aspects of your syllabus. Make sure that the information in your syllabus is consistent with the catalogue information and properly reflects the school's curriculum. Besides basic information such as the course number, title, and description, you will want to determine important details from the catalogue such as whether your course would be a core course for the school's degrees or an elective. Core courses may require curriculum-specific objectives and assignments while electives can be more flexible and creative. Be ready to pay attention to the school's terminology and labels in the catalogue that pertain to your course, starting with the header.

Course Description

Another place that you should plan to utilize the school's catalogue is for the course description, which is often the first paragraph in your syllabus. The description in the catalogue will be linked to the school's mission and curriculum. If the syllabus is for a core course, you will want to follow the description and wording in the course carefully, and any specific information given about the content of the course will guide you in making necessary adjustments in the subsequent objectives, assignments, and topics of the course.

If the syllabus is designed for an elective, you will have more freedom in developing your course description. Design an attractive personalized description for your course that summarizes main themes, objectives, and emphases in your course. Work at combining a description that reflects the school and you as an instructor.

Course Objectives

Forming course objectives is covered in another chapter of this book. In summary, the ideal course objectives in your syllabus should be specific, student-centered, and measurable. The McMaster Divinity College paradigm for course objectives of knowing, being, and doing will be helpful in forming course objectives for any school—they are a helpful development and organizing tool that assists in specifying a more educationally constructive range of goals. This is particularly true for courses at seminaries that are training men and women for professional ministry—the objectives should communicate relevance for the outcomes of not only the course, but the degree. When formulating your objectives, make sure that they correlate with the assignments, course content, and reading, so that it is clear that the components of the course are designed to fulfill the objectives. The final composition of your syllabus allows you to think critically about how these components fit together and places you in a position to make adjustments.

Course Requirements

PhD students and recent graduates need to pay particular attention to designing course requirements that are appropriate to the education level, and the specific school, where the course is being offered. PhD students and first-time professors are notorious for having unrealistic course requirements. This is usually because: (1) they are used to the workload of a PhD course and have not adjusted their expectations; (2) they are overoptimistic about how much they and their students can accomplish in one semester; and/or (3) they received their education from institutions that were more demanding in their course requirements than the professors tend to be at the school at which they are teaching. If you are offering an elective course, overestimating the work load could be the kiss of death for the survival of your course.

Some schools and seminaries pride themselves on being "more academic"—they expect a student to spend a higher number of hours on the course: they expect a large minimum number of pages read per week for a course, and typically want a comparatively larger number of research papers with high expectations for research and documentation. Other schools reflect different expectations, and offering a "more academic" course will frustrate both the professor and the students. Therefore, it is important to determine the school's suggestion for the appropriate workload for your course, including how many total hours the average student should spend on the course, how many pages of reading a week would be appropriate, and what variety of assignments is commonly given.

It is advisable to consult with the academic dean as well as to study the syllabi of courses that have been offered. Recognize that there may be a difference between what the academic dean suggests and what is actually being done in the classroom at a given school, because the academic dean may be trying to raise or relax the standards, so that he or she may be attempting to set a new level in your discussion. A careful approach to your course requirements will be important in creating the maximal classroom experience, and you will want to have the appropriate tension in your workload.

When designing the requirements, determine the variety of assignments and activities that you will require and clarify the basis of your evaluation in regards to the assignments and activities. Requirements for a course may include the following:

1. Participation/discussions
2. Reading
3. Papers
4. Projects
5. Tests and exams

Specify the requirements for the course, and give necessary and helpful detail such as additional details concerning the assignment, page requirements, any style guide used, and the due dates (perhaps in bold). Additional material on assignments, such as criteria for grading or check lists, may be included in appendices. Be sure to include late policies and penalties.

Assign percentage values to each course requirement (some requirements may be given 0%, such as participation and discussion). Provide a grading summary, making sure the percentage values add up to 100%.

Textbooks and Supplementary Reading

List the textbooks required for the course, and any recommended reading. Make sure that the text is appropriate for the level of the course in terms of content and length. Some schools are urging professors to give careful consideration to the price of the text, in order to reduce the student's expenses.

Determine if there will be supplementary reading and whether the research requirements of the course will strain the library's resources. Plan at this time to place necessary materials on reading reserve in the school library so that your students may have access to the materials they need to succeed in your course.

You may wish to require textbook reading and/or supplementary reading for each course session, or even in advance of the course or after the course has finished meeting in the case of modular courses. You may place the reading schedule with the daily course schedule, marking any required reading that comes before or after the course.

Classroom Policies

You may wish to include a section on classroom behavior that reflects your personal requirements and the requirements and culture of the school. You could cover issues ranging from attendance and excused absences to cell phone use and eating in class. You may wish to ask the students to give consideration and respect to views that differ from their own. It may be advisable to require gender inclusive language in all discussions and coursework.

You can use this section to set the tone for your course and it may provide the basis for certain judgment calls that you may feel compelled to make in the evaluation of a given student. This section may reflect some of the "being" objectives for a seminary student, and give some definite criteria that are not covered in the other areas. It is impossible to anticipate every issue that could arise in your course, but this section allows you to set some guidelines for how students interact with each other and you.

Daily Schedule

Your course schedule is an essential tool not only to inform the students but also to assist you in your lesson plans. Obtain the school's academic calendar as well so you will be equipped to plan your schedule around any special dates or school events. Be sure you account for holidays, other special dates such as reading weeks, and have the correct beginning day and ending day of the class.

On your course schedule, you may want to include:

1. Topics for each class
2. Reading due for each class
3. Assignments with their due dates
4. Tests

There are different formats by which you can organize this material, and you may pick up ideas from various syllabi.

As a new teacher, you will have to make a profound decision as you conduct your course. You will always have more to say on any topic than you are able to cover in the time that you have planned in your course schedule. From the first week, you will need to decide whether you will stick with your timetable and skim over some important aspects in each session, or whether you will take the time to cover what you consider to be important and allow yourself to fall progressively farther and farther behind in your plan. As a professor, I have done it both ways, and I far prefer making a careful plan in the beginning and following it. Sometimes I know that one topic will spill into the next session, but I plan to "catch up" so that each topic gets time and attention. I have decided, for example, that I do not want to teach a survey course in New Testament that fails to cover Hebrews, the General Epistles, and Revelation.

Bibliography

Many professors opt to offer a bibliography for their course, though in European education, that is considered to be the student's responsibility. If you choose to offer a bibliography, you will usually be able to build your bibliography on bibliographies in syllabi that you have collected and key texts in your subject. Be sensitive to the dates when the bibliographies were composed so that you may update them with newer works on your topic. You may update your bibliographies with abstracts and even searches in your library catalogues and Amazon. You may indicate books important to certain research topics that students will be asked to write about.

CONCLUSION

While you are a PhD student, developing a repertoire of syllabi that reflect your grasp of your field as a generalist and a specialist is highly advisable. At the end of each course you take as a student, you could make a habit of preparing a syllabus to teach that topic at the college and/or graduate level. However, recognize that you will eventually want to customize your syllabi for the specific schools at which you wish to teach. When it comes time to apply to teach an adjunct course or to apply for a position, your syllabus will be an indicator as to whether you "fit" into the culture of the school. You should demonstrate that your syllabi and your course reflect the school's curriculum and further the school's mission. If the school places the syllabi online before registration, your syllabus may also be essential in "marketing" your course to the student body and drawing new students to the school.

EXAMPLE OF A SYLLABUS

The following syllabus is designed to teach a course in the introduction to the New Testament at the masters level for professional ministry students at McMaster Divinity College, a seminary located in Hamilton, Ontario, Canada. The syllabus "borrows" certain formatting from courses taken and taught at Denver Seminary in Denver, Colorado, but reflects the culture of McMaster Divinity College, particularly in the header labels and terminology, the name of the course, the description, and the objectives as well as the classroom policies.

McMaster Divinity College
NT1A03: New Testament Literature and History
Cynthia Long Westfall, PhD
Phone: Ext. xxx
Email: xxx@xxx.xx
Fall 2010 (Term 1)
Wednesdays 8:30—10:20 a.m.

Course Description

An introduction to the basic features of New Testament study. This involves acquaintance with the background, nature, and content of New Testament documents; the concept of historicity; and an introduction to the central issues in contemporary New Testament scholarship.

Course Objectives

Through reading, lectures, discussion, and assignments, the following goals are set for the student:

A. KNOWING: Grasp the content of the New Testament as a whole within its first-century context and in terms of its component parts, including its growth and development, major themes, and genres.

B. BEING: The formation of the identity of the ministry and the minister by the study of, meditation on, and imaginative participation in the literature of the New Testament.

C. DOING: Apply the text to personal discipleship, and community and ministry formation, and consider strategies for its re-presentation in contemporary contexts.

Course Requirements

A. CLASS PARTICIPATION: Student participation in interactive lectures and class and group discussions is expected, based on your readings for the week.

B. READING: (10%)
See the Daily Schedule at the end for the precise dates and pages.
1. Read the pages for the required reading prior to class on the due dates, omitting the Exegetical skills and special articles—these are excellent resources but not required (see Daily Schedule at the end). Be prepared to interact with the main issues in group discussions. During class time, reading groups will compose peer evaluation for each individual in the group.
2. Reading the entire New Testament and the course text will comprise 10% of your grade, however only a maximum of 85% (value of an A) for 100% of the reading will be possible.
3. At the time of the final (*December 16*), each student will submit a reading report, stating a percentage of the reading completed on time.

C. RESEARCH AND PROJECT ON THE HISTORICAL JESUS (30%)
   a. Each student will write a paper on the historical Jesus. You may choose any topic on the historical Jesus to research in order to design a project for a ministry context. It is due *October 27, 8:30 a.m.* in electronic form. Late papers lose 2% each day.
   b. Length and style: The research section should be no more than 1,500 words (about 6 pages) of text, excluding footnotes and bibliography. For all matters of style and form, see the McMaster Divinity College Style Guidelines for Essays and Theses: www.mcmasterdivinity.ca/sites/default/files/documents/MDCStyleGuideMarch0413.pdf
   Consult at least 6 academic sources (not including the course text).
   c. Project: Based on your research, briefly outline (1 pg.) a study or presentation that you can use in your ministry. This is your opportunity to show how the study of the Bible informs your philosophy and practice

of your ministry—whether counseling, youth, pastoral, cross-cultural, academic, etc.

d. Recommended: Research the presentation of the historical Jesus in *The DaVinci Code* by Dan Brown (reading the entire novel would not be a requirement). Approach: The paper would consist of an examination of the book's representation of the historical Jesus, particularly in terms of the sources utilized and the interpretation of the sources. Be sure that you consult the primary Gnostic sources (Gospel of Mary, Gospel of Thomas available online). Utilize the continued interest in the *DaVinci Code* in ministry.

e. See attachment for criteria for grading.

Optional: Attend the optional *Workshop on research and writing a paper*, Wednesday, Sept 22, 12:30—1:20 p.m.

D. RESEARCH PAPER (30%)

a. Each student will write a research paper. *It will be due November 24, 8:30 a.m.* in electronic form. Late papers lose 2% each day.

b. Length and style: It should approximately 3000 words (about 12 pages) of text, excluding footnotes and bibliography. For all matters of style and form, consult the McMaster Divinity College Style Guidelines for Essays and Theses: www.mcmasterdivinity.ca/sites/default/files/documents/MDCStyleGuideMarch0413.pdf. There should be a minimum of 15 sources used in the footnotes and bibliography.

c. Approach: Choose a topic in New Testament studies from the list below or in consultation with the professor (however, do not overlap material with your paper on the historical Jesus):

- Some aspect of New Testament era (Roman, Greek, Jewish) culture or customs (e.g. marriage, slavery, Roman law, dress)
- Josephus, the Jewish historian
- Formation of the NT Canon (but consult with the professor first before proceeding)
- Pseudonymity and the New Testament Writings
- Synoptic Problem and Source Criticism
- Textual Criticism
- Parables and Preaching of Jesus
- Meaning of the Kingdom of God in the Gospels

- The Formation and Care of Congregations in Acts or Paul
- The Delay of the Parousia in Paul or the General Epistles
- Typology and Symbolism
- Structure of a New Testament book
- Exegesis of a New Testament problem passage

d. See attachment for criteria for grading

E. FINAL EXAMINATION (30%)

a. The examination is scheduled for *December 16* during class time. The main purpose of the final examination is to help the students master basic knowledge of the Bible, identify major themes, and see the big picture.

b. The final will consist of 105 points:

Short essays (40), short answer and objective questions (60), and the books of Bible (5)

c. See below for people and places that you will be expected to know for the final.

1. You will be asked to identify certain people by filling in the blanks
2. You will be asked to identify certain places on a map
3. You will be asked to identify the book and chapter of key passages
4. You will be asked to list the New Testament books in order

F. GRADING SUMMARY

1. Reading 10% (value of 85% maximum)
2. Research and Project 30%
3. Research Paper 30%
4. Final exam 30%

All assignments must be handed in to avoid failing the course, and must be completed by the time of the final.

Textbooks and Materials

A. Required

1. deSilva, David A. *An Introduction to the New Testament: Contexts, Methods and Ministry Formation.* Downers Grove, IL: InterVarsity, 2004.
2. The New Testament (modern version such as NRSV or TNIV)
3. The Greek New Testament (for those with Greek competence). Students with facility in Greek or who are beginning Greek are encouraged to use their Greek Bible.

B. Recommended

1. The *IVP Bible Dictionary Series* (4 vols.)
2. Keener, Craig. *IVP Bible Background Commentary: New Testament.* Downers Grove, IL: InterVarsity, 1994.
3. Access to good maps online or a Bible Atlas including first-century Palestine and Jerusalem and the three missionary journeys of Paul.

C. Textbook Purchase

All required textbooks for this class are available from the College's book store.

D. Additional Materials

1. Handouts for lectures and class discussion will be made available during class and/or online at the instructor course link. Further information will be provided in class.
2. Procedures and guidelines for assignments will be given in class and/or online.
3. Optional Workshop: Writing a research paper, September 22, 12:30—1:30.

Classroom Behavior

A. Attendance

1. Students should be on time to class or be prepared to offer an explanation to the professor.

2. Students are expected to stay for the entire class session, unless arranged in advance.

3. Except in extreme circumstances, more than two absences from class will result in grade penalties; four or more absences from class will result in failure of the course.

B. Participation

1. Please respect the opinions of others without disrespect or ridicule, even if you do not agree with them. However, feel free to respond logically and critically in an orderly manner.

2. Students are not expected to be doing work on any other subject except that which is appropriate in the course outline.

3. Students are not to carry on off-topic conversations in class.

4. Students may eat or drink in class if they do not distract others and they clean up their desks.

Students who fail to respect these guidelines will be dismissed from the class with consequences.

C. Academic Honesty

Academic dishonesty is a serious offence that may take any number of forms, including plagiarism, the submission of work that is not one's own or for which previous credit has been obtained, and/or unauthorized collaboration with other students. Academic dishonesty can result in severe consequences, e.g., failure of the assignment, failure of the course, a notation on one's academic transcript, and/or suspension or expulsion from the College.

Students are responsible for understanding what constitutes academic dishonesty. Please refer to the Divinity College Statement on Academic Honesty: www.mcmasterdivinity.ca/programs/rules-regulations.

D. Gender Inclusive Language

McMaster Divinity College uses inclusive language for human beings in worship services, student written materials, and all of its publications. In reference to biblical texts, the integrity of the original expressions and the names of God should be respected. The NRSV and TNIV are examples of the use of inclusive language for human beings. It is expected that inclusive language will be used in chapel services and all McMaster Divinity College assignments.

Disclaimer on Syllabi posted on the web and at the bottom of each syllabus:

Please Note: This syllabus is the property of the instructor and is prepared with currently available information. The instructor reserves the right to make changes and revisions up to and including the first day of class.

Appointments

Contact me via email if I can assist you in any way.
Office hours: TBA
Also available by appointment.

NT1A03 Daily Schedule

Date	Class Session Topic	Reading in deSilva due	Reading in New Testament and other reading due
Sept 15	Introduction to course and the study of the NT		
Sept 22	Context of the Gospels *Workshop on research and writing a paper 12:30—1:20*	pp. 37–143	
Sept 29	The 4 Gospels and the Historical Jesus Critical methods for the study of the Gospels	pp. 145–93	MaClean's Magazine, March 31, 2008, pp. 38ff
Oct 6	Narrative, Mark and Matthew	pp. 194–297	Mark, Matthew
Oct 13	Synoptic Issues, Luke-Acts	pp. 298–390	Luke-Acts
Oct 20	John	pp. 391–448	John
Oct 27	The Pauline mission begins Genre of letter/epistle Introduction to Paul Issues emerge *Historical Jesus project due 8:30 a.m.*	pp. 475–554	Galatians and James 1 and 2 Thessalonians
Nov 3	Pauline controversy and issues clarified	pp. 555–639	1 and 2 Corinthians Romans

Nov 10	The Pauline mission operated from prison	pp. 640–732	Philippians Colossians and Ephesians Philemon
Nov 17	Research and Review day		
Nov 24	The torch passes from Paul	pp. 733–75	1 and 2 Timothy, Titus
Dec 1	*Research paper due at 8:30 a.m.* The early church in crisis	pp. 776–884	Hebrews. James 1 & 2 Peter & Jude
Dec 8	Ultimate perspectives on early church problems	pp. 449–74 pp. 885–931	1, 2, 3 John Revelation
Dec 16	*Final Examination Submit reading report*		

People, Places, and Passages to Know/Locate for the Final

People: Ananias (1); Ananias (2); Anna; Annas; Apollos; Aquila; Barabbas; Barnabas; Caiaphas; Cornelius; Elizabeth; Eutychus; Felix; Festus; Gallio; Gamaliel; Herodias; Jairus; Junia; John Mark; Joseph of Arimathea; Judas Iscariot; Lazarus; Levi; Lydia; Martha; Mary Magdalene; Mary of Bethany; Nathanael; Nicodemus; Philip; Priscilla; Salome; Sapphira; Silas; Simeon; Simon Magus; Simon of Cyrene; Simon the leper; Simon the Pharisee; Stephen; Theophilus; Timothy; Titus; Zaccheus; Zebedee.

Places: Antioch (of Syria); Antioch (of Pisidia); Asia (minor); Athens; Capernaum; Bethlehem; Bethany; Caesarea (Maritima); Colossae; Corinth; Crete; Cyprus; Damascus; Dead Sea; Decapolis; Emmaus; Ephesus; Galatia; Galilee; Italy; Jericho; Jerusalem; Jordan River; Judea; Macedonia; Mediterranean Sea; Nazareth; Perea; Philippi; Rome; Samaria; Sea of Galilee (Genessaret); Syria; Tarsus; Thessalonica; Troas; Tyre.

Key Passages: Matthew 1:18—2:23; Matthew 5–7; Matthew 13; Matthew 16:13–20; Matthew 24–25; Mark 9:14–32; Mark 16:9–20; Luke 1–2; Luke 4:14–30; Luke 10; John 1:1–18; John 3; John 11; John 13; John 14–16 (general content); Acts 2; Acts 9; Acts 15; Romans 1:16–17, 18–32; Romans 5:12–20; Romans 8; 1 Corinthians 7; 1 Corinthians 12–14 (esp. chap 13); 1 Corinthians 15; 2 Corinthians 4:7–12; 2 Corinthians 12:1–10; Galatians 3:28; Galatians 5:22–26; Ephesians 5:15—6:9; Ephesians 6:1–10; Philippians 2:5–11; Philippians 4:4; Col 1:15–20; 1 Thessalonians 4:13–18; 1 Timothy 2:11–15; 1 Timothy 3:1–12; 2 Timothy 2:2; 2 Timothy 3:16; Hebrews 6:4–8; Hebrews 5–10; Hebrews 11; James 1:2–8; James 2:14–26;

1 Peter 4:12–19; 1 John 2:16; 1 John 3:11–15; Revelation 2–3; Revelation 17–18; Revelation 20.

Ten people and ten places and ten passages will be chosen for the exam. For character names and passages, the question will involve a one-phrase description and you will supply the correct name. For places, on blank maps of Israel (for the Gospels list) and the Roman Empire (for the Acts list) you will write in the names at the correct locations.

5

Sculpting a Lesson

The Art of Preparing a Classroom Learning Experience

LEE BEACH

INTRODUCTION

If you were to take a poll on the question, "What makes for a good classroom learning experience?" you would inevitably receive a broad range of answers. One person would say it is a great lecture from a knowledgeable professor, another might say a stimulating class discussion, others would say the opportunity to work with others in a small group, still others would say the inclusion of media such as movie clips or YouTube videos. How students answer that question would be influenced by a number of factors such as past experience, learning style, cultural background, and personal preferences. Likely if the question was explored more deeply, most students would agree that it is a combination of things that makes a classroom experience meaningful. Their answers would, of course, reflect the subjective nature of classroom learning and serve as a reminder that what students value in a learning experience varies greatly. However, while there are many variables in effective teaching, are there some things that can be considered foundational to the preparation and presentation of great lessons?

Ultimately the classroom should be a dynamic place where the possibility for genuine learning is created by the teacher each time students enter the class. This means the teacher must be someone who is engaged and working hard to present lessons that draw students into the act of personal and intellectual exploration. Those of us who are given the privilege of teaching have to believe that the classroom experience is a unique opportunity for students to engage in personal reflection that will lead to new knowledge, new possibilities for living, and ultimately personal transformation. The following diagram is adapted from a variety of models presented by educator David Kolb. While it is based on an experiential learning model it also holds true for traditional classroom learning as well.[1]

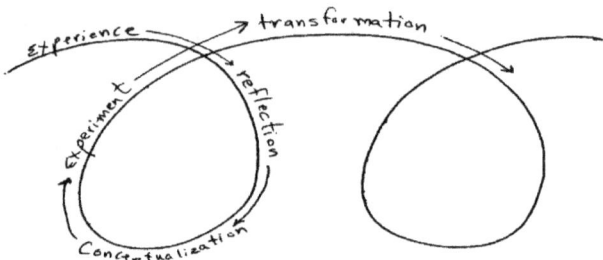

As teachers we seek to invite people into the experience of the classroom so that they can reflect on new information that will be presented in the hope that this will lead them into the acquisition of new ideas or concepts. These new concepts lead to suggestions of how they can be applied in practice, and thus students are encouraged to experiment with these ideas. As they do, new ways of understanding and living bring about genuine transformation, which then invites students back into the classroom to continue the process. This is the potential that the classroom holds and that we as teachers must prepare for every time we set foot into our classrooms.

While learning experiences are subjective, and the uniqueness of each student can never be ignored, there are some common components that go into developing meaningful learning experiences. In this chapter we will consider some of those key ingredients and how we can develop classroom lessons that stimulate learners in a way that leads to an optimal classroom experience.

---

1. See Kolb, *Experiential Learning*. This model is reflective of Kolb's ideas, but may also have the ideas of others wrapped up in it as well as I do not recall exactly how it has developed over the years.

PREPARATION

The highly regarded preacher and teacher of preaching, Haddon Robinson, makes this statement about preparing to preach: "Someone suffers every time you preach. Either you suffer in preparing it, or the listener suffers in hearing it."[2] The same can be said about teaching in the classroom. Great classroom experiences take preparation. My experience is that the better prepared I am the greater the chance that the class will have energy, direction, and a clear focus. When I am not as prepared the whole class suffers. It lacks clarity, the kind of content that engages the group, and the creativity that adds color to a lesson. The hard work of doing good preparation is a necessary part of good teaching and great classroom experiences. There are rarely any short-cuts or ways around this reality. With this in mind we must understand that preparation is a two-fold endeavor.

First, preparation for effective teaching begins with research and gathering material that will provide the basis for learning. No great classroom experience is exclusively the result of great techniques. The only way transformative learning happens is if the lesson offers students truly good content. All the engaging techniques you come up with and employ will not bring about great classes on a consistent basis. Ultimately great classes are about content, and great content is usually the result of preparation. This involves mining notes from our previous study or courses that we have taken, doing the necessary reading on the topic, and spending time reflecting and developing ideas that become the primary content that we are going to offer to our students in a given class. These are key ways that we develop our content for a lesson and it rarely comes without some major effort on our part. But when we invest the time and do the work to develop good content we are laying a strong foundation for a great learning experience for our students.

The second aspect of preparation is deciding how to deliver the lesson in an engaging way. This takes the same amount of thought and development as the content side of the equation, because the idea that we can just present our content in a straightforward, unvarnished way is quite misguided. As teachers we easily fall in love with our content and we assume that our students will too. On one hand this is not bad. When we research and discover great ideas that are worth sharing, it creates passion in us and this is a key part of great teaching and classroom experiences. However, it is not uncommon for us to become enamored with our ideas to the point

---

2. Haddon Robinson, as quoted in Johnston, *Preaching to a Postmodern World*, 172.

that we believe that all we have to do is share them verbatim from our notes and this will capture our class as deeply as we have been captured by these thoughts. This leads us to believe that delivering the content will be easy, we just have to speak it out in a lecture and the students will fall under the spell of our deep thoughts. This is usually a big mistake. Don't make that mistake. Lesson planning is not simply putting your research into lecture notes, it is also deciding how to present your ideas in a creative and stimulating manner. How we do this can take many forms and will employ a variety of techniques, but it is an essential aspect of lesson planning that can take almost as much time as the developing of our content.

Both the research that develops content and the thinking that provides engaging methodology for delivery are necessary components of great classroom experiences. You will not succeed at cultivating great classes without working hard at both. At my wedding the minister who performed the ceremony (actually my father-in-law) spoke to my bride and me about the idea that great marriages don't just happen, they are created by two people who give themselves to the cause of developing a mutually fulfilling marriage relationship. Like great marriages, great classes don't just happen. They are created by teachers who give intentional effort, spending time in preparation to create the kind of classes that provide space for students to be transformed as a result of their learning.

DEVELOPING A MAIN IDEA

Every lesson needs a main idea or guiding theme, an overarching thought that defines what the point of the lesson really is. The wisdom of developing a main idea for every lesson can be summed up in the old adage, "If you don't know what you are trying to say there is a good chance those listening to you won't know either." Main ideas help us to be clear about what we are talking about so that those we are talking to will also know what we are talking about. A main idea organizes your lesson and gives it direction. When we can define our main idea clearly it produces clarity for us and our students.

As a youngster I had a good friend whose family owned a sailboat. I recall one day being with them on the boat when my friend's dad summoned me to the stern and told me that it was my turn to steer the boat. Up until this point, I had thought of my friend's father as a reasonable man. Now I was sure that my early impressions were misguided. Nonetheless he handed me control of the rudder and I was charged with the responsibility of guiding the ship toward our destination across the lake (luckily for other boaters it was a big lake). As the boat cut across the water empowered by a stiff wind I struggled to keep the boat on course; after a few minutes my friend's dad offered me a tip. He told me to pick a point on the horizon near the place that we were heading for. He told me to keep my eyes fixed on that point and on the tip of the ship's bow. As long as I kept those two points aligned I would know that I was on course. With this advice I was able to keep us on course (more or less) and help to guide us to our ultimate destination. The main idea of a lesson is like that point on the horizon. It is the destination of our lesson, and as we keep it in focus throughout the journey it will assure that our lesson delivers what we want it to for our students.

In preparing to teach a lesson, after we have done our initial research and we have a general sense of what it is that we want to teach, we need to start further developing our main idea. It is at this point that we begin to try to articulate the main theme of the lesson. A good main idea should be articulated in one or two sentences, and is clear enough to keep the lesson tight but also broad enough to accommodate the various aspects of it. For example a lesson on how to develop effective classroom lessons may employ a big idea such as this:

> The idea of this lesson is to help participants think about some key elements that go into a meaningful classroom learning experience so that their own future teaching will be affected by this input.

This statement of the big idea is broad enough to allow for a multi-faceted exploration, but clear enough to provide a general focus for an introductory lesson.

The development of a big idea for your lesson is not a science; there is not necessarily one specific way to do this. What is essential however is that your lesson has a clear idea that is guiding it, an idea that is clear enough to keep you focused on what it is that you are trying to communicate to your students.

WHAT ARE THE OBJECTIVES?

Objectives are an important corollary to the development of the main idea of the lesson. Objectives specify how and what you will teach in order to achieve your main idea. Further, objectives also identify desired outcomes of the lesson. That is, they help you to articulate what it is that you hope your students will take away from the lesson that you are about to teach them.

The objectives connected to the big idea expressed above for a lesson on how to develop effective classroom lessons may look something like this:

- Help the group think reflectively on their own experience in the classroom
- Identify and explain some of the key elements that go into a successful class lesson
- Give participants the opportunity to identify and articulate at least one key point of new (or renewed) learning.

These objectives provide clarity for the content that I would develop for the lesson. They provoke questions to ask and applications to offer. As these take shape early in the lesson planning they guide the ongoing preparation in a way that helps to bring overall cohesion and lucidity to the lesson. While it is beyond the scope of this chapter to deal comprehensively with the art of developing objectives for a lesson, William Yount offers an important perspective for this task: develop objectives from the student's point of view. How will this lesson affect their understanding of the subject and what impact will it make on their behavior?[3] In considering this important factor, McMaster Divinity College has adopted a three-pronged rubric for developing course objectives that can also be adapted for crafting specific lesson objectives. The rubric employs three categories to develop objectives under knowing, being, and doing.[4] Each of these categories is student-centered, as they call for course and/or lesson objectives to be shaped around what knowledge the student will acquire, how that will affect how they live, and how it will ultimately impact their professional practice. Making sure that our objectives are student-centered and outcome oriented will add to the effectiveness of our classroom teaching.

As your preparation evolves, objectives can be adjusted or further clarified as necessary; however, they are an essential element of good planning. I skip this step to my (and my students') detriment too many times. Identifying my objectives before I actually prepare my lesson always clarifies my approach and strengthens my overall presentation. It helps to keep me on track and focused on what really matters in the presentation of my material, and it also forces me to be clear about what I want my students to take away.

---

3. Yount, *Called to Teach*, 142–43.

4. This rubric comes from the Association of Theological Schools, who employ it as a standard for assessing curriculum effectiveness at member schools.

These two steps, developing a main idea and clear objectives for the lesson, are crucial steps in preparing to teach. While they can initially seem peripheral to the real task of gathering material and figuring out how to present it, in the long run they offer tremendous benefit to your teaching in the classroom and are well worth the time that you invest in them.

MAKING THE CLASSROOM A COMFORTABLE PLACE

A typical classroom, particularly in a postsecondary setting, can be an intimidating place for students, especially on the first day of class. Think about your own experiences. We can all remember entering a classroom for the first day of class hoping to see a familiar person to sit with, wondering what the teacher would be like, what the expectations would be, what the other students would be like, whether we would be able to succeed, and maybe fretting about who our competition would be! Many times the class would be almost silent as students filtered in and found a seat. Were you comfortable with that? I know I never was. Even as the semester unfolds, if a classroom has not developed some level of comfort there can be an underlying tension in the room every time the class meets together. This is hardly conducive to effective teaching. Tense, quiet classrooms make for tense, quiet lessons and that is why making the classroom a comfortable place for students is as much a part of sculpting an effective lesson as all the other elements are.

The central element in cultivating a comfortable classroom environment is hospitality. Offering hospitality to your students is not only an act of genuine academic friendship but will go a long way toward creating an atmosphere that is conducive to learning. It helps to decompress inevitable tensions that are a part of the academic environment and it establishes rapport between you and your students that you can build on as you seek to lead students in considering the material that you bring to them from class to class.

For some of us this is more of a challenge than for others, as some of us are more naturally relational than others. However, making the classroom a comfortable place does not depend fully on personality type. Even someone who tends toward being more introverted can do things that will be interpreted as an attempt at hospitality, which will immediately help to make the classroom a warmer, more personable place. In some ways it is helpful to think of our classrooms as our home where we are welcoming guests. What kinds of things do we do when guests come to our home?

Clearly we cannot duplicate all the things that we do in our home to welcome students in our classroom, but some of the basic things we do can certainly be practiced. First, we can show up early to class, ahead of most students, so that we are present when they arrive. This signals an interest in relationship and a desire to connect with the students relationally, at least on some basic level. As students come in we can greet them and welcome them to class and even tell them it is good to have them there. I often play music before class starts and also during the breaks in order to remove the uncomfortable silence that often prevails, especially early in a semester. I have found that the sound of music alone can make people more at ease and less awkward, especially if they do not have anyone to sit with or talk to. Prior to the first class I often send a short email to the class as a whole introducing myself, welcoming them, and inviting them to share with me some expectations that they have for learning from the class. This begins the professor/student relationship even before the first day of class. Of course, one can even go so far as to bring some food to class from time to time as a way of showing hospitality. One of my colleagues is known for her home baked cookies that make appearances in class several times a semester and tell the students that the professor wants to relate to them as people as well as students. Efforts like these help the classroom to soon feel less ominous to students and maybe even a bit more like a home to them. We can't guarantee a comfortable classroom but we can make efforts to try and bring it about. This is an issue of effective teaching and it raises the possibility that better learning will occur.

BRIDGING IN

Creating a welcoming context is important but it does not assure that when we are ready to start teaching students are ready to start learning. When students come to class they are coming from somewhere else and their minds may still be there too, or somewhere else completely. They may be occupied with an issue they discussed in their previous class, or with the boyfriend they just said goodbye to, or the spouse they had an argument with that morning, or the bills that need to get paid. While some, perhaps on a good day even most, of the students are fully present and ready to engage when you start class, one cannot assume that this is the case for all of your students. In fact, I think that it is better to assume that they all need a little help to get focused at the beginning of the lesson. This requires the building of a bridge from where they are to where you want to take them in the lesson that you have prepared.

Bridging in can be done in a variety of ways but usually involves two key things: the statement of the main idea of the lesson along with some or all of the objectives, and an engaging opening that helps to focus students' attention.

The best way to start a lesson is never with a dense, extended discourse on a difficult concept that you know is unfamiliar to the majority of your students. Of course you may have to do that at some point, but never start there. Think of the first five to ten minutes as a bridge from where your students are to where you want them to go. The questions that you have to answer are: "Where do I want them to go?" and "How can I get them oriented in that direction and on board for the trip?" Bridging in is an act of orienting students to the topic of the lesson by getting their attention and stimulating their interest. This can be done by presenting a case study and discussing it in order to identify the issues that are at stake; it could be by presenting a movie clip that contains the issue to be considered, or by raising a key question for discussion in small groups. It could be by taking a class poll to garner opinions on an issue that is relevant to the topic of the lesson. There are numerous ways to build a bridge from where students are to where you want them to be for the period of time that you are together as a class, but taking the time and making the effort to build this bridge and invite students to cross it is an important part of getting the lesson off to the right start as it raises key questions, creates a need to learn in the students, and captures their interest to proceed.

ASSESSING KNOWLEDGE

Connected to the step of bridging in, as it is usually a helpful early step in the lesson, is the act of assessing what students already know about the topic that you will be discussing as a class. This does several things to help make the lesson effective. First it helps us determine where students are in terms of the content that we have planned. In assessing their level of knowledge we may discover that they lack even a rudimentary knowledge of the topic, and it may cause us to add some basic introductory content in order to help orient the students more fully before proceeding. On the other hand it may reveal to us that the class already possesses much of the knowledge that we want to teach. This does not necessarily mean that we should not proceed with what we have planned, since knowledge of a subject almost always varies in a classroom of students, but it may mean that we will alter our approach in order to include more opportunities for students to discuss points and offer their own knowledge to the group. Second, inviting students to reflect on what they already know about a topic is an empowering approach to classroom learning. It says to students that you believe that they already have knowledge of this subject to offer to the class. This sends a message that you are not the only one who knows something about this, and it encourages learners to become engaged in sharing what they know and asking questions about areas of the topic that they may not know as much about. This act of assessing student knowledge before class discussion, not just as an evaluative tool at the end, is a highly empowering and helpful tool for developing a dynamic classroom where students believe they can contribute to the knowledge of their peers and receive from them as well. It immediately starts to level the classroom (at least as a start) and give students a place where they can share comfortably because they are sharing something that they know.

The main way, although certainly not the only way, we can begin to assess student knowledge is by asking questions. Usually it is best to begin with broad questions that allow for a variety of possible responses. From here the questions can be narrowed slightly in order to ascertain how deep the knowledge of the lesson's subject already goes in your class. As an example, I teach a course called "The Mission of the Church," and one of the early sections of that class involves teaching a biblical theology of the subject. Early in that first lesson I begin by asking, "Are there any themes, stories, or passages that you can think of in the Bible that may indicate to us that God is interested in reaching out to humanity?" This is a fairly broad question for a class of seminary students. I make the assumption that all of them could potentially offer one or two answers to this question if pressed. It always yields numerous responses, many of them quite predictable, but without exception some students offer answers that reflect significant prior engagement with the topic. Sometimes some students even offer ideas that I had not considered. I often follow this with a question about the place of mission in the Old Testament, as some people may not perceive that mission has any place in that part of the biblical story. This question generally generates less response, although some students do offer insight and reflection on it that helps me know where they are in terms of their knowledge of the subject. This then allows me to continue my lesson, which starts with a consideration of the place of mission in the Old Testament. As a result of these discussions I then refer back to answers that have been offered by the class, picking up on points that respondents made or questions that they raised, sometimes even asking them to comment further if it is appropriate.

This act of knowledge assessment gets people involved by giving them opportunities to share what they know and it helps the instructor to proceed with some sense of the level of knowledge that is already present in the class.

MAINTAINING MOMENTUM IN THE LESSON THROUGH THE USE OF DISCUSSION

Great novels and movies have a distinct rhythm to them. They begin with an interesting opening, they acquaint you with interesting characters, immediately start building tension, then move to a moment of dramatic significance that creates disequilibrium of some sort, there is something in the plot that needs to be resolved, then new information starts to come out that leads to new tension being built, then a significant event occurs within the story that leads to the tension being resolved and the story is concluded. While this description is a bit contrived, it is at least recognizable to many of us. It is a standard story-telling formula. In a certain sense, classroom lessons need to follow a similar rhythm. Interest can be generated.

A key component of this formula in the classroom setting is the use of discussion as a way of maintaining the student's attention and cultivating ongoing student engagement. While the dynamics of leading good classroom discussions are numerous let us consider at least some of the basic elements of leading discussions that enable dynamic learning experiences.

In most cases good interaction begins with knowledge assessment kinds of questions that invite people to share their own knowledge of a subject based upon a question that allows them to draw from a broad base of experience. This means that the best way to begin a class discussion is with a broad question (or several broad questions) that don't force students to share their own thoughts or opinions too personally. These are questions that are not hard for students to answer because the answers come out of their own experience. Their answers do not even have to reflect their personal opinion on the issue—they are simply a reflection on their experience. Sometimes the question can even be posed in a way that asks for input based on what the student has heard others say about a particular topic. This keeps the question even broader and less personal but still invites students to share what they know. Approaching a discussion like this can create a level of comfort, and allow everyone to participate if they want to because the answers are based on experiential knowledge—there are no right or wrong answers. It also gives you as a teacher an opportunity to get a sense of what the class already knows about the topic you are going to teach, which is helpful as you proceed with the lesson.

In "The Mission of the Church" course that I teach, I begin the first lesson by asking the question "What are the obstacles to sharing the gospel with people in our country today?" This is a very broad question; there are many possible answers and it is based on the students' own experience or on what they have read. It assesses their knowledge of the subject and invites many students to participate if they choose to.

From here discussions generate learning and insight when you ask students to answer questions that are more personal in nature in that they require some introspection, deeper reflection, and self-disclosure. It is worth noting that a master teacher like Jesus employed a similar method as recorded in the Gospel of Matthew. In Matt 16:13–16 we see Jesus engaging with his disciples over the crucial topic of who they think he is. Early in the discussion he begins with a broad question that invites the disciples to share their knowledge based upon their experience. "Who do people say the Son of Man is?" Jesus asks them. In response, the disciples give a number of answers that they have heard people offer: "John the Baptist, Elijah, Jeremiah, maybe one of the other prophets," they say. From here, Jesus asks a much more personal question that requires the disciples to reflect on what they really think. "What about you?" Jesus quizzes the twelve, "Who do you say I am?" This is the essence of leading a lively classroom discussion, moving from the general to the specific so that once students are brought into engagement with questions that are not too hard to answer they are further challenged to share much more personal opinions or ideas. At this point the potential for a deep exchange and the discovery of new knowledge is at hand.

Of course the ultimate goal in leading discussions is to get the students beyond simply responding to questions from the instructor and instead get them responding to each other. When the students start engaging with one another's answers and start looking at one another when they talk, you know that you have helped to create a genuine exchange of ideas that will bring a tremendous amount of momentum to the classroom.

How do we do that? In her book, *Improving Your Classroom Teaching*, Maryellen Weimer offers several helpful suggestions for setting the tone for good classroom discussions.[5]

Give students time to think. Often we are uncomfortable with the silent pauses that follow a question we pose to the class. Weimer reports that research done in the K–12 area shows that teachers, on average, wait less than five seconds for responses to their questions before moving on.[6] This does not always allow time for reflection on the question so that students can form a genuine response. Effective discussion can depend upon our ability to tolerate silence while our students consider the question and formulate a response. Silence does not necessarily mean disinterest, so be patient, don't panic, and give students time to offer their thoughts.

Be careful not to intimidate. It is sometimes hard to imagine ourselves as intimidating, but to students we sometimes are. If we, through non-verbal communication, tell our students that we are not satisfied with their answers or that we are not genuinely interested in their answers, it will be detrimental to the cultivation of class discussion. For good classroom discussion we must visibly, through verbal and non-verbal communication, value our students' participation. This means listening closely to responses, inviting further comment when warranted, asking for clarification when needed, being gracious when a student's comment is not that helpful, and thanking students for their input regularly. When we behave in this way as a teacher we create a safe atmosphere for students to participate in.

Handle wrong answers with sensitivity. Wrong or bad answers are inevitable when we open our class up to discussion. How we handle these answers is critical to maintaining a positive atmosphere for discussion. At the core of the issue is ability to address the answers and not the students themselves. That is, when a wrong or improper answer is given we must always take care to address the idea that is being shared not the student. This means thanking the student for their input and then engaging with what they said without indicting them for saying it. While this can be tricky, it is essential that we maintain a distinction in our responses to bad answers between the student and the answers.

---

5. Wiemer, *Improving Your Classroom Teaching*, 50–55.
6. Ibid., 50.

Get students talking to each other. When students start looking past you and begin to address one another directly, a genuine class discussion is taking place. There are moments when this happens naturally; unfortunately it is all too rare in most classroom settings. One way to make this happen is by inviting students to answer one another's questions or offer comments on a comment made by their classmate. If a student asks a provocative question, rather than answering it yourself invite the class to reflect on it together. If a student makes an interesting comment ask the class to reflect on the comment. This is a way to empower students and demonstrate to them that what they have to share has value to the class. Students will pick up on this and it will encourage them to engage in the discussions you try to create.

This creates momentum in the lesson as we begin to invite participation and discourse on the topic at hand. A discussion is often the best way to stimulate interest and make room for genuine participation in classroom learning that is truly mutual. When we help to facilitate the process of self-discovery or participative learning we help students feel like they have discovered the answer for themselves. This leads the student to a sense that he or she has come to a personal realization that makes the learning go deeper in a way that provides it with a greater sense of ownership. Again, in terms of momentum, when a discussion breaks out, classroom momentum is always high and this creates a wave for the rest of the class to ride upon.

The new information that you as the teacher have to present can best be introduced as contributing toward answers to questions raised in the discussion. Student interest is usually high when the information comes in this context.

ASSESSING LEARNING

The conclusion of the lesson should give students the opportunity to assess or apply what they have learned. Here some key questions may be in order. It may be appropriate to ask the class some questions that invite the student to consider how the lesson may impact them in the future. You may ask the question, "How is this going to affect your life and/or your ministry or work?" This question is a direct attempt to get students to consider the implications of the lesson on their lives and future vocation. Another key question may be, "What questions do you have?" This offers an opportunity for the students to assess what areas they may have for further exploration in the future. It is not always necessary or possible to answer all of the questions that are raised. The point is to help students assess their learning by articulating what they still do not fully understand. For some this will help them clarify future pursuits in a particular area. Another approach may be to invite the students to write a "one minute essay." Sometimes, at the end of class I distribute a 3x5 card and invite students to write one or two things that they will remember from today's lesson. This is an opportunity for them to assess and articulate what they have derived from the lesson and how it may apply to their lives as they go on from here.[7] After distributing the 3x5 cards I literally give the students one minute to write before I dismiss the class. This is a quick but concrete way to help students solidify what they have learned in class that day.

Giving students a chance to reflect on what they have learned is a key part of closing the loop and helping them to consider what new ideas they have gained and how they may apply them. Many times it is at this point of reflection that things come together and a new nugget of knowledge is genuinely discovered. It is also through this time of assessment that the possibility of knowledge retention is increased as students identify their specific points of learning after engaging with the content of a lesson. This part of the classroom experience is an important part of assuring the effectiveness of your overall approach to the lesson as a whole.

CONCLUSION

What makes for a good classroom learning experience? As we noted at the beginning of this chapter, it is usually a combination of things, but good preparation, a clear sense of your main idea, and some specific objectives are foundational. From here, making the classroom a comfortable place, offering a good introduction that bridges the students into the material, assessing the students' prior knowledge, and maintaining momentum through the use of discussion are also significant components. Finally guiding students in an assessment of their learning helps to make for a good classroom experience.

---

7. This learning tool was originally brought to my attention in a workshop entitled "Effective lesson planning for diverse learning styles and intelligences" presented by Dr. Lovaye Kajiura at McMaster University, 28 Oct. 2009.

Teaching effectively is an evolving skill that requires continuous adaptation, ongoing training, and a lot of trial and error. However, the things offered in this chapter are some of the foundational practices that will enable you to sculpt effective lessons on a consistent basis. Practicing them will help to assure that your students will never have to "suffer" through your teaching. In fact they will find themselves engaged and fulfilled as learners as they experience many satisfying learning experiences in your classroom.

BIBLIOGRAPHY

Johnston, Graham. *Preaching to a Postmodern World: A Guide to Reaching Twenty-First Century Listeners.* Grand Rapids: Baker, 2004.

Kolb, David A. *Experiential Learning: Experience as the Source of Learning and Development.* Upper Saddle River, NJ: Prentice Hall, 1984.

Weimer, Maryellen. *Improving Your Classroom Teaching.* Newberry Park, CA: Sage, 1993.

Yount, William R. *Called to Teach: An Introduction to the Ministry of Teaching.* Nashville: B&H, 1999.

6

Teaching Introductory New Testament Greek

Lois K. Fuller Dow

Congratulations if you get to teach Greek! You will learn a lot. It was not until I started teaching Greek that I really got some of the grammar issues sorted out in my head. Teaching will keep your own Greek fresh and useful, and help it to improve. If you hope to become truly competent in Greek, a proven strategy is to teach it to others.

THINKING ABOUT THE TASK

Goals

Most teachers have it as their goal for an introductory language course that by the end, with the aid of a lexicon and a reference grammar, students will be able to read (even if slowly) and understand all but the hardest New Testament texts and be able to use their reading in studying the Bible for themselves and to inform their teaching and preaching.

Teaching a biblical language can be very fulfilling if we see ourselves empowering people to enjoy direct access to the biblical text. Students, too, need to see learning Greek as empowerment rather than as a difficult imposed requirement, so tell them up front that this is what the course is about and entice them with examples of the benefits.

Responsibilities

Teachers and students each have their responsibilities. It is the teacher's responsibility to make sure that the student *understands* the grammatical concepts and how the language works. Teachers are also responsible to help *motivate* students by showing them the value of what they are learning. It is the student's responsibility to *memorize* the necessary vocabulary and endings, and to *practice* using what is taught by doing the exercises and assignments.

Kinds of Students

Many Greek classes have three kinds of students. There are those who easily grasp linguistic concepts and generally enjoy Greek. Then there are those who have less natural ability, but with hard work can do quite well. Finally, there are those who find language concepts opaque. Any of these students will lack motivation if they think Greek will not be needed in their contemplated ministry, and just want to pass the course so they can graduate. You need to find ways of engaging and motivating all three kinds of students. The gifted students can be challenged by extra information and I have even kept some of them engaged by having them teach a bit of the class. Struggling students need extra help, advice on learning strategies, and experiences where they succeed. All of them need to see how Greek is useful for reaching their own goals.

CHOOSING A TEXTBOOK

Sometimes teachers are required to use a certain textbook by the institution or supervisor where they teach. But there are dozens of books available. You can easily find most of them by looking at the website of an online bookseller. A short list is given below. If you are allowed to choose the textbook you will use, there are a number of things to consider about any book:

1. In what order is the material introduced? Do you prefer to do all the work on substantives before beginning verbs, or do you think it better to start with a mixture, or with verbs alone? How soon do you think things like contract verbs, -μι verbs, and participles should be introduced?

2. Does the book teach deductively (learning grammar first, then applying to Bible passages) or inductively (starting from Bible passages and learning grammar needed for each verse as you go along)?

3. Is the material divided into chapters that can easily be divided into the number of teaching sessions scheduled for your class?

4. Does the book require the students to learn all Greek accents, or none, or just those essential to distinguish words that look alike? What is your philosophy about this?

5. Do you agree with the book's treatment of things like number of cases (5 or 8) and the meaning of tenses (aspect or time)?

6. How much vocabulary does the book require the students to learn, and how long are the vocabulary lists to be learned with each lesson? Do you think the vocabulary lists are of a suitable length for your students?

7. How detailed are the glosses supplied with the Greek words (too many to start with or not enough to give the range of meaning)? Does the book give English words related to Greek vocabulary to help students remember the words or will you have to supply these?

8. What exercises are available for students to practise? Do you expect students to learn to translate from English into Greek, or only from Greek to English? Are there preliminary exercises to use during the lesson as each point is introduced, or only exercises that require knowledge of the whole lesson? Is an answer key available?

9. How soon are biblical texts introduced? Can the student start reading biblical texts in Greek quite early in the course? Are there other features that help students use Greek outside of class?

10. How much technical grammatical terminology is used? Is the level of technical language and the way it is explained (or not) appropriate for your students?

11. How long and detailed is the material? Does the book just cover the commonest forms or does it include a lot of "exceptions" and forms or words rarely used in the New Testament?

12. Does the textbook come with electronic aids such as a CD or internet resources? Most textbooks now have something like this. Try to have a look at the electronic resources supplied.

13. Does the book point out exegetical or devotional applications of what is being learned? Do you think this is useful and well done, and do you agree with the way the applications are made?

14. Is the book easily available and affordable for your students?

15. Are the pages laid out clearly, with the right amount of explanation?

No book will suit you perfectly. (Maybe that is why so many Greek teachers end up writing their own?) But these are some things to think about as you choose a book. Some classes or situations need one kind of book and others need another. Many people want to teach out of the book they learned from, and this has the advantage of familiarity. But remember too that by using a different book, you are likely to learn new things about Greek. I have used six different textbooks over the years, and each one has taught me new things. Using various textbooks also helps you discover the advantages and disadvantages of different strategies for presenting the material.

Some Available Textbooks

Many textbooks on New Testament Greek are available in English. You can easily find many of them using an internet search. However, here is a short list to give you an idea of the variety.

Beetham, Frank J. *An Introduction to New Testament Greek: A Quick Course in the Reading of Koine Greek*. London: Duckworth, 1992.

Black, David Alan. *Learn to Read New Testament Greek*. Nashville: B&H, 2009.

Countryman, Louis William. *Read It in Greek*. Grand Rapids: Eerdmans, 1993.

Croy, N. Clayton. *A Primer of Biblical Greek*. Grand Rapids: Eerdmans, 2007.

Dobson, John H. *Learn New Testament Greek*. Grand Rapids: Baker Academic, 2005.

Duff, Jeremy. *The Elements of New Testament Greek*. Cambridge: Cambridge University Press, 2005. Updates and replaces Wenham.

Hadjiantoinu, George, and James A. Gee. *Learning the Basics of New Testament Greek*. Chattanooga: AMG Publishers, 1999.

Hewett, James Allen. *New Testament Greek: A Beginning and Intermediate Grammar*. Revised and expanded by C. Michael Robbins and Steven R. Johnson. Peabody, MA: Hendrickson, 2009.

Jay, Eric George. *New Testament Greek: An Introductory Grammar*. London: SPCK, 1987.

Kunjummen, R. D. *New Testament Greek: A Whole Language Approach*. Chicago: Emet, 2009.

Machen, J. Gresham. *New Testament Greek for Beginners*. New York: Macmillan, 1923. Revised ed. by Dan G. McCartney. Upper Saddle River, NJ: Prentice Hall, 2003.

Macnair, Ian. *Teach Yourself New Testament Greek*. Nashville: Thomas Nelson, 1995.

Mounce, William. *Basics of Biblical Greek*. Grand Rapids: Zondervan, 2003.

Penner, Erwin. *A Guide to New Testament Greek*. Toronto: Clements, 2002.

Porter, Stanley E., Matthew Brook O'Donnell, and Jeffrey T. Reed. *Fundamentals of New Testament Greek*. Grand Rapids: Eerdmans, 2010.

Summers, Ray, revised by Thomas Sawyer. *Essentials of New Testament Greek*. Nashville: B&H, 1995.

Wenham, J. W. *Elements of New Testament Greek*. Cambridge: Cambridge University Press, 1965.

CLASSROOM ATMOSPHERE

Because many students are afraid of Greek, or at least are not looking forward to studying it, creating a warm and attractive class atmosphere is very important. New Testament Greek is often taught in institutions where it is appropriate for class members to share their stories with each other and pray for each other. When community is built in the Greek class, and students care about each others' success, learning Greek can be a wonderful experience. I am always excited when I hear that students have organized study groups, are sharing study aids they have discovered with each other, and are praying for each other to succeed.

I have also found that most students, even graduate students, are susceptible to the attractions of snacks and treats to ease the pain, and rewards (even stickers!) for good work.

Try to include some games, films, and interesting activities for variety. Here are a few:

1. Show the Vision Video film "God's Outlaw: The Story of William Tyndale." It is useful for getting students to think about Tyndale's work of figuring out the English equivalents for various Greek words.

2. Bring in someone working today in Bible translation for a discussion about the meanings of biblical words and constructions, and the challenges of translation.

3. Let students work in pairs or groups at in-class exercises before presenting their answers to the class.

4. Hold parsing contests in teams. Making the team responsible for the parsing rather than an individual helps to avoid shaming individuals who can't parse as well in front of others.

5. Have students make posters/pictures. These could depict some New Testament pericope, labelled with the Greek vocabulary used in the pericope, illustrate some environment such as the home or a landscape, do a Greek alphabet with a New Testament word for each letter, or illustrate words in the same semantic domain, such as plants or animals in the New Testament, parts of the body, or people's occupations.

6. Let students share their experiences of using Greek outside class.

7. Have students try to figure out clippings from Greek newspapers.

8. Find or develop crossword puzzles and word search puzzles using vocabulary items.

9. Find or develop interesting stories or fables to read, with mixed English and Greek, using Greek words the students know so far.
10. Take a field trip to a Greek-speaking church and observe the use of Koine Greek going on there.

TEACHING AIDS AND STRATEGIES

Understanding Basic Grammar Concepts

Students start Greek at various levels of linguistic understanding. Some need help with basic grammar concepts, which they can probably learn best by starting with English as an example. There are various resources that can help them, such as:

Lamerson, Samuel. *English Grammar to Ace New Testament Greek.* Grand Rapids: Zondervan, 2004. Introduces English Grammar in the order needed for Mounce's textbook.

Long, Gary A. *Grammatical Concepts 101 for Biblical Greek: Learning Biblical Greek Grammatical Concepts through English Grammar.* Peabody: Hendrickson, 2006. Contains parallel English and Greek examples.

It is usually useful to start any lesson that introduces new grammatical material with a review of the parallel English grammar, pointing out similarities and differences. If your students know or have some experience with other languages with helpful parallels, bring those in too. It is always good to start the course by asking what languages besides English each student has some experience with, so you can use any of those languages familiar to you to illustrate Greek.

Handouts

I have found that few students can learn Greek from the textbook without the help of a teacher to illustrate and explain. For this reason, having students read the textbook ahead of your teaching the lesson is not always useful. Slides and/or handouts, and work on the board are very important. In my experience, if students have to take too many notes, they are distracted from listening and thinking, so it is worth while giving handouts or electronic versions of your notes that they can add to. Present the material in the way you find clearest, but be aware that not all students share your learning style. All along, refer to the sections of the textbook that treat the material you are teaching. You do not need to go through the lesson in the order the textbook does it. You may have to simplify or elaborate on the textbook, depending on the book and your students.

In-Lesson Exercises

Many textbooks, even those with workbooks, do not have preliminary exercises to drill just one point and you may have to make these up to use in class. For example, when you teach the idea of case, have a little story in English in which the students have to find all the nouns and pronouns and tell what case they would be in Greek before they try to recognize cases and their uses in Greek text. Or when teaching the augment, have an exercise for putting augments on various verb stems before attempting to recognize them in text. Unless most students see a grammar point in action, and have to recognize it in text, they won't understand or grasp it. Try to do an exercise as part of every point you teach.

Helping Students Memorize

Since students have to do so much memorization to succeed at biblical languages, they need strategies for helping them memorize the technical terms, alphabet, vocabulary, and endings involved. Try to use and suggest a wide variety of strategies, because people have different learning styles. Some remember better if they write and see, others if they hear or speak.

1. Compose or ask students to compose songs to sing the alphabet, paradigm endings, and other things, such as the list of cases or the information needed in parsing. I like to sing the alphabet to the tune of "Yankee Doodle" but there are other good ways of doing it.

2. Assigning students to sing or memorize biblical passages (short ones at first) will help fix vocabulary and grammar in their minds. Craig A. Noll has written a good article on the use of memorized Greek Scripture: "Biblical Meditation: A Forgotten Resource in Learning New Testament Greek?" *McMaster Journal of Theology and Ministry* 11 (2009–10) 62–67 (http://www.mcmaster.ca/mjtm/pdfs/vol11/articles/MJTM_11.3_NollMeditation.pdf).

3. Ask students to share with each other some of the mnemonic devices they use to remember words and terms, the funnier the better!

4. Demonstrate the use of vocabulary cards. Another way to review vocabulary is to have all the words on one sheet, grouped by part of speech or in some other useful way.

5. Do aural/oral drills of greetings and commands like "Stand up," "Sit down," "Give it to me," "What is your name?" etc.
6. Always point out words that share a root, and English borrowings and cognates of vocabulary and grammar items. Bruce Metzger's *Lexical Aids for Students of New Testament Greek* (Grand Rapids: Baker, 1998) is a great resource for this.

The more a student has to use a word, the more he or she will remember it, so the games and activities listed above are a help. There are internet sites that feature many activities. Some of your students will enjoy finding them. Of course, you need to make sure you look at them before encouraging everyone to use them, because they might have errors. Learning to recognize errors is also part of the learning process for your students.

Reading the Greek New Testament

The sooner students have their own copies of the Greek New Testament and a lexicon or dictionary, the better. Help them learn to recognize the names of the books of the New Testament in their copies, and to find verses that interest them. Give enough helps that students can read a New Testament passage almost every class. Before Christmas, read the Christmas story from Matthew or Luke, and before Easter, read one of the Gospel passion accounts.

Helping Stragglers

In most Greek classes there are a few students who fall behind. This is usually because something has disturbed the time they need to devote to learning Greek, and they have not been able to master a lesson before subsequent lessons are piled on top. You need a fairly comprehensive test every three or four weeks to alert you to who is struggling. These people may need a private tutor to help them catch up. Try to recommend a good current or former Greek student as a tutor, because tutoring will help the tutor solidify his/her knowledge of Greek as well as aiding the student who is behind. Sometimes offering a student a way to re-take a failed test or hand in work late without penalty can revive hope and allow the student to renew effort. Since our objective is to get everybody to actually learn Greek, not just to maintain some kind of class "discipline," we can be merciful if we think mercy will produce the desired result.

Deductive, Inductive, or Immersion?

There are three main strategies for teaching languages, and all three have been used to teach New Testament Greek.

The first, most widely used, is the *deductive* method. In this method, vocabulary and grammar are presented to the student and once these are learned, the student is asked to find and interpret them in texts. For example, students learn about the cases of Greek nouns, memorize some nouns and the case endings, and then are asked to identify the instances and uses of cases in some sentences, and to translate the nouns appropriately. The advantage of this is that students are immediately presented with the whole pattern of a kind of usage. The disadvantage is that it delays the use of actual texts (of, say, the New Testament) because not all forms used in a typical text have been covered until near the end of the course. Also, learning paradigms and vocabulary lists without the context of actual usage is tedious and seems unnatural.

Using the second method, the *inductive*, students are presented first with a text and are given help to read it. They learn just what they need to interpret that text. Then they learn another text, and build up their knowledge of vocabulary and forms text by text. The advantage of this method is that students start using texts right away, and they learn vocabulary and forms in the context of a text. One disadvantage is that it takes a long time for patterns to emerge and for students to get the whole picture of any aspect of grammar. The student has to deal with a lot of incomplete accounts of many different types of information until any type is completed. Some students find this overwhelmingly frustrating and some find it too confusing. Another disadvantage is that the course starts out very slowly because there is so much to learn in order to be able to interpret just one text in Greek that students feel they are stuck on that text for too long.

I have sometimes used a combination of deductive and inductive, that is, using a deductive method to teach the first half of the course, then switching to inductive for the second half. This means that students already have some complete patterns mastered before they go on to inductive learning so it goes much faster and they learn the second half of their grammar in the context of texts using it.

The third method is *immersion*. This method is more often used with living languages. Students learn phrases needed to survive and interact with others first, and add to their knowledge as new experiences and environments requiring use of further language are encountered. The emphasis is on hearing, then speaking, and only later on reading and writing. There are some people who advocate using immersion for learning New Testament Greek. This is certainly an interesting way to do it, and students who are better at hearing/speaking than reading/writing will find it easier. If we lay aside for a moment the objection that we are not sure exactly how Greek was pronounced in the New Testament period, the first disadvantage of this method is that it takes a lot of time, much more than the typical college or seminary course allots. We could, of course, advocate for more time being allowed for the course, though to get more credits for it because of the greater time spent might be harder to argue for. The second disadvantage is that the method requires more time learning vocabulary seldom or never used in the New Testament, and less time on words used most in the New Testament, since the New Testament is full of theological and ethical concepts used less frequently in survival and interaction contexts. Thus the method does not quickly prepare students to read the target text, the New Testament.

All of these methods have been used successfully to teach New Testament Greek. A student or class with linguistic experience and ability might find the inductive approach stimulating. The immersion approach can be interesting if rapid progress in ability to read the New Testament is not an issue. But the average college or seminary class will probably do best using the deductive method, at least for the first half of the course.

Introducing the Tools

One of the important tasks of a Greek teacher is to get students familiar with the tools they will need for continuing to use Greek after the introductory course. The sooner they get acquainted with such tools, the better. Most students can get a Greek New Testament from the Bible Society (*UBSGNT*, latest edition). Help students to find their way around in it, and demonstrate the use of the three kinds of footnotes.

Explain the various kinds of lexicons available (e.g., short lexicons with reading glosses, those for scholarly use like BDAG and Liddell-Scott, and how the Louw-Nida works) and give practice in using them. Students also need information about theological dictionaries and wordbooks (e.g., *TDNT, NIDNTT*), and the major commentary series that use the Greek text.

As the course goes on, introduce some of the major descriptive grammars, and demonstrate how to use them, especially when, while trying to translate a New Testament text, you find something unexpected happening in the grammar.

MARKING SCHEMES

Your marking scheme for the course needs to motivate students to spend time on the material you want them to master. I like to give a generous amount for memory-work quizzes (a quiz each class) so that students are motivated to keep memorizing new material. This also helps people pass who work faithfully, but for any reason don't function well on a final exam. You can also include brief translation on the daily quizzes. Certainly you need to test comprehension ability more than just in a mid-term and final exam. This is so that you can quickly spot students who are getting bogged down and act to help them. It also forces students to do more comprehensive review than they may otherwise do before regular classes. I have two or three long tests of an hour and a half each, spaced evenly through the semester with the final examination at the end. There should be some marks for special assignments (such as posters). Sometimes you can just deduct marks for uncompleted smaller assignments, such as exercises. You need a final exam so that students review again, and can demonstrate their ability to comprehend, using all the material taught so far.

When marking, I like to give a lot of partial marks. For example, when a student has to translate a Greek sentence into English, I give some marks for correctly identifying the vocabulary items, some for interpreting the cases of the nouns or pronouns correctly, for making them plural if necessary, for getting the subject of the verb right, for translating with the correct voice, and so on. This encourages students to write down anything they recognize in the sentence even if they can't translate the whole thing. I don't mind if initially the grades are very high. The first few weeks, everyone should be getting A+. Set reasonable standards for what you think the outcomes should be in terms of ability to understand Greek text, and don't try to grade on the curve. In a small class, it is quite possible for most of the students to do well.

AFTER YOUR COURSE: KEEPING GREEK ALIVE

Finally, as your course ends, students who are going on to exegesis classes as well as those who hope to use Greek in any way in the future need some advice on how to keep all the Greek they have learned from leaking out of their minds over the next few weeks! The Porter, Reed, and O'Donnell text has a program for continuous review that involves 20 minutes a day (p. xiii). If that kind of regimen looks daunting, I sometimes encourage students to translate just three to six verses a week from some of the Johannine books, maybe as part of their daily devotions. Any continued use of Greek will keep knowledge of it alive and gradually add to it. Some, and hopefully most, of your students will actually be able to use their Greek for the rest of their lives!

REFERENCE WORKS MENTIONED

BDAG—Bauer, Walter. *A Greek-English Lexicon of the New Testament and Other Early Christian Literature.* Translated by William F. Arndt and F. Wilbur Gingrich. Chicago: University of Chicago Press, 1979. Revised and edited by Frederick William Danker. Chicago: University of Chicago Press, 2000.

Liddell-Scott—Liddell, Henry George, and Robert Scott. *A Greek-English Lexicon.* Revised by Henry Stuart Jones. Oxford: Clarendon, 1968. Supplement by P. Glare, 1996.

Louw-Nida—Louw, Johannes P., and Eugene A. Nida. *Greek-English Lexicon of the New Testament, Based on Semantic Domains.* 2 vols. New York: United Bible Societies, 1988.

TDNT—*Theological Dictionary of the New Testament.* 10 vols. Edited by Gerhard Friedrich and Gerhard Kittel. Translated and edited by Geoffrey W. Bromiley. Grand Rapids: Eerdmans, 1964–1976.

NIDNTT—*New International Dictionary of New Testament Theology.* 4 vols. Edited by Colin Brown. Grand Rapids: Zondervan, 1986.

7

Teaching Biblical Hebrew

Practical Strategies for Introductory Courses

PAUL EVANS

Teaching languages is part art and part science. The science is in the grammar and syntax[1] while the art is in pedagogical practice. Unfortunately, there is actually little research dedicated to ancient language pedagogy[2] and this essay does not claim to bring such research to bear.[3] The purpose of this chapter is to make available to those who will teach introductory Biblical Hebrew a range of practical teaching strategies that I have found effective in my experience as an instructor. I do not mean to suggest that my approach to teaching Biblical Hebrew is the only way or even the best way (as in the words of that somewhat macabre saying, "There is more than one way to skin a cat"). Since individual teachers each have different personalities, strengths, and weaknesses, each instructor's approach will necessarily differ accordingly. The focus here is on the

---

1. Though even at this point language mechanics are not pure science either.

2. As noted by Halabe, "Ancient Languages." However, she refers the readers to the Department of Ancient Languages in Moscow State University (Russia), which has "Theory and Methodology of Teaching Ancient Languages" as one of its primary fields of research. Unfortunately, one needs to know Russian to access that resource.

3. For some good resources for further reading, cf. Halabe, "Introduction to Biblical Hebrew" and Griffin, "Killing a Dead Language."

practical side of pedagogy. Rather than simply pointing to underlying theory or generic learning strategies and techniques,[4] I will share specific strategies I have used in the classroom so that the reader may add them to their teaching repertoire if they wish.

TEACHING GOALS

How one goes about teaching Biblical Hebrew will be determined by the goals for the course. If instructors set out to duplicate themselves, creating academic biblical scholars, then that would entail having students master the minute detail and idiosyncrasies of the language. While this is obviously a teacher-centered approach, I believe that the goals of an introductory Biblical Hebrew class should really be student-centered. After all, the vast majority of students who take Biblical Hebrew do not intend to be—and never will be—scholars.[5] A class in introductory Biblical Hebrew should try to assist students to meet *their* goals. The goal in my introductory Biblical Hebrew class is to enable students to be able to read and translate the Old Testament in Hebrew as well as it is possible given the limited time allocated to the learning experiences. The ramifications of this goal will be seen throughout this essay.

CLASS ATMOSPHERE

I have found that it is vital to create an enjoyable class atmosphere when teaching Hebrew.[6] The material can be dry and the workload tremendous, but there is no need for the class atmosphere to be dull or sterile. Each instructor will find their own ways to create an enjoyable atmosphere, but here I share some of the ways I have found to create a fun class atmosphere.

---

4. Adapting generic learning activities to fit the actual content of different courses can be quite challenging, due to the complexity of the process. As Weimer, *Learner-Centered Teaching*, 70, points out, "The process is rarely addressed in active learning material or workshops." Thus this essay will attempt to be as specific as possible.

5. If I have a student whose goal is to continue on in graduate studies in Bible, I sometimes have student-specific goals for that individual. I may tell them to master some material that I do not require the rest of the class to master. However, in fairness to the student and the class, I do not test on the additional material, but I make sure to make myself available to help this student understand the material.

6. In his blog on teaching biblical languages, John F. Hobbins notes one Bible translator who argues that the way biblical languages are often taught makes the experience "so achingly boring" that the only person who could enjoy it has "to either be steeped in self-deception or a masochistic moron." Cf. Hobbins, "Sadistic Approaches."

Games

Playing games in class can be helpful not only in terms of class atmosphere but also for helping students use the information they have been learning in a different way. (Such instances can actually help improve future recall of material.) For example, after students learn the alphabet (first class) we play Hebrew Bingo. Bingo cards can be created by hand, by using a word processor, or by downloading the free program that creates Hebrew bingo cards to be printed out and used in class.[7] After students have learned the vowels I spell out famous phrases/sayings, or lines from popular films[8] using Hebrew characters and vowels and either hand out print copies or project them on a screen using a digital projector. I get the class to work in teams at deciphering the phrases based on how the word sounds (this gets them to practice pronouncing words written in Hebrew characters). After students have progressed through Hebrew grammar to an appropriate point, it can be fun to play Hebrew Scrabble® or Boggle®.[9] This often works well on the last day of class of the semester and/or the year. It can be fun to have some type of token prizes to offer the winners, remembering not to create a super-competitive atmosphere, but an enjoyable one for all.[10]

Songs

Another way to liven class atmosphere is to sing Hebrew songs. In my experience, regardless of the students' ages, they find the use of Hebrew songs enjoyable (part of the enjoyment is hearing the professor attempt to carry a tune when teaching the songs to them). I usually begin with singing Deuteronomy 6:4 (the *Shema*) which is very simple. After the class has learned it, I teach them to sing Psalm 133:1, which is relatively simple but has a great tune and can be sung in a round (usually a student hit). Of

---

7. Online: http://www.learnbiblicalgreek.com/free_bingo. This program can run on Windows or Mac OS. Be sure to install the Teknia Hebrew font, which can be found on the same webpage.

8. The possibilities for phrases to use are endless. E.g., a phrase I have used is the opening words in the Star Wars movies (אָה לוֹנג טִים אָגוּ עֶן אָה גָלֶעֲחִי פַר פַר אָוֵי) "A long time ago, in a galaxy far, far away."

9. I first was exposed to Hebrew Scrabble® in a Hebrew class by Tyler F. Williams (The King's University College, Edmonton, AB) and Hebrew Boggle® by Mark J. Boda (McMaster Divinity College).

10. When I studied Hebrew I participated in a "parse-off" contest, but found that it turned quite competitive and was basically discouraging for some students while allowing others to show off. Therefore, I steer clear of games of that nature.

course there are many different songs one could choose to sing. A great song to sing with students comes from the movie *The Prince of Egypt*. In the film, just before[11] Moses leads the people across the Red Sea, Miriam sings a short song in Hebrew, the lyrics of which come directly from Exodus 15.[12] Students often enjoy learning this song as they are aware of the movie, and if they remember the song, are unaware that every word comes directly from the Bible.

Regardless of whether one plays these or other games or teaches Hebrew songs or not, I think it is important to find a way to keep the class somewhat lighthearted in contrast to the workload. The vast majority of students will find the assigned homework in a Hebrew class very heavy, so if the instructor can create an enjoyable atmosphere in the class itself it can be very beneficial in terms of motivation.

Supportive Environment

I find that students learn well in a supportive environment where they can learn, ask questions,[13] and actually contribute to the learning itself. Student contributions often aid classroom learning and can even teach instructors a thing or two. Sometimes I find that students formulate better ways of explaining something than I have. If this happens to you, acknowledge it! Tell the student that it is a great way of looking at it or a great idea. This can be quite thrilling for students, and you can add such ideas and illustrations to your own instructional arsenal. Also, do not be afraid to say you do not know. Sometimes instructors put pressure on themselves to appear infallible and always know the answer. While it is important that the instructor

---

11. It is interesting that in the movie they sing this before the Red Sea crossing, while in Exodus the song is sung after the crossing. Just remember that chronological change if you go to look for the song in the movie.

12. The song quotes from Exod 15:1b (אָשִׁירָה לַיהוָה כִּי־גָאֹה גָּאָה) repeating it twice, then quotes Exod 15:11a (מִי־כָמֹכָה בָּאֵלִם יְהוָה מִי כָּמֹכָה נֶאְדָּר בַּקֹּדֶשׁ), then concludes by quoting Exod 15:13a (נָחִיתָ בְחַסְדְּךָ עַם־זוּ גָּאָלְתָּ). It can be found on "The Prince of Egypt: Music from The Original Motion Picture Soundtrack" (Track 14—the version sung by Michelle Pfeiffer and Sally Dworsk—contains the Hebrew part, while Track 1—the pop version sung by Mariah Carey and Whitney Houston—does not) or in the film itself as part of the song "When You Believe."

13. It is very important that students ask questions. I would encourage them by reminding them that if they have a question about something chances are that others in the class have the same question but are afraid to speak up. To ensure everyone is following sometimes I have actually had students put their heads down and raise their hand if they are not following. Surprisingly, this somewhat juvenile method can be quite effective.

knows the material well, sometimes it is beneficial for students to hear that you still use a lexicon, or that you still struggle with a form from time to time. Hebrew can be quite intimidating and often students are in awe of instructors and their command of the language. It is tempting to play up on that and try to maintain that image of Hebrew guru. Sometimes instructors "show off" to students to further their image, as when they mention how many ancient languages they know (even if their knowledge of say, Moabite, is limited to the one Moabite text that exists). I think it is better to be honest with students and encourage them that they too could gain mastery of the language, rather than build up an untouchable façade. Humility rather than ego will draw students to you. We should honor our students and always seek their best interests—and appearing as the untouchable Hebrew expert, whose status they could seldom hope to reach, is of no benefit to them.

ENGAGING AND MOTIVATING STUDENTS

Language courses risk being boring and repetitive and disconnected from students' interests and goals. Yet, recent research has shown clear links between students' motivation and engagement with their success in learning languages.[14] Teaching Hebrew is a balance between communicating information and conveying passion. If students get too discouraged, they lose their engagement and motivation, which then limits their success. While the rules of grammar and rote memorization cannot be avoided, instructors must seek to avoid student discouragement or disillusionment.

Connecting with Students' Reasons for Studying Hebrew

Instructors must find a way to connect with the reasons why students are taking the class in the first place. I recommend beginning the first day of class with student self-introductions and asking each one to provide some reason why they are taking the course. Even though some will only be taking the course to fulfil degree or elective requirements, most are quite interested in the Bible and/or theology. Whatever the level of interest, it is the instructor's goal to further cultivate that interest rather than stifle and dishearten it through the difficulties of Hebrew grammar.

---

14. Gardner et al., "Role of Attitudes." Cf. Dörnyei, *Teaching and Researching Motivation*.

Choosing Meaningful or Interesting Hebrew Passages

Therefore, the instructor should give examples where knowledge of Hebrew significantly impacts one's understanding of a biblical text, has theological implications, or is interesting in some other way. I recommend having in each class (or at least in each week) some interesting exegetical or translation issue that they can now engage due to their new knowledge of Hebrew.[15] In fact, it is important to have some in place for the different levels of knowledge throughout the course. Here are some examples:

1. After learning the alphabet and vowels, have students read the Shibboleth passage from Judg 12:6 where the fate of people is decided on how they pronounce a Hebrew word. Students newly armed with knowledge of Hebrew pronunciation can see that the difference in pronunciation is due to one Hebrew letter.[16]

2. After learning about the definite article in Hebrew, look at *Adam* (הָאָדָם) in Genesis 2–3 and *Satan* (הַשָּׂטָן) passages in Job 1–2 and Zechariah 3 to see that there is a definite article on the noun—making it a question of whether we should understand these as proper names.

3. After learning how the definite article combines with prepositions (losing its ה) read Gen 1:1. They will be surprised that there is no definite article in בְּרֵאשִׁית.

4. After learning about adjectives, read 1 Sam 16:7, 12. God states that he does not look on the outward "appearance" (Hebrew לַעֵינַיִם) as humans do, yet when David is introduced, it says he is "beautiful of appearance"(Hebrew יְפֵה עֵינַיִם).

5. After learning the singular and plural demonstratives, look at Exod 32:4 and 2 Kgs 12:28. Some translations (e.g., NKJV, JPS) of Exod 32:4 read, "This is your god O Israel" even though the demonstrative is clearly plural (and should read "These are your gods").

6. After learning pronominal suffixes, read Judg 8:22–23 in English where Gideon says he will not rule over the people and neither will his son, then note Judg 8:31 where Gideon names his son "Abimelech" (אֲבִימֶלֶךְ). Students who recognize the first person common singular pronominal suffix will be able to translate the name "my father is king."

---

15. Some textbooks may offer exegetical insights with each chapter, but it is still helpful to provide brief motivating examples in class (these could even be drawn from the textbook).

16. Another good passage to read after just learning how to pronounce is Isa 5:7 and the rhyme/play on words at the end of the verse (לְמִשְׁפָּט וְהִנֵּה מִשְׂפָּח לִצְדָקָה וְהִנֵּה צְעָקָה).

7. After learning the Qal imperative, read Gen 12:2 and note the imperative to be a blessing (וֶהְיֵה בְּרָכָה) which is not reflected in most English translations.

8. After learning about jussives and the Hithpael verb (with its reflexive meaning), read Jonah 3:8 and ask students to identify the subjects of the verb. The command is given to both men and animals to "cover themselves" (וְיִתְכַּסּוּ) with sackcloth. This can be humorous as we try to picture cows dressing themselves.

Many other passages could be employed to similar ends. It is worth noting that I do not choose these verses to promote a certain interpretation of any of these passages but to pique the interest of students. If desirable, the instructor can briefly sum up debates of interpretation and offer reasons for their own view. Sometimes I find it best not even to offer my own view but just to show them the text and refer them to commentaries to dig in deeper. Knowledge of Hebrew becomes empowering as they now have access to debates in ways that they did not before.

Grade Guarantees

In my experience, the most common reason for students to drop Hebrew early in the first semester is discouragement about low scores on some of the initial tests. While frequent quizzing is necessary from the outset, instructors can alleviate some of the worries about failing that such students have by offering grade guarantees.[17] Despite having a rough start to the semester in terms of grades on quizzes and grammar tests, any student who attends *every* class, completes *all* homework *on time* and *passes* the final exam will be guaranteed a "C" in the class.[18] I think you will find that any student who does all three of those requirements will score at least a "C" on the final exam. Whether students pick up Hebrew quickly or catch on more slowly, if they "get it" in time to pass the final exam, they can pass the course.

CHOOSING A TEXTBOOK

I believe that choosing a Hebrew textbook should be done with caution. While it may be tempting to simply choose the text from which you learned Hebrew, I believe four things are worth considering when choosing a textbook.

17. Isbell, "Hebrew Teacher."

18. When such an offer is made, the instructor must emphasize that there are no exceptions to these conditions or the grade guarantee is lost.

Less is More

First, I believe you should choose a textbook that is less technical.[19] In light of the stated goals for the class (not producing scholars but students who can read Hebrew fairly well) I prefer a textbook that focuses on the most common constructions, rather than consistently highlighting idiosyncratic ones. Unfortunately, Hebrew textbooks invariably give too much detail for beginner students to successfully absorb.[20] They try to teach too much too fast.[21] Compared to most language introductory texts, Hebrew textbooks spend inordinate amounts of space on technical issues of grammar and often attempt to account for every idiosyncrasy found in the Hebrew Bible.[22] Though I have not found my "ideal" text in this regard, some are better than others and I would encourage instructors to preview a text and judge for themselves how it balances necessary and advanced information.[23]

On that note, do not be afraid to tell students to skip a section of the textbook if you do not think it will benefit beginner students. Each year, I have instructed my students to skip certain sections of the text (sometimes just a paragraph, occasionally an entire chapter). For example, sometimes a textbook lists in a paradigm a variant form that occurs less than ten times in the entire Old Testament. In my opinion, any focus at all on that form is counter-productive, as students need to master the common forms. After all, if they run into one of the ten occurrences in their reading of the Hebrew Bible they can look up the aberrant form in a lexicon and move on. The ability to recognize a rare form does not outweigh

---

19. Of course there is no consensus as to what material should go into a language grammar textbook. As Halliday, *Functional Grammar*, xxx, has observed, "there is usually a trade-off of breadth against depth: we need both highly specialized machines that will do just one job perfectly, and less specialized machines that will do a broad range of jobs effectively."

20. As Greenspahn ("Hebrew Textbooks") has observed, "Hebrew texts tend to inundate students with far more detail than a beginner could possibly absorb, much less master. Moreover, all this is done using unfamiliar terms and with reference to tools that are frequently in languages such as French and German . . . that students also do not know."

21. As Vail, "Hermeneutics and Homiletics," 372, commented long ago, "Our writers of Hebrew grammars have aimed to write for scholars rather than for students. They have been ambitious on most points to say all that could be said, without studying to say only that which is needed to be said."

22. As Halabe, "Ancient Languages," comments, "one of the problems with introductory textbooks and courses is the difficulty they have in presenting a program whose clear objectives are compatible with realistic expectations from students."

23. Sometimes more detailed information is found in an excursus or in a section for advanced information, which is helpful.

the potential /probable negative feelings of being overwhelmed that most beginning students feel.

On the same note, if a lexicon is assigned to the class (perhaps in second semester), one should avoid choosing a lexicon that gives too much information.[24] For this reason I require my students to purchase Holladay's lexicon[25] rather than BDB.[26] The latter gives considerably too much information for beginning students, and of course, the words in BDB are organized around roots rather than listed alphabetically, making Holladay more user-friendly for beginning students. As well, if a Hebrew Bible is to be purchased for the class, I do not require that it be *Biblia Hebraica Stuttgartensia* (though of course that is more than acceptable).[27] Since my course is focused on learning the language—not learning about textual variants and textual criticism—it is not necessary to have the textual apparatus. If the student goes on to further study there will be time for learning to use the apparatus, but in introductory Hebrew the focus is on learning the language and I do not wish to complicate things (e.g., by having them struggling to understand the Latin used in BHS to decipher the notes in the textual apparatus).[28]

A Good Workbook

I recommend choosing a textbook that has a corresponding workbook *and* includes an answer key.[29] Most textbooks have exercises at the end of each chapter, but some do not give actual space for the answers to be written out in the text itself. I prefer that there be an actual workbook that leaves appropriate space for student answers because: (1) it does not require students to have their own paper (many study at Starbucks etc.);

---

24. Halabe, "Ancient Languages," argues that students in an introductory course should be given just "a minimal list of the most common interpretations of any verb form and encourage the students to use context and common sense while reading a straightforward text."

25. Holladay, *Hebrew and Aramaic Lexicon*.

26. Brown et al., *Hebrew and English Lexicon*.

27. I usually encourage those who intend to go on in Hebrew and Old Testament studies to purchase BHS so that they do not have to buy two different Hebrew Bibles.

28. I believe that there could be some introduction to the tools for further study of Hebrew and textual criticism perhaps at the end of the course. However, there is no reason why students need to gain familiarity with the most technical texts and lexicons in the course itself. The course should focus on learning Hebrew and not lexicography, textual criticism, etc.

29. Either on an accompanying CD or answers printed at the back of the workbook.

(2) it requires less organizational skills than keeping their homework on separate sheets (otherwise many lose or misplace their homework;[30] (3) it makes checking student homework easier as the answers are written on the same sheet as the questions.[31] Some texts include a built-in workbook, providing space for students to write in but not answers to the exercises.[32] However, since not all exercises can be discussed and corrected in the classroom (due to time constraints), the availability of an answer key gives students instant feedback, which can greatly increase their learning away from the classroom. I think a workbook separate from the actual grammar textbook is best (and allows students to hand in exercises more easily), but a built-in workbook with space provided for student answers, and an answer key provided at the back or on a CD, is sufficient.

Print Size Matters

Though smaller texts have the advantage of being lighter and easier to pack around, texts with larger print are to be preferred. Generally students are already struggling with learning the new, foreign script, so having it printed in a small font only exacerbates the difficulty. The larger the font, the easier it is to read.

Less Transliteration

Lastly, I prefer a textbook that prints the Hebrew characters and does not use transliteration. Unlike the situation some decades ago, today's books are always able to print the Hebrew characters and rarely use transliteration, so knowledge of transliteration is not as important as it once was. Though in some instances (such as comparing Hebrew to other Semitic languages or proto-Semitic) knowledge of transliteration is necessary, that type of study is outside the scope of an introductory Hebrew course. Again, keeping in mind the goals of the students (learning to read Hebrew, not become scholars) transliteration will not be too useful for most. Therefore,

---

30. Sometimes otherwise brilliant people are hopelessly unorganized—professors included.

31. When students merely write out answers on a separate sheet, checking their progress is more labor intensive on the instructor, as you have to make sure they did not miss any questions, pages etc.; if their answers are written on the actual page where the questions appear, this is much easier.

32. E.g., Kittel et al., *Biblical Hebrew*. Though a separate answer key can be purchased, e.g., Williams, *Answer Key*.

in introductory Hebrew it is best to leave transliteration behind early in the course and focus on the printed Hebrew characters.

PRACTICAL HINTS

While an instructor's approach may be limited to, or at least connected with, the approach of the chosen textbook, I believe the following suggestions are extremely beneficial regardless of the chosen textbook.

Oral Mastery of the Qal Strong Verb

While the memorization of all paradigms (especially the *binyanim*/derived stems) is not that useful, I believe that memorization of the Qal is essential. Most textbooks suggest that students be able to reproduce these paradigms exactly in written form. However, in addition to this what I have found extremely beneficial is having students learn to orally recite the Qatal and Yiqtol paradigms for the strong verb.[33] Just as many of us still recite the ABCs song when looking up something alphabetically (e.g., in a dictionary, or contacts list), so students who can recite the Qal strong paradigms will find that this ability helps them when tackling different verbal forms (during tests or in personal reading) as they can recite the paradigm mentally or verbally (quietly) and then recognize the correct parsing for the form they are studying. In order for this to work, students need to know the oral recitation of the paradigm extremely well. Therefore, I regularly dedicate time in class to reciting the paradigm orally. To assist in memorization of these paradigms I record myself reciting them on a computer and produce an electronic file (m4a, mp3, wma etc.) that I can either post on a course website or email directly to students who are interested in using it.[34] Students can then put it on their iPod or other mp3 player, or burn it on CD or some other device, and listen to it anywhere they like. Students have found this to be very effective in memorizing the paradigms orally.

Focus on Recognition

In light of my goal (to facilitate reading of the Old Testament in Hebrew) and the necessity of engagement and motivation, my approach is to fo-

---

33. By Qatal and Yiqtol I mean the Qal perfect/affix paradigm and the Qal imperfect/prefix paradigm using קטל.

34. Creating these files is quite easy to do as most computers allow you to plug in an external microphone or already have one built in.

cus on recognition and translation of Hebrew rather than on a thorough knowledge of *why* things change (that is, ability to explain the rule).[35] Sometimes such explanations are necessary to know,[36] and I naturally teach the class reasons why things change when they are helpful for recognizing the forms.[37] However, in testing, the focus is on recognition. That is, even if a student cannot remember *why* a form differs as it does from the Qal strong paradigm, if the student can recognize the form enough to parse it and identify its lexical form, that is enough. After all, most of us in our native languages cannot always explain why some forms differ the way they do (though we can recognize and understand such forms without effort)[38] so why should it be any different in Hebrew?[39] What is important is whether a student can recognize, parse, and translate Hebrew forms, not whether they could compose a passage in Hebrew or even give me the explanation for why a form diverges from the norm.[40]

In keeping with this focus, even early on in the year, I regularly expose my class to biblical passages that are not in the textbook or workbook. By either having them use their Hebrew Bibles or displaying the Hebrew text on a digital projector, I walk them through several biblical passages throughout the semester in order to expose them to the text again and again. I have found that constant exposure to the text proves more beneficial than emphasizing rules.[41]

---

35. Some research has suggested that such rules are "neither realistic nor desirable in learning/teaching situations." Cf. Westney, "Rules."

36. Of course, some knowledge of rules is necessary in order for students to predict and recognize changes. However, we must ensure that the rules we teach are really relevant to student needs. As Westney, "Rules," has asserted, rules should be relatively simple, non-technical, and more "rule of thumb" in form.

37. Sometimes the reasons for the changes are too complex to be worth explaining and I simply say, "Don't worry about why, just know that it changes."

38. As Westney, "Rules," asserts, language users "know" that "language is like this" without knowing the rules.

39. Similarly concerned with too many rules in introductory Hebrew, some have actually advocated teaching Biblical Hebrew without pointing. Cf. Griffin, "Killing a Dead Language."

40. As Habale, "Ancient Languages," asserts, students "can internalize higher levels of grammar through massive exposure . . . without necessarily knowing the rules."

41. As Halabe, "Ancient Languages," has asserted, "massive intake of straightforward authentic ancient language texts during and following the introductory course may be more effective in absorbing the way that language 'is' than going through innumerable high-level rules during the introductory course."

Assessment Methods

Unlike some courses where students can "cram" late in the semester and still pass, in a course like introductory Biblical Hebrew it is essential that students keep up with the material. The best way I have found for ensuring this is regular, frequent testing. Specifically, I have a test *every* class. Sometimes the test is purely vocabulary, other times it is vocabulary and grammar.[42] Each test must be cumulative (potentially covering material dating back to the beginning of the first class) to ensure that students do not merely learn things temporarily. Frequent testing allows instructors to know who is falling behind so that they can attempt to help such students before it is too late. I also assign part of the course grade to homework completion and have students hand in their workbook/homework assignments regularly to ensure they are keeping up.[43] I have found a direct correlation between those who fail to complete their homework and those who either struggle with the course or actually fail.

Memorization Aids

Naturally most of the drilling and reading has to be done outside of class time, so instructors need to give "advice about *how* to explore the system independently."[44] Instructors must encourage successful learning strategies and study habits.[45] First of all, instructors must emphasize that students should review Hebrew *every day*. Skipping days will only make things harder. Make it clear that cramming does not work and that only regular daily study will result in mastery of the language. That being said, time spent learning Hebrew vocabulary can be made more efficient through the use of memorization tools and study hints. It is essential that instructors not only offer students multiple tools to help in memorization but also give students some guidance as to the best way to use them.

---

42. If class meets twice a week, I have one vocabulary test and one grammar test per week. If class meets once a week I have one vocabulary and grammar test per week.

43. Alternatively, you could mark the assignments, though if students have access to an answer key this may not be worthwhile.

44. Odlin, "Introduction," 14.

45. Halabe, "Ancient Languages."

Vocabulary Cards

Hebrew vocabulary cards are a tried-and-true method and can be bought for a relatively small price[46] and some grammars even sell vocabulary cards that pair with the grammar.[47] Alternatively, students can create their own cards, which actually might be the preferred method as it allows them further practice in writing Hebrew characters. Regardless of whether they purchase or create cards, some instruction on good ways to use the cards is vital to student success. I suggest that students initially pull out a limited amount of vocabulary flash cards (5 to 10 words) at a time and initially quiz themselves using only those cards. Once those words are mastered, they should pull out (or create) another stack and learn them. However, it is essential that students do not confuse the different stacks of cards but keep multiple distinct stacks: (a) a stack of cards for words the student has mastered; (b) a stack of cards for words they occasionally or frequently get wrong; and (c) a stack of cards containing new words the student is learning for the first time. These stacks are not immutable piles but must be changed frequently. As the student masters words from stack B or C, these are then transferred to stack A. Stack A continually changes as new words are added and stack B continually changes as new difficult words are added to it. I suggest that students review stacks B and C more often than stack A. While this or a similar method may appear self-evident to you, it is not always so for students. I have been consistently surprised by how some instruction on using the cards in this way has transformed test scores for students who were already using flash cards but in a haphazard manner.

Computer Programs or Apps

Free computer programs are available for students to quiz themselves.[48] Also, various Apps are available that can allow students to use digital flashcards

---

46. E.g., Dillard, *Biblical Hebrew Vocabulary Cards*. These usually sell for around $20 or less.

47. E.g., Zondervan sells vocabulary cards (Van Pelt, *Old Testament Hebrew Vocabulary Cards*) that pair with a particular Hebrew Grammar (Pratico and Van Pelt, *Basics of Biblical Hebrew*).

48. Teknia has an excellent program called FlashWorks that can run on Windows or Mac OS. Online: http://www.learnbiblicalgreek.com/flashworks. Similarly, Christopher Heard has created a series of flash cards using iFlipr, which can be used for free. Online: http://iflipr.com/deck/search?query=Cohelet. There is also an iFlipr iPhone App for purchase. Another website for Hebrew vocab drilling that allows you to choose lists of words by frequency is http://home.earthlink.net/~vikn/hebrew.htm. Another website has short vocabulary quiz videos with the Hebrew word both shown and read out loud

on their iPhone or iPod touch.[49] I have seen great student success through the use of these programs, with some students dramatically improving after using such programs. Some students are simply more likely to use their computer than paper or cardboard flashcards. This is simply a reality today as many spend more time with their computer (be it a desktop, laptop, or Smartphone) than anything (or sometimes anyone) else.

Word Association Hints

One additional tip I give my students is to come up with a hint based on an English word or phrase to associate with the sound of that Hebrew vocabulary word. I then suggest they write the hint on the back of the flash card (if they are using them) or beside the word in the vocabulary list in the textbook, in order to help them remember the word. While memorization of Greek vocabulary is greatly aided by the frequency of English cognates, in Hebrew this is extremely rare.[50] Therefore, I suggest creating funny or otherwise memorable hints to remind them of the Hebrew word. For example, the word נָשָׂא means "to lift" (among other things), so on the back of the flash card for נָשָׂא I suggest writing "NASA—lift off!" underneath with the proper definition. By way of example, here are a few of the hints (word association mnemonics) I have used:

- שַׂר—Czar (ruler) (the word actually derives from the word 'Caesar')
- זָקֵן—old / elder—old people use 'za cane'
- חָכָם—wise, skillful (wise people know 'how come'?)
- סֵפֶר—book/scroll (a book 'is a fair read')
- הֵיכָל—someday I'll see John Calvin in the Heavenly temple and say "hey Cal"
- זָהָב—gold—(zey have ze gold)[51]
- חַיִל—strength, army—(heil!)

(and includes pictures and/or word association hints). Online: http://www.freechurchseminary.org/Vocabulary%20Videos.html

49. E.g., *HebrewFlash Biblical*, by Paul Avery, available through the iTunes store. As well you will find a handy App for learning the Hebrew alphabet: *iStudy: Hebrew Alphabet*. There is also an iFlipr iPhone App that you can buy. There are several Modern Hebrew Apps as well. E.g., *WordPower—Hebrew/*.

50. Sometimes connections can be made with words or phrases students already know (e.g., יוֹם *Yom Kippur*/Day of Atonement or שָׁנָה - Rosh Hashannah—New Years festival in Judaism) but this is rare.

51. Works best with a German accent.

- אָרוֹן—Ark (Aaron was the priest of the Ark)
- "Can't walk? Take לָקַח"[52]

Initially, I give students these types of hints for words, but have found that eventually, after they get the hang of it, students come up with the best hints themselves. Many times the hints work for one individual and not another, so it is best for them to come up with their own (though I encourage sharing any hints with others).

One other hint that can help students remember what the *mappiq* is and how it functions is to refer to it as "the Feminine Period." This term was coined by the (all female) authors Bonnie P. Kittel, Vicki Hoffer, and Rebecca A. Wright.[53] They write, "Because the mappiq in a final ה is always the sign of a feminine singular suffix, we call it the 'feminine period' as a reminder of both its use and its position in a word."[54] I have found this term to be quite useful for students in recognizing *mappiq*.

Rhymes

Along these same lines, I teach my class a couple of handy rhymes. In order to help students keep Hebrew pronominal suffixes straight I teach them this rhyme.

נִי is me
מִי is who
הוּא is he
הִיא (הוּא) is she
and דָּג is fish

Similar to having paradigms committed to memory orally, students can recite this rhyme in their head when they come across one of these pronominal suffixes to assist them in coming up with the right translation. Another short rhyme I use to aid in remembering when to pronounce a *shewa* goes like this:

> When two shewas go a'walkin'
> The second one does the talkin'

The rhymes are fun and are actually quite useful mnemonic aids for students.[55]

---

52. Kittel et al., *Biblical Hebrew*, 105.

53. Ibid., 357.

54. Ibid.

55. The first rhyme I learned in a Hebrew class with Tyler F. Williams at North

USING THEIR HEBREW BIBLES

Once students have purchased or received their Hebrew Bibles I encourage them to use them. After explaining how to find things in the Hebrew Bible, I begin having periodic "sword drills"[56] in class where they attempt to look up a verse faster than other students. To get them familiar with using their Bibles I occasionally have them look up verses to show them interesting features of the text or passage. For example, I get them to look at: (a) the Song of the Sea in Exodus 15 because it is written with extra blank spaces to make the text resemble waves; (b) the Shema in Deut 6:4 because the first ע and the last ד are both enlarged (forming the word עד, the significance of which students can then debate);[57] (c) the final form ם in a medial position in Isaiah 9:6 (לְמַרְבֵּה); and (d) Gen 4:8 which appears to have some dialogue missing.[58]

I also encourage students to look up verses they are familiar with or perhaps memorized as a child.[59] If they attend church, encourage them to take their Hebrew Bibles with them and look up any reference to the Old Testament mentioned in the sermon or Scripture reading (though such references may not be as common as you might hope). Students will be surprised how many words they can recognize. This type of use of their Hebrew Bible raises their level of interest and allows them to apply their knowledge of Hebrew in other settings.

INTEGRATING ORAL LANGUAGE

Research has shown that learning experiences that involve one language process (reading, writing, speaking, listening, viewing) contribute to one's development in others.[60] In fact, oral language has been found to

---

American Baptist College (Edmonton, AB, Canada). The second I learned from Jerry Shepherd in a Hebrew exegesis course at Edmonton Baptist Seminary (Edmonton, AB, Canada). I am not sure who originally composed these rhymes but would express my debt to these two great teachers in this regard.

56. Classic sword drill rules: 1. Students hold Bible by the binding in the air at least at head level. 2. The Instructor reads a biblical reference (e.g., 1 Sam 1:1) then says "draw" (as in draw your swords); 3. Students look up the reference as fast as they can and the first to read the verse wins.

57. Is the word עֵד "witness" or is it עַד "until" as in "forever and ever" (וָעֶד לְעֹלָה)?

58. It appears the dialogue has been lost. It reads "and Cain said to his brother . . . and it happened when they were in the field."

59. Recommended by Isbell, "Hebrew Teacher."

60. Cf. Jeroski, *Reaching Readers*.

be the foundation for development not only in writing but also in reading.[61] Integrating oral language when studying a dead language can be difficult. However, given the potential positive impact on student learning, the instructor should find some way to have an oral component in the classroom.

In Class Reading and Reciting

Obviously, instructors should make some time in class for students to read Hebrew aloud. However, due to time constraints and the amount of material that needs to be covered, student oral reading may have to be somewhat limited.[62] As I mentioned above, I frequently have students recite paradigms orally in class. Also, I always have my class memorize a Hebrew psalm and spend some class time memorizing and reciting it together. Such recitation proves beneficial in terms of both oral practice and student enjoyment.

Audio Recordings

In addition to recording myself reciting paradigms and making the recordings available to students (as mentioned above) I have also recorded myself reading a Hebrew passage slowly, and make the audio file available to students so that they can follow along in their Hebrew Bible. There are many resources available for such use, some of which are free downloads online.[63] Another option is to purchase recordings of people reading Hebrew.[64] If you choose to have your class memorize a Hebrew passage it is helpful to record yourself reading the passage and offer the audio file to the class to aid in memorization.

---

61. Cf. Fountas and Pinnell, *Guiding Readers*.

62. Most students are very slow readers at the beginning, making extensive in-class reading problematic for time constraint reasons.

63. These websites contain the Hebrew Bible recorded in mp3 format with files broken down into chapters and placed in separate folders. Online: http://www.audiotreasure.com/mp3/Hebrew/Hebrew.htm. See also, Online: http://www.aoal.org/hebrew_audiobible.htm.

64. Some resources are available in connection with textbooks. E.g., Kittel et al., *Biblical Hebrew: An Audio Cassette*, is designed as a companion to Kittel et al., *Biblical Hebrew*, and helps students pronounce vocabulary and the lesson sentences. It also has Gen 22:1–19 read and chanted. There is also a newer edition on three CDs that includes songs (Hoffer, *Biblical Hebrew*).

Video Recordings

There are many videos in Hebrew that instructors could integrate into a classroom exercise. One I have used is Mel Gibson's film, *The Passion of the Christ*. This movie was, of course, quite controversial, and very gory; however, the scene I use from the film is neither. Immediately after the opening scene in which Jesus is arrested in Gethsemane, the scene switches to his mother Mary's home where she awakes and has a brief conversation with Mary Magdalene. Though the film is in Aramaic, this scene is in Hebrew. Have students listen to the scene with the English subtitles turned off (the DVD has this feature) and see if they can make out any words. Some of them will be very familiar words (e.g., יְהוָה; בְּמִצְרַיִם; הַלַּיְלָה; אֱלֹהֵינוּ). If you do this exercise late in the year you can even have students parse the various verbs used. After you have guided them into discerning most of the words, write out all the words on the board (alternatively you could add Hebrew subtitles to the video clip as I do) and translate into English. Finally show them the clip with the English subtitles on. They will be very interested to see how the English does not match up with the Hebrew. Specifically the words "in Egypt" and "Yahweh our God brought us out" are not even translated! Interestingly, the short conversation between the Marys is actually a recitation of part of the traditional Passover Seder. Upon realizing this students often discuss how and why the film is associating Jesus' passion with the Passover Seder.

Youtube.com has many videos in Hebrew that could be integrated into the classroom, including scenes from the Hebrew version of the film, *The Prince of Egypt*, that can be fun for the class to watch. One fun exercise is to have the class view the opening seven minutes of the film[65] and listen for Hebrew words they can pick out. The feature song in this clip is "Deliver us" but in Hebrew it is "Hosanna"—but do not tell students that; let them figure that out for themselves. Discovery is part of the fun.[66] Not only do these videos remind them that Hebrew was once a living language, seeing and hearing the language spoken can be motivating and can allow them to connect their knowledge of one language process (hearing Hebrew) with another (reading Hebrew).

---

65. http://www.youtube.com/watch?v=TsVej9neGmQ&feature=related.

66. Another great one is when God first talks to Moses. See the clip in Hebrew at http://www.youtube.com/watch?v=z84BJctyPuE&feature=related.

USE OF CLASSROOM TIME

Practice

I believe each time new concepts or points of grammar are covered, it is essential to illustrate by putting them into practice right away. For instance, if a class or grammar chapter covers multiple topics, immediately after teaching one concept I have students turn to the workbook to put into practice what we just learned. I prefer to do some practice after each concept—even if it is only brief—rather than wait until all concepts for the day are covered, then turning to the workbook.

Use Visuals

Each student has his or her own learning aptitudes and style. It is therefore vital to incorporate different methods and learning strategies to assist students in learning Hebrew. In class I have students read from the grammar, and listen to me lecture, and I also write on the board and display Hebrew words and concepts from a digital projector. Do not simply lecture or refer students to the text or workbook in class. Write out Hebrew on the board, or project the Hebrew text from a computer using a digital projector. If a digital projector is available, I find projecting the Hebrew text from a Bible software program on my computer is very helpful.[67]

It is also helpful to illustrate how letters are lost or how words inflect by writing out the forms on the board. First write out the lexical form then erase or make the changes and step-by-step draw out the changes to illustrate what happens. Never underestimate the value of writing it out—even when the same form is on the page of the textbook.

Using a Bible software program with some basic searching capabilities can be very helpful. For example, when there is a form that, out of context, is ambiguous because it is identical with another form, by using Bible software you can search for the form in the Hebrew text and show students how context really makes clear which form it is. While you can always *tell* them this (and I often do), *showing* them can make a greater impact as they can see for themselves that the form is not as ambiguous as it looks removed from its context.[68]

---

67. You can usually split the screen so that students see only the Hebrew and on your laptop screen you can see translations, parsing etc.

68. For further visuals, some clever comic books on the book of Jonah are available. Online: http://www.animatedhebrew.com/jonah/index.html. These are written in unpointed Hebrew but are fun to read with students in class.

Translate in Every Class

Regardless of how much material must be covered in a class, I believe it is imperative to spend some time every class translating with students. The theory and grammatical rules are well and good, but it is in coming to terms with the written Hebrew text that students finally start to "get" the language. In class you can model ways of deciphering the text and ask questions leading them towards answers. When working through translations it is helpful to call on different students to translate and parse. This also allows you to gauge how well individuals are doing.

The goal in spending time translating with students is to prepare them for independent translation on their own. If you model how to translate, they will be able to use some of the same strategies you demonstrate in class on their own. As they attempt to translate on their own, remind them to take risks while translating—they do not always need to be sure. Encourage them to tolerate ambiguity and vagueness.[69] This will be frustrating for some who want things in black and white, but it is a necessary skill.[70] Encourage students to look at the context and make educated guesses. Often students lack the confidence to do this, but through watching the translation process in class they will begin to see how it is done.

CONCLUSION

Those of us who teach Hebrew are really privileged individuals. Some of the practical benefits of teaching the language are immediately obvious. First, by continually going over the fundamentals of the language, Hebrew instructors are able to keep the language fresh in their own minds much more easily than they would otherwise. Of course, most of us use the language regularly in our research and preparation for other courses, but constantly teaching the grammar can actually produce further fruit in one's scholarship. Second, as a Hebrew instructor you get to see immediate results.[71] You can actually see how students are improving day by day, rather than waiting for a midterm or final exam. This allows you to adjust your teaching throughout the semester according to class aptitudes and progress. Finally, one of the greatest benefits of being a Hebrew instructor occurs when you see a student fall in love with the language.

---

69. Westney, "Rules." So Halabe, "Ancient Languages."

70. I refuse to answer questions by using the words "always" or "never" in regards to Hebrew. Languages do not work that way.

71. Isbell, "Hebrew Teacher."

Though you as a teacher of Hebrew can take or leave the advice proffered in this essay, I hope that no matter which style or approach you take, you will aim to make Hebrew enjoyable. One of my goals, beyond reading and comprehension, is that students come to know the joy of reading God's Word in the original language. Reading the Old Testament in Hebrew is a privilege that statistically very few people are able to have. So whether students set out to become scholars or pastors, or anything else, aim to make reading the Hebrew Bible a joy, so that they will say with the psalmist:

מָה־אָהַבְתִּי תוֹרָתֶךָ כָּל־הַיּוֹם הִיא שִׂיחָתִי:

Oh, how I love your teaching! It is my meditation all day long. (Ps 119:97)

BIBLIOGRAPHY

Brown, F., S. R. Driver, and C. A. Briggs. *A Hebrew and English Lexicon of the Old Testament.* Oxford: Clarendon, 1907.

Dillard, Raymond B. *Biblical Hebrew Vocabulary Cards.* Springfield, OH: Visual Education Association, 1981.

Dörnyei, Z. *Teaching and Researching Motivation.* London: Pearson Education, 2001.

Fountas, I., and G. Pinnell. *Guiding Readers and Writers: Teaching Comprehension, Genre, and Content Literary.* Portsmouth, NH: Heinemann, 2001.

Gardner, R., R. Lalonde, and R. Moorcroft. "The Role of Attitudes and Motivation in Second Language Learning: Correlational and Experiential Considerations." *Language Learning* 35 (1985) 207–27.

Greenspahn, Frederick E. "Why Hebrew Textbooks Are Different from Those for Other Languages." *SBL Forum* (July 2005). No pages. Online: http://sbl-site.org/Article.aspx?ArticleID=420.

Griffin, P. W. "Killing a Dead Language: A Case against Emphasizing Vowel Pointing when Teaching Biblical Hebrew." *SBL Forum* (May 2007). No pages. Online: http://sbl-site.org/Article.aspx?ArticleId=675.

Halabe, Rahel. "Ancient Languages Are Still Around, but Do We Really Know How to Teach Them?" *SBL Forum* (Feb 2008). No pages. Online: http://sbl-site.org/Article.aspx?ArticleID=756.

———. "The Introduction to Biblical Hebrew the Practical Way." *Hebrew Higher Education* 12 (2007) 101–19.

Halliday, M. A. K. *An Introduction to Functional Grammar.* 2nd ed. London: Edward Arnold, 1993.

Hobbins, John F. "Sadistic Approaches to Teaching Biblical Languages." Online: http://ancienthebrewpoetry.typepad.com/ancient_hebrew_poetry/2008/02/sadistic-approa.html.

Hoffer, Victoria. *Biblical Hebrew, Second Edition (Audio CD).* Yale Language Series. New Haven, CT: Yale University Press, 2005.

Holladay, William Lee. *A Concise Hebrew and Aramaic Lexicon of the Old Testament: Based upon the Lexical Work of Ludwig Koehler and Walter Baumgartner.* Grand Rapids: Eerdmans, 1988.

Isbell, Charles D. "The Hebrew Teacher: Guru, Drill Instructor, or Role Model?" No pages. Online: http://www.sbl-site.org/assets/pdfs/ isbell.pdf.

Jeroski, S. *Reaching Readers: Canadian Biographies*. Teacher's Guide and Transparency Pack. Toronto: Pearson Educational Canada, 2005.

Kittel, B. P., V. Hoffer, and R. A. Wright. *Biblical Hebrew: A Textbook and Workbook*. New Haven, CT: Yale University Press, 1989.

———. *Biblical Hebrew: An Audio Cassette*. Yale Language Series. New Haven, CT: Yale University Press, 1989.

Odlin, Terence. "Introduction." In *Perspectives on Pedagogical Grammar*, edited by Terence Odlin, 1–22. Cambridge: Cambridge University Press, 1994.

Pratico, Gary D., and Miles V. Van Pelt. *Basics of Biblical Hebrew Grammar*. Grand Rapids: Zondervan, 2001.

Vail, S. M. "Hermeneutics and Homiletics." *Methodist Review* 48 (1866) 371–86.

Van Pelt, Miles V. *Old Testament Hebrew Vocabulary Cards*. Grand Rapids: Zondervan, 2004.

Weimer, Maryellen. *Learner-Centered Teaching: Five Key Changes to Practice*. San Francisco: Jossey-Bass, 2002.

Westney, Paul. "Rules and Pedagogical Grammar." In *Perspectives on Pedagogical Grammar*, edited by Terence Odlin, 72–95. Cambridge: Cambridge University Press, 1994.

Williams, Tyler F. *An Answer Key for Biblical Hebrew: A Supplement to the Text and Workbook by Bonnie T. Kittel, Vicki Hoffer and Rebecca A. Wright*. Yale Language Series. New Haven, CT: Yale University Press, 1996.

8

Leading Intentional Theological Reflection in the Classroom
The Merging of Mind and Heart

WENDY J. PORTER

INTRODUCTION

Seminary is one of those places where you train your mind to process, evaluate, think, and write, and where you develop the skills to evaluate others' thinking and writing at the same time. You might be tempted to train your brain just in order to pass an exam, to get a good mark on a paper, to get credit for a class, or just to get that degree that will help move you towards a further educational, career, or ministry goal. Or the subject itself may be so stimulating and rewarding that you can't seem to get enough information about it, and so you just keep gathering more and more.

The life of the mind is fascinating and intriguing, compelling and exciting. The more you learn about something, the more you can interact with others about it. It can be heady to discover that you know more about a subject area than your peers do. As you research your area and begin to formulate your own thoughts and ideas about it, there is something almost addictive in the thrill of the chase, getting your ideas worked out, interacting with scholars who have published in the area—though their publications are most certainly not as relevant and exciting as your own discoveries, of course. You may experience endorphins when you are running or working out in the gym, but there is an equal or greater endorphin-rush when you find yourself deep in an investigation of the mind.

But here's the thing. Unless you pay close attention, unless you are on active guard-duty, unless you are absolutely attentive to that still small voice and the quiet probings and whispers of your heart in the midst of all this, you will end up with a mind-heart dichotomy that can leave you with something worse than a lobotomy. It can result in something that I have tentatively named a "heart-onomy" (which you will not find in your dictionary, although you can find "cardialectomy"). Perhaps a better term—also not found in your dictionary—is "heart atrophy."

Heart atrophy is where you end up with a massive brain, able to digest and process and distribute great quantities of information, but where your heart shrivels up from lack of use. The more education, knowledge, or information a person has about a particular topic or subject or discipline, the more likely they are to rely on that education, knowledge, or information. And this is where the challenge lies: We must have a *merging* of mind and heart, rather than an *emerging* of one over the other. In the academic sphere, it is usually the mind that wins out. In the everyday workplace and in the average church, it is probably the heart that wins out. Neither is entirely acceptable. There needs to be a merging of the mind with the heart, and strong resistance to the emerging of heart or mind above the other, although almost everyone tends to lean towards one or the other.

This is where intentional theological reflection becomes crucial to our lives. Learning to do theological reflection and then to actually lead intentional theological reflection in the classroom is one way in which we bring together these two aspects of our lives into a useful and meaningful communion.

If it is not attended to, the *informational knowledge* that results from a head-only accumulation of data can begin to separate our intellectual minds from having a meaningful connection to the heart. *Transformational knowledge*, on the other hand, is a kind of knowledge that involves both heart and mind. Theological reflection can help move us more in the direction of transformational knowledge.

The term "theological reflection" is becoming increasingly familiar in churches, Christian universities and colleges, seminaries, and other Christian and broadly-defined religious circles. Many people agree that it is good to engage in it.

But what it really is still seems to remain something of a mystery! People have trouble defining it. Ask the average church-goer, maybe even the average seminarian, what theological reflection is and you will hear some ambiguous answers. Mind you, this does not prevent people from having strong opinions about theological reflection, even if they can't tell you what it is exactly. Impressions range from the vague notion that theological reflection is something that makes your Christian life better, which somehow seems appealing and attractive, to the more specific (yet still remarkably vague) notion that it is a bunch of people sitting around talking about their feelings about theology and life, which is often perceived as quite unappealing and unattractive. It is generally agreed that, whatever it is, it is supposed to be good for you, just like bad-tasting cough medicine. Then when people discover that it does require some hard mental work, and can cause some emotional distress at the same time, they often become less fascinated with the notion, and quickly decide that they probably did not really need it after all. Subsequently, that also means that they do not and cannot teach others anything about it either.

However, there is good reason to believe that understanding and engaging in the process of theological reflection is vital to one's spiritual life, that it is an essential skill that every Christian should develop. Why? Because it is through the thoughtful experience of actively looking for God's presence in the events and experiences of our individual and corporate lives that we encounter greater depth and breadth as Christian individuals and communities. Essentially, the act of theological reflection is the ongoing search for God, and for spiritual—that is, Spirit-led and Spirit-filled—wisdom. Knowledge without this spiritual wisdom is simply knowledge. Knowledge *with* this spiritual wisdom is something incredible that brings us into communion with God at every level, a merging of our own heart and mind with the greater heart and mind of God.

For this reason, every Christian teacher should attempt to practice theological reflection and to integrate it into their class sessions. This is true whether their subject matter is obviously related to theology and faith or not, and perhaps *especially* if the subject matter is not obviously related to theology and faith. But even teachers of Bible and theology and the practice of ministry need to learn the art and skill of leading theological reflection in the classroom, because it is all too easy to accumulate knowledge or develop skills, even in these areas, without learning how to integrate them into the deeper spiritual aspects of one's life. For all of us with Christian principles and values, including teachers, it is critical that we learn how to work out those Christian principles and values in every area of our lives and to challenge and teach our students to do the same.

Before we move on, let's begin with a working definition of theological reflection.

WHAT IS THEOLOGICAL REFLECTION?

In some ways, the instinctive questions that people ask when something bad happens are the questions that invite us into the initial stages of theological reflection. Questions like "Why did this happen?" "Why did God let this happen?" or even "If there is a God, why would he let this—or cause this—to happen?" all direct us to consider God's presence in our lives or in the world around us, even if we don't know quite what that means. These are intellectual conundrums. They are also heart conundrums, because they touch us at the deepest parts of our lives where things do not always seem to make sense.

But theological reflection is not something reserved only for those most troubling and traumatic moments in our lives. Meaningful theological reflection should be a way of life long before those large-scale problems come. In fact, without practicing this skill on the small things, we find ourselves unprepared to navigate the larger troubling issues in times of crisis and trauma. The excellent patterns and habits of theological reflection that we practice and teach provide foundations for thinking about and dealing with life. They help us to be more fully integrated Christians, allowing Christ to permeate every aspect of our lives and ministry, our careers and callings and relationships.

Apart from the major crises in life that prompt even the normally *un*reflective person to ask some questions about God's presence in the world and in our lives, there are many everyday observations and ideas that can and should prompt us to engage in intentional theological reflection. The key word is "intentional." To engage in meaningful theological reflection requires a conscious decision to enter into it, to take it seriously, and to develop the "muscles" of working in this way. We all know that we do not develop physical muscle while we sit on our couches and watch endless hours of television, that it is only when we get out and exercise and challenge those muscles that they develop any tone or strength. In the same way, it is only when we actually exercise and challenge our theological reflection muscles that we develop any strength and tone in them, because real theological reflection requires intentional activity.

There are many ways of describing and defining this activity of theological reflection. Howard Stone and James Duke, in *How to Think Theologically*, define Christian theological reflection as the "process of thinking about the meaning of faith in the Christian message of God,"[1] or "serious thinking about the meaning of Christian faith."[2] They go on to describe it thus: "To engage in theological reflection is to join in an ongoing conversation with others that began long before we ever came along and will continue long after we have passed away."[3] This notion of a conversation is one that is used by many of the recent writers on theological reflection.

James D. Whitehead and Evelyn Eaton Whitehead, in their *Method in Ministry: Theological Reflection and Christian Ministry*, write: "Theological reflection in ministry is the process of bringing to bear in the practical decisions of ministry the resources of Christian faith."[4] The resources of Christian faith that they refer to are Christian tradition, personal experience, and cultural information.

Others that have contributed to defining and describing the notion of theological reflection include Raymond Collins,[5] Elaine Graham,[6] Patricia O'Connell Killen,[7] Robert Kinast,[8] Stephen Pattison,[9] John Patton,[10] and Judith Thompson,[11] to name a few. None of these defines theological reflection in exactly the same terms, of course. Some are fairly broad in their definition, and their definitions reflect their own theological backgrounds, but each is very intentional about engaging in—and helping to lead others to engage in—meaningful theological reflection.

Theological reflection is a process of actively exploring the ways of God, the ways of people, and how these intersect. In fact, I would say that theological reflection is active engagement with God in response to God's invitation, not only to learn more about God, but to know God more

---

1. Stone and Duke, *How to Think Theologically*, 138, see also 2.
2. Ibid., 4.
3. Ibid.
4. Whitehead and Whitehead, *Method in Ministry*, 1.
5. Collins, *Models of Theological Reflection*.
6. Graham et al., *Theological Reflection: Methods*.
7. Killen and de Beer, *Art of Theological Reflection*.
8. Kinast, *What Are They Saying about Theological Reflection?*
9. Pattison, "Some Straw for the Bricks."
10. Patton, *From Ministry to Theology*.
11. Thompson et al., *SCM Studyguide to Theological Reflection*.

deeply, and therefore to know ourselves more fully, and to understand and love our neighbor more effectively. Theological reflection is a process by which we seek after God, and by which means we discover that he is already seeking after us.

Theological reflection involves both our left brain more-rational thinking *and* our right brain more-creative thinking, which creates a synergy that is not produced with only one or the other. Theological reflection originates with God, although most people engage in theological reflection as a result of something happening to them, so it *looks* like it begins with us. God has already revealed himself to us through creation, through Scripture, through Jesus Christ, through his Spirit, through our consciences, through our own spirits responding to him even when we aren't quite sure that is what we are doing. Through this revelation of himself, he invites us to notice him. He invites us to begin a mind-and-heart conversation with him that allows us—on our own and with others—to understand more deeply every aspect of him, to recognize what he has shown or revealed to us about himself, and what he is showing us about ourselves.

Theological reflection is an intentional, focused, and imaginative process of actively responding to God's revelation of himself. This revelation invites and challenges us to search for him, to actively look for the evidence of his presence and work in events, interactions, and intersections of life around us and within us. Our goal in responding to this invitation to engage in meaningful theological reflection is that we will be deepened and transformed in our hearts, our minds, and the way we live. As we train our hearts and minds in this discipline of theological reflection, we become increasingly more attuned to who God is, and where he is working in and around us. As we move forward in this discipline, we become increasingly shaped and formed like him, just as Paul indicates in his letter to the Romans (12:2): "Do not conform to the pattern of this world, but be transformed by the renewing of your mind. Then you will be able to test and approve what God's will is—his good, pleasing and perfect will." This, ultimately, is the motivation for serious theological reflection.

As I have outlined above, theological reflection is, in part, an activity that is *intentional*. It doesn't happen without some effort. Theological reflection is *focused*. It requires attention and time and space devoted to really concentrating on the issue or problem or idea. Theological reflection is *imaginative*. One of the factors that challenges some people in beginning to engage in theological reflection is that it requires activating our right-brain thinking, while a lot of standard education and learning seems to be centered in left-brain thinking. Theological reflection is a *process*. It doesn't all happen at once; it requires starting somewhere, and then moving forward, step by step. Theological reflection requires an *active response to*, and an *active search for* God's revelation of himself. If we seek, we will find, because it is by God's invitation that we enter into this conversation, or step into this journey. Every day—and in this case, every class—provides numerous opportunities for meaningful theological reflection, but we have to notice one, we have to stop and pick it up, we have to do something with it. God *is* with us—and theological reflection is the means by which we begin to see how "with us" he really is. In actively responding to him in this way, we are saying that we are open to being deepened and transformed, because we desire God to be "with us," and to be actively present "within us." So, there is some risk involved in theological reflection, because God's truth may—in fact, probably will—change us in ways that we were not expecting or desiring. But openness to this risk is absolutely worth it. As our minds and hearts are opened, they are also changed, re-formed, transformed. As we persist in active and thoughtful theological reflection, we are shaped by the working out of these spiritual conversations, these spiritual journeys, until we are refined and re-shaped into individuals and communities that more closely reflect Christ.

There are three foundational keys or starting points for meaningful theological reflection. The primary *grounding* for theological reflection is *Scripture*. The primary *catalyst* for theological reflection is the *Holy Spirit*. The primary *attitude* for theological reflection is *prayer*. Many who write about theological reflection would not place these as centrally, but I believe that the essence of deep and meaningful theological reflection is the result of this triad.

There are a number of sources or lenses that help us to engage in meaningful theological reflection. Again, not all who contribute to the growing body of literature on the subject of theological reflection would include all these. However, my colleague Lee Beach (who has co-taught a class on this with me for several years) and I are increasingly convinced that they should include *Scripture* (which I have noted above is foundational), *Christian Tradition* (which could also be called *Christian History*), *Experience*, *Culture*, and *Reason* or *Logic*. A final one could be called *Discernment*, or perhaps just an acknowledgment that the Holy Spirit must guide us in determining where we end up. Each of these sources or perspectives can help us to be more comprehensive and grounded in our thinking and reflection about any given topic or issue. We will look at some further examples of this below.

WHO NEEDS THEOLOGICAL REFLECTION?

Every growing and maturing Christian benefits from, and even needs, theological reflection. We find examples throughout Scripture of men and women who were involved in deep and active theological reflection, starting with Adam and Eve in the garden and ending with John's account of his spectacular and troubling vision of something yet to come. Read the biography of any truly great woman or man of God throughout history and we see that they each engaged in various forms of deep and ongoing theological reflection, regardless of what it was called at the time. This ongoing activity of theological reflection is part of the working out of our salvation with fear and trembling, as Paul puts it (Phil 2:12).

To be more specific, let's consider who it is that needs theological reflection:

Individuals need theological reflection. It deepens our spiritual lives and causes us to become more thoughtful, and more *heartful*, in our Christian faith.

Marriage-partners need theological reflection. We learn a great deal about how to meaningfully contribute to our marriages by engaging in personal theological reflection alone with God about our own marriage, as well as in active exploration with our spouses, as we develop the discipline of theological reflection in the center of our marriage relationships. The troubling issues of decision-making, careers, moves, challenges in communication, merging different family traditions, child-rearing, and empty-nesting are but a few of the possible entrees into potentially meaningful theological reflection. So also are the simple moments of observant appreciation for the beauty of God's creation on a walk together or sitting quietly outdoors in the coolness of a summer evening.

Families need theological reflection. Theological reflection as family members helps us to remember God's place in our individual lives and how we grow together as a family. Family theological reflection helps to sort out the things that happen in families, the changes that take place—everything from discipline issues at home to problems at school to changes as children grow and develop into young adults, and the difficulties related to choosing friends, dealing with deaths in the family, choosing higher education, moving to a new place, family budget struggles, choosing a spouse, etc. Each of these can provide excellent entry points into meaningful theological reflection, where every participant, young and old, can learn and grow in faith.

Church leaders and ministers need theological reflection. The busyness of church life and ministries and meetings can keep us from actually stopping to think about and engage with God in our lives and ministries. Without theological reflection, we can miss out on God's presence working in and through us while we are busy doing the things that we think or presume are ministry.

Church members and attenders need deep theological reflection. Some church leaders might even be tempted to deter their congregations from developing this important discipline, but it is crucial for Christians to learn how to engage their own hearts and minds in deep matters of faith and life, and to search for how God reveals himself in their own faith and lives—not just waiting for the pastor to give them the right answers.

However, even if you agree that individuals, marriage-partners, families, church leaders, ministers, and church members and attenders all need theological reflection, you may still remain unconvinced that theological reflection belongs in the classroom. Is that honestly a place for theological reflection?

The Classroom Needs Theological Reflection

Admittedly, the classroom is not where most people tend to imagine theological reflection taking place. But why not? Why shouldn't students learning biology or chemistry or philosophy or math or literature or writing composition or the history of music or computer science or cooking or woodworking or systematic theology or biblical knowledge (or any other subject) be challenged to engage in meaningful theological reflection about God's work and presence in their lives and in the world around them? Why shouldn't they develop into more fully integrated Spirit-filled human beings by considering scenarios or challenges of how God relates to his world through their own subject area? Why shouldn't they learn to explore how intentional theological reflection in the context of any discipline can cause us to think more deeply about God and his ways?

But, we may respond, how could we include theological reflection in a class on biology or chemistry or philosophy or cooking, etc.? How can we stop for theological reflection, when we must cover certain material? Perhaps the better question is: Can we afford *not* to stop for theological reflection? In some cases, it may actually help us to cover more material and more fully learn that material in more efficient and beneficial ways than any other approach. No, it won't take the place of our lesson plans, but it can certainly supplement them in valuable ways. And it will help our students in *in*valuable ways.

If our teaching environment will not permit the exercise of engaging the entire classroom in theological reflection (though, keep reading below), we can certainly engage individual students in one-on-one conversations before and after class. These are the kinds of life-changing conversations that a student remembers long after they have forgotten all the specific material that we teach in the formal class.

Starting with Ourselves

During the time that we lived in London, England, my husband and I would sometimes see a particular man in the Waterloo train station. He was noticeable because he was extremely hunched over. He was so hunched over, in fact, that he could not look forward to see where he was going, because his face was parallel to the ground, and he could not lift his head up from this position to be able to see where he was going. So, he carried a small mirror. He would position this mirror in such a way that he could look down into it and see what was up ahead. The bravery of this man going through that train station in such a manner was astonishing to see.

Perhaps this man is more like each of us than we at first realize. Because we can stand upright and use our own eyes to see (though perhaps with the help of glasses or contacts or even surgery), we can be lulled into thinking that we can automatically "see." But we each have mis-shapen aspects of our lives and character that can prevent us from "really seeing," that require us to be intentional about "really looking," and that require some tools to assist us in "really seeing." Sometimes the families or churches or cultures that we grew up in formed us in ways that were actually more de-formed than we knew at the time, and now it is difficult to see God in and around us.

Before we can introduce theological reflection into the classroom, we need to engage in it ourselves. We can do this with colleagues or fellow-students or friends or family members. And we should each actively engage in intentional theological reflection that specifically relates to our own specialized subject areas.

We can begin by identifying an initial question that relates to our area, and perhaps an area that we may also be teaching. How has God revealed himself through some area of our own discipline? How has God revealed himself to us as we have studied and learned our discipline? What large troubling problem or small niggling problem in our discipline prompts us to ask where God is at work in it, or in the world, or in us? As we begin to develop thoughtful internal conversations with God about these concerns, we begin to become more observant of all the possible valuable conversations that we could have with our students that could be deep and meaningful, challenging and life-changing.

Even learning how to invite God into the middle of our class-time would be an excellent illustration of our awareness of God's presence. In a Christian institution, it is not unusual for a teacher to *begin* a class with prayer. But why don't we stop and pray in the *middle* of the class, when there is something troubling being discussed or something difficult to teach or learn? Why don't we invite the entire class to stop for a minute, to be silent as we center our attention on being in the presence of God, and then ask him to focus our hearts and minds in the details of an exploration or examination of something, whether big or small? Why not stop mid-stream, and publicly invite God into the process? He's there anyhow, so why don't we acknowledge it and, by doing so, teach our students to do the same?

God's ongoing revelation to us invites us to respond to him. Why don't we make a point of actually doing that, even if it is the briefest moment in the middle of a class?

BUT HOW DO WE REALLY DO THEOLOGICAL REFLECTION?

We do need practical instruction and tools to do theological reflection. There are many possible ways of doing theological reflection, whether individually or in a group, but here are some basic guidelines.

First, we begin with an attitude of prayer. We consider God's revelation to us of himself, and begin to ask where God has revealed himself in a particular scenario or situation, perhaps prompted by an issue or question, a troubling problem or crisis. We can imagine that God himself is hosting the conversation and that he is warmly inviting us to engage honestly with him in it.

Second, with a prayerful heart, we can choose a scenario that will be the focus of our classroom theological reflection. There is no limit to the possibilities here, but some general suggestions are included below.

Third, we begin by describing the situation, scenario, or question, and we try not to interpret anything at this point or give "answers." This helps everybody to learn how to observe, to notice, to determine the facts of a situation, separate from any kind of interpretation.

Next, with an ongoing pervading attitude of prayer, we begin to discuss our topic through the following perspectives or lenses: (a) *Scripture*, (b) *Christian Tradition* or *History*, (c) relevant *Culture*, (d) personal *Experience*, (e) our use of *Reason* or *Logic*. One question that is frequently used as a starting-point in theological reflection is: "Where can we see God in this?" This can provide a thoughtful beginning to the conversation. As we consider these various perspectives or lenses, it might look something like the following.

We might begin by considering *Scripture* passages that speak of a similar troubling scenario or raise a similar problematic question. Perhaps we search for a passage that gives us insight as to God's perspective on the situation. What passages do we discover, and what do they say? What truths do we learn related to our particular discussion? Would we need more time and research to really explore what Scripture has to say on our topic or how it might speak into our situation? Should this investigation be an ongoing discussion that we carry on throughout a semester or year?

We then could begin to consider things that others have already struggled with or already learned, and perhaps shared (e.g., through literature, church traditions, creeds and liturgies, poetry, the arts, etc.) throughout *Christian Tradition* or *History* that has something valuable to contribute to this conversation. Have others already been where we are, and can we learn something from their wisdom—or their mistakes?

Then we could turn to discussion of what the surrounding *Culture* has to say about this topic or problem. Are there aspects of our specific current and local culture that conflict with or confirm what we have seen in Scripture and church history? We can be challenged by how God has influenced—or been shut out of—our current cultural perspective, and perhaps how we have similarly been blinded or dulled by it.

Then we can turn our attention to consider how personal *Experience* is related to our topic. Does our own or someone else's well-selected experience bring insight and wisdom to the discussion? Does it challenge our perceptions and beliefs in some way? What do we do with that challenge?

As we note each of the above factors, we must then begin to use *Reason* or *Logic* in relation to our topic. What that means is that we now need to weigh the issues, look at the facts, compare *Scripture* with someone's personal *Experience*, compare *Christian Tradition* with what we have noticed in our current and influential *Culture*, and so on, to determine how to come to a conclusion on where God is revealing himself through this problem or event. What are the truths that we can hold on to (yes, even for a so-called post-modern culture that pretends that "truth" doesn't exist)? What is it that God is communicating to us through our thoughtful interaction with one another and with these various perspectives?

As we are using the resources of *Reason* and *Logic*, we must return to Scripture in an attitude of prayer. We hold all of our findings and musings and experiences up to what we know and understand about the Word of God and ask the Holy Spirit to give us the *Discernment* necessary to see what God wants us to know about himself through this process.

As we look back on our theological reflection, we begin more fully to see and absorb what we have learned through this process, and then we determine what personal or group change needs to happen as a result of our learning, for all deep theological reflection will result in some kind of change, whether internal or external.

HOW TO LEAD THEOLOGICAL REFLECTION IN THE CLASSROOM

In bringing theological reflection into the classroom, it is crucial to plan for it in advance and to designate a specific period of time (no matter how short) in at least one class, with the goal of engaging the class in a discussion or project. This is best, though not absolutely essential, if the topic or subject area is pre-assigned, so that students have at least some opportunity to prepare for it.

A Theological Reflection Class Project

Introduce a scenario or topic that is relevant to the class members, and give this to them in advance of the class discussion. Divide the students into five groups, and assign each group to contribute several significant examples from their assigned source or perspective, as outlined above (*Scripture*; *Christian Tradition/History*; *Culture*; *Experience*; *Logic/Reason*).[12] Students

---

12. Note that depending on the age and maturity of the students in your class, and unless they are exceptionally quick at assessing ideas as they are being presented, you

in the first group would bring several significant *Scripture* passages that relate to the topic. The second group would have several important contributions from *Christian Tradition/History* that have something important to say about the topic. The third group would bring examples from contemporary *Culture* that raise questions or contribute answers to the discussion topic. The fourth group would have gathered evidence of personal *Experience* that confirms or questions the topic. The fifth group would be prepared to put forward *Reasoned or Logical arguments* that weigh the various contributions and help the group to come to a conclusion about God's presence in the situation.

Ideally, plan on at least 20 to 30 minutes to guide this discussion. Have students sit with the others of their group, so that everyone can visually identify who represents what resource (though there will inevitably be overlap among the groups). Keep your eyes on the clock. Elicit responses from each group, one by one, even while inviting some participation from the various groups throughout. Leave a few minutes for each group to bring their findings.

In the process, some of those who didn't think they understood what was going on will begin to engage in the topic. At the very least, it will prompt some of them to begin to think more deeply on the topic. Summarize the findings at the end of the designated time, but encourage students to continue thinking and talking about it. Invite students to talk personally with you about it if they are interested. If possible, build some kind of longer-term project or assignment around this kind of discussion, or a similar or equally relevant topic for the next time.

Most of all, encourage students to become observant about the intersection of God in the world and the lives of people around them, as well as the intersection of God within the particular discipline that is being taught in that classroom. It is worth noting that you may well find that this is the most productive class of any you have ever taught. If that is the case, it may be worth considering more ways of engaging in similar kinds of discussion throughout the duration of the course.

---

may plan to guide the class as a whole to draw on the fifth source, *Logic/Reason*, *after* the other four have been presented. The use of the fifth category largely rests on what is presented in the first four. In a seminary-level class, it is reasonable to have all five categories presented by various groups; in an undergraduate class or high school class, however, it might be necessary for the teacher to guide discussion of the fifth source.

In a Class on Any Subject?

Many of us may wonder how a teacher of a subject other than formal theology can effectively guide students to learn how to engage in meaningful theological reflection. Even if we haven't really systematically studied theology, we can be convinced that it is important to help students to be conscious of this important aspect of their development and theological integration, and want to help them to gain these tools. How do we help students to learn how to be aware that God is present and somehow at work in the world around us and even in the interactions of our own day-to-day learning and life, no matter how difficult they may be?

What if every one of us as teachers of every subject area were to build into our teaching plans intentional moments of God-reflection? What if we were to regularly build in moments that draw attention to where our subject matter converges with the things of God? What if we were to think of it as one of the lookout-points that we find on a highway through the mountains: a spot where we can pull our car away from the speeding traffic, get out of our car, walk to a specific spot that has a magnificent view, and simply stop for a moment to take in and appreciate this spectacular expanse of creation? This can be a moment of pure re-creation, where we connect however briefly with the Creator, and are re-energized, re-ignited as one of his created beings through experiencing his presence. We breathe. We take in the beauty. We notice the colors. We feel the breeze. We hear the trickle of a spring or the rush of a waterfall. We feel the spray of water or the touch of a breeze on our face. We feel the warmth of the sun or the freshness of the rain. We consider the works of God's hands. We hear the whisper of the Spirit as we take it in. We consider passages of Scripture that speak of his majesty and his handiwork. We think of a book or poem or piece of art that has compelled us before to think about God in a similar way. We think about the speeding cars behind us that might represent our culture, all so busy, not bothering to stop and take in the beauty. We realize that we are now adding to our own personal experience of finding God in the middle of a frantic trip somewhere, anxious to get there quickly, yet realizing that in our hurry, we almost missed this moment of tranquility and of sensing God's presence. We weigh all of these factors and come to a conclusion that we are going to be more intentional in the future about stopping—no matter how busy we are and no matter how little time there seems to be—in order to notice God and to commune with him in other similar moments.

So it is in our class. We are hurtling along a road to somewhere, on a high-speed information highway, with specific goals in sight, things our students need to learn and must know, things that are important to our discipline and for this particular class. We have a syllabus and we are trying to accomplish the goals set out in it. We have an Academic Dean or a Headmaster, a Principal or a President, that we must give an account to, so we need to accomplish a great deal in this class. We have students preparing for careers or further academic pursuits, and we are certain that they need each moment of our prepared material for their own futures.

Even if this is true, it does not mean that we cannot—or should not—find moments in our class for reflection on God, inviting God or God-awareness into our discussions. These will be refreshing, motivating, inspiring, and they will help to put everything else into perspective and right balance. These moments are important, possibly even more important than the prepared lecture. These moments help us, and our students, to remember why it is that we do what we do, and why it is important to teach what we teach or to learn what we need to learn. One small detail in each class could be highlighted in this way.

We can personally begin by doing some of our own homework, searching out what Scripture has to say and teach us about our own subject area or discipline—not just the noted scholars that we normally read or study. As we do this, we can begin to incorporate more of these insights into our regular lesson plans. We can teach our students how to think theologically in all subjects, to ask questions like: Where is God in this?

In creating syllabi and lesson plans, could one assignment have to do with seeing and understanding God through the lens of our subject-area or discipline? As we develop students in our own discipline in the areas of Knowing, Being, and Doing, can we incorporate Imagination by asking how our students can be godly representatives in this area of study, learning to discover where God is at work in it? If we have not been asking ourselves those same kinds of questions, then this is an excellent place and time to begin. As we personally discover answers, we will want to include our students in this theologically reflective and insightful journey as well. For instance, where *do* we see God in our discipline? Where *have* we observed him at work in our subject area? What role *does* our subject area have in God's large-scale drama? If there are troubling issues in our fields of study, what potential discussions would provide opportunity for meaningful theological reflection, even if we cannot arrive at a final "solution" or "answer"? As we discover evidence of God working in some aspect of our discipline, we can bring these into the discussion.

It would be easy to assume that the obvious place to include theological reflection is when teaching at a seminary, but even at a seminary you must be pro-active in order to accomplish the important task of teaching and leading theological reflection in the classroom. One of the best solutions is to assign our students to do it throughout the duration of the course, because then they are fully engaged in it (at least on the day for which they are responsible), and it allows the unique creativity of the individuals in the class to be explored. Almost any class could have room for a student-led 5 or 10-minute "devotional" or "theological reflection" or "God-awareness moment" at the beginning of the class. Students could present a thoughtful question to consider or an insight into the connection of God with humans or with subject areas. Encourage students to be creative, but also require depth of thought and insight. Assignments could include such things as:

- an interactive skit that several students act out, dealing with a theological issue or problem that has relevance to the subject matter of the class
- a collection of poems or readings that speak thoughtfully to the topic
- a newly-written poem or song that brings insight to the class
- a thoughtful presentation incorporating a music recording
- a news item that prompts theological reflection on the theme of the class
- creative interaction with a biblical/historical character that prompts the class to weigh issues and think theologically.

Regardless of the subject matter of the class, there will always be issues, themes, topics, problems, questions, and current events that can engage everyone in thinking more deeply about God, his ways and revelation, and how he intersects with us where we didn't expect or can't explain or just don't like.

In being willing to explore theological reflection in our own lives, and then risking finding ways to bring it into our classrooms, we can develop more compassion for our students and more commitment to their own developing spiritual maturity. As we grow in Christ-like love for our students, we become interested not only in the areas of their academic pursuits, but also in helping to foster a maturing integration of their spiritual lives within that discipline, learning how to process ideas, articulate thoughts, and convey solid arguments through speaking, writing or other media—all tempered with the wisdom and discernment of the Holy Spirit. As Henri Nouwen writes, the person "who can articulate the movements of his inner life, who can give name to his varied experiences, need no longer be a victim of himself, but is able slowly and consistently to remove the obstacles that prevent the spirit from entering. He is able to create space for Him whose heart is greater than his, where eyes see more than his, and where hands can heal more than his."[13]

Moments of Contemplation

As we develop our own personal capacity for deep theological reflection, we will begin to see possibilities all around us for wonderful and challenging moments of spiritual insight and spiritual growth. If we are engaged in the close detailed work of learning and teaching some subject area, we can challenge ourselves to learn to step back for a moment from whatever we are learning and teaching, and to look for evidence of God in the bigger picture. Or, if we are constantly looking at the big picture, we can also discipline ourselves to take the time and effort to stop and look more closely at the intricacies and details that will reveal God's handiwork. In either case, we can share our personal insights and learnings with our students.

For instance, if music is my subject area, and I spend my time analyzing musical formulas, recognizing the composer's creative genius in the details, but never stop to just sit there and listen to the music—what is the point? I have not understood or experienced the music at all.

However, if I normally just listen to excellent music as background to whatever else I'm doing, but never stop to appreciate the intricate details of a brilliant and masterful composition, and perhaps the genius of the composer behind it—again, what is the point? I have missed out on the greatness of the music by neglecting to really stop and notice it.

Now, if I consider God as the Composer, is there some "music" out there that requires that I do some more intentional and focused listening? And is there a background piece that he has created that requires some diligent investigation to see what tiny and marvelous miracles are hidden beneath the surface of those incredible sounds and melodies and rhythms?

---

13. Nouwen, *The Wounded Healer*, 38–39.

IN CLOSING

No matter what the subject area, there are dozens, even hundreds, of topics, themes, and questions that could result in meaningful and challenging classroom theological reflection, inviting us to respond to God's presence in the world, in our world, in our subject area. And we have the privilege and the responsibility as teachers of looking for meaningful ways of engaging in this personally and then teaching our students to do the same by building it into our classroom time. Don't let this opportunity pass you by, because as a teacher, you will inevitably discover that a student is not usually around for long. The opportunities for this kind of valuable learning are gone in an instant if we don't make the most of them while we can.

SELECT BIBLIOGRAPHY FOR FURTHER INVESTIGATION OF THEOLOGICAL REFLECTION

Collins, Raymond F. *Models of Theological Reflection*. Lanham, MD: University Press of America, 1984.

Garrido, Ann M. *A Concise Guide to Supervising a Ministry Student*. The Concise Guide Series. Edited by Kevin E. McKenna. Notre Dame, IN: Ave Maria, 2008.

Graham, Elaine, Heather Walton, and Frances Ward. *Theological Reflection: Methods*. London: SCM, 2005.

———. *Theological Reflection: Sources*. London: SCM, 2007.

Killen, Patricia O'Connell, and John de Beer. *The Art of Theological Reflection*. New York: Crossroad, 1994.

Kinast, Robert. *What Are They Saying about Theological Reflection?* New York/Mahwah, NJ: Paulist, 2000.

Nouwen, Henri. *The Wounded Healer: Ministry in Contemporary Society*. New York: Image, 1979.

Pattison, Stephen. *The Challenge of Practical Theology: Selected Essays*. London: Jessica Kingsley, 2007.

———. "Some Straw for the Bricks: A Basic Introduction to Theological Reflection." In *The Blackwell Reader in Pastoral and Practical Theology*, edited by James Woodward and Stephen Pattison, 135–45. Oxford: Blackwell, 2000.

Patton, John. *From Ministry to Theology: Pastoral Action and Reflection*. Nashville: Abingdon, 1990.

Stone, Howard W., and James O. Duke. *How to Think Theologically*. 2nd ed. Minneapolis: Augsburg Fortress, 2006.

Thompson, Judith, with Stephen Pattison and Ross Thompson. *SCM Studyguide to Theological Reflection*. London: SCM, 2008.

Whitehead, James D., and Evelyn Eaton Whitehead. *Method in Ministry: Theological Reflection and Christian Ministry*. New York: Seabury, 1980.

Woodward, James, and Stephen Pattison, eds. *The Blackwell Reader in Pastoral and Practical Theology*. Oxford: Blackwell, 2000.

9

From Doctoral Program to Classroom

Steven M. Studebaker

The transition from my doctoral program to my first full-time teaching position was a mixed bag of excitement and frustration. On the one hand, I was brimming with anticipation and delight because I had secured a position and was now able to begin a career as a professor of theology—the fruit of those long years spent in graduate school. I was Assistant Professor of Theology in the School of Christian Ministries at a Christian liberal arts college. It was a dream come true. On the other hand, I had a bit of consternation, especially as I made my way through the first couple of years of teaching. Several problems confronted me.

First, I quickly realized that the academic skills that impressed my graduate school colleagues and professors were less appreciated by my students. I wanted the classroom experience to be like the graduate seminar, a robust conversation between the professor and students based on an intimate understanding of the issues at hand. But such was not to be.

Second, the necessity of preparing and teaching four courses per semester (all new preparations for the first year and rarely multiple sections of the same course thereafter) left little time to revise my dissertation for publication and pursue new research programs.

Third, I earned a PhD at Marquette University. Marquette is a Catholic university and the Theology Department has an ecumenical faculty and student body. This context fostered vibrant interaction among faculty and students and the cross-pollination of theological ideas. Discussions in class were sometimes intense, but always charitable. However, my first teaching position was at a college with a strong denominational connection. The school was not anti-ecumenical and parochial, but it expected its professors to teach material that represented and respected the tradition of the school. In other words, I moved from an ecumenical setting of a free exchange of ideas to a confessional one.

This essay offers advice for making the transition from the graduate school experience to the context of the classroom. It addresses three challenges in this transition: (1) teaching for the class and not the graduate seminar; (2) pursuing research through the means of teaching; and (3) teaching within a confessional context. The assumed teaching setting for the advice in this essay is undergraduate Christian colleges and universities, and seminaries that focus on preparing people for various forms of Christian ministry.

TEACHING TO THE CLASS AND NOT THE SEMINAR

In graduate school, students hone vigorous academic research skills. They develop the art of crafting, demonstrating, defending, and presenting the results of their research in order to impress their fellow graduate students and professors. They also begin to present the fruits of their research at academic conferences and publish it in refereed journals. The graduate school experience is very exhilarating and rewarding. Moreover, it is a very practical experience for producing the apex of formal theological education—the dissertation—and for preparing for and participating in the arena of academic scholarship. Unfortunately, the graduate school experience and the habits learned therein do not instill practical skills suited to teaching, especially teaching in an undergraduate context, where many newly minted biblical, theological, and church history scholars will have their first opportunity to employ their craft. This section offers several points of advice for making the transition from the graduate seminar to the classroom. These recommendations touch on pedagogical techniques, but focus more on the broader attitudinal and cultural values related to the classroom.

First, the successful transition from graduate school to the classroom requires you to embrace the distinct culture of the classroom. Unless you secure the rare opportunity of going directly from graduate school to teach advanced graduate seminars in a research-oriented university setting, classroom teaching calls for skills that differ from those of the graduate seminar. Even professors at seminaries and universities often teach introductory courses in their respective fields and teach electives that, although they segue with their doctoral research, also go beyond it. The challenge in most teaching settings is to embrace the reality that the talent that led to success in the graduate seminar may lead to failure in the classroom.

The reason for this disconnect is the different cultural expectations and values between the graduate seminar and the classroom. The culture of the graduate seminar prizes erudition on the fine nuances of ancient languages, historical texts, and contemporary theologies and scholarship. Copious footnotes that demonstrate mastery of the primary and secondary literature impress graduate student colleagues and professors. They recognize the value of scholarship for the sake of scholarship because it contributes to an ongoing field of scholarly discourse and to developing a trajectory of inquiry. Most undergraduate and seminary students who sit before you could not care less about these things. You need to grasp the fact that other than the people who comprised your dissertation committee and a few scholars sprinkled here and there around the world, no one much cares about the ground breaking advance in scholarship proffered by your dissertation. This disconcerting situation is especially true of the hurly burly group of undergraduates you will encounter in the classroom. As much as this might offend your scholarly sensibilities, the sooner you get over it the better. Moreover, you should not fault these students; after all, why should they care about such things as the distinctions between Thomas Aquinas's theory of primary causes and his theory of secondary causes?

Most students at Christian liberal arts colleges and universities take courses in Bible, theology, church history, and ethics because the curriculum requires them to do so and not because they see any value in them. Of course, the classes do have value and that is why schools include them in the core requirements for degree programs; nevertheless, the students themselves often do not recognize their importance. This reality is true even for students in ministry degree programs. They want to learn "how to do ministry" and not to waste time studying what to them are the esoteric and attenuated intellectual rabbit trails of biblical and theological scholars. Thus, the first step in the transition from graduate school to the classroom is to accept the distinct cultural context of the classroom.

Second, the primary expectation of the classroom is to give students a credible introduction to the field of study and to do it in a way that makes sense to, and has some feel of relevance to, students preparing for diverse professions. These cultural values of the classroom are a product of both the expectations of the institutions and the students. The institution did not hire you to air the intricacies of your dissertation and latest journal article to its students. The school and its students want you to answer questions like: "What does the doctrine of the Trinity and Paul's letter to the Roman Christians mean for a nineteen-year-old preparing for a career in nursing or elementary school education?" The school that pays your salary and the students that pay the tuition that enables the former to pay your salary expect you to answer such questions and concerns. Moreover, this expectation is appropriate. Answering scholarly questions and making innovative contributions to scholarship are valuable too, but at an academic conference and not at 8:00 a.m. on a Monday morning to a group of undergraduates in an introductory course on Christianity.

Third, do not expect undergraduates to operate at the academic level of the graduate seminar and the dissertation oral defense. They are undergraduates who have probably never thought much about the intellectual issues of the Bible and the Christian faith beyond Sunday School and Youth Group. Their minimal ability to conduct theological reflection and research is not a moral failing. Rather, it is a result of the broader Christian culture in North America that focuses on personal piety and church activities and tends to marginalize the life of the mind.[1] They also come from disparate educational backgrounds. Some of them will be able to articulate their research and their viewpoints with finesse. But many of them will not even know what a thesis is, let alone have the ability to write a thesis paper. Moreover, though writing a thesis is a very practical activity for a graduate student, for most of the students in your classes it may have little utility. You should endeavor to develop assignments that require students to delve into the academic field of the course and enable them to reflect on this material in a way that can help them better understand what it means to be a Christian in the context of their personal lives and careers.

Fourth, you should endeavor to remove unnecessary impediments to students' success. Based on my graduate school experience and especially at the doctoral level, in that context professors could expect students to learn the ropes more or less on their own by talking to their colleagues who were further along in the program. Professors could do this because graduate students tend to be motivated and have a strong desire to succeed because their future in and beyond the program depends on it. We

---

1. For two excellent essays that describe the neglected life of the mind in North American Evangelicalism, see Stackhouse, "Perpetual Adolescence," and Stackhouse, "The Christian Church in the New Dark Age."

do not want the person we ask for a letter of recommendation for our first teaching post to think that we are inept dupes. Undergraduates are more concerned with getting through the class with a grade that will not hamstring their overall GPA. With this reality in mind, the professor should accept that their students need more direct guidance, instruction, and help in order to succeed in their classes.

One way to accomplish this task is to provide student friendly syllabi. The syllabi I received in doctoral seminars were often one page (excluding the bibliography) with very Spartan assignment descriptions: such as, research paper 80% and book review 20%. If you try this with undergraduates, you may as well plan for a meeting with your department chair and/or academic dean, who will then duly disabuse you of the propriety of such practices. Why? Because undergraduates go into an apoplectic fit when they see that the majority of their grade rides on one assignment. Furthermore, what on earth do you mean by "research paper"? What topics are acceptable? Yes, appropriate topics are obvious to you; after all, the class is an introduction to Christian theology. However, your students may not even know what Christian theology is and thus not have the slightest clue as to what a suitable topic might be. You should endeavor to de-mystify the course and the assignments as much as possible. What is clear to you is ancient hieroglyphs to them. Students are from earth; academics are from another galaxy.

Professors can also help their students by remembering that teaching is a student-focused activity. With that in mind, teachers should let the nature of the course shape the content of lectures and the approach to the class. Courses of an introductory nature should provide the "big picture" of and broad orientation to the subject and not the arcane minutia that is of interest mostly to specialists in the field. However, upper level electives can delve into the more sophisticated and technical issues of the subject matter. The nature of the course should drive the content and approach to the material presented in the class, although hopefully professors can achieve an alignment between their research interests and their teaching areas.

The classroom is also the place to empower students. I believe that paternalistic and condescending attitudes should be rejected. For example, some professors refrain from incorporating student presentations and projects into classes because they think such assignments produce only a collaboration of the ignorant. To be sure, students will not usually present material at the level of an academic conference, but so what? We should expect them to operate at the level they are at and not at that of a professional conference. Some courses are more suited to the more traditional lecture format due to size and the content focus of the course. However, I believe that professors should give students the opportunity to practice the art of the discipline of study. After all, they will never learn to do so without mentored assistance and practice. Students are like flowering plants. Early on they appear awkward and gangly, but without these first seasons of sparse blooming and pruning, they will never become beautiful flora.

Teachers should also remember that the classroom is a place where students can achieve vocational clarity. My college Theology and Old Testament professors were inspirations to me. Their inspiring example, their enthusiasm, and their genuine concern for their students helped shape my vocational calling; I wanted to be what they were. Teaching is a privilege—a privilege that includes not only dispensing data (though that is important) but also shaping the lives of students. I am not suggesting that professors assume delusions of grandeur in terms of their influence over students; nevertheless, they play a real and sometimes decisive role in shaping the lives of students and that reality should influence what is taught and the way it is taught. Which of your professors would have guessed that when you were in his or her introductory course, you would catch a vision for the field and eventually make the transition from student to teacher?

TEACHING, A CONTINUATION OF RESEARCH BY OTHER MEANS

One of the most significant challenges that new professors face is to find time to conduct research as they create lectures for new classes. The transition from the graduate school context to the teaching one is stark. The former not only encourages, but demands focused and sustained specialized research, while the latter calls for canvassing and summarizing the notable highlights of multiple areas of theology. For example, my doctoral research focused on the trinitarian theology of Jonathan Edwards. I spent several years delving into the intricacies of the Augustinian trinitarian tradition, arcane early Enlightenment philosophies and criticisms of the Trinity, and the internecine squabbles among scholars over the interpretation of Edwards's trinitarian theology. Three months after graduating with the doctoral degree, I moved to my first full-time teaching position. For that first semester, I had to prepare lectures for four new courses—New Testament History and Literature, Gospel of John, Christian Ethics, and

God and Revelation. Of these four courses only the last one had anything to do with my area of specialized research. Although I had taken graduate courses in biblical studies and ethics, they were not my areas of expertise. My experience, especially for those who begin their career in an undergraduate setting, is not unusual.

The challenge for the new graduate and professor is to meet the twin challenges of becoming an effective teacher and an excellent scholar. Compounding the challenge is the reality that many liberal arts colleges that take pride in their student focus and identity as teaching institutions may not value research and scholarly activities. Scholarship is not explicitly denigrated, but simply may not be a cultural value for the institutions. The focus on teaching is appropriate because it coheres with the mission of these institutions to educate students for a variety of professional fields. Nevertheless, it does mean that professors who seek to serve their schools and contribute to the academic guild have an added task. Despite the formidable challenges to pursuing scholarly research and contributions, new professors need to traverse them and achieve a scholarly identity and voice. I am not suggesting that you subordinate teaching to research or give your teaching short shrift; however, I do want to encourage you to retain and develop your scholarly habits as you expand your repertoire to include the art of teaching. For inspiration, I turn to an unlikely source, Carl von Clausewitz's theory of war.

Carl von Clausewitz (1780–1831) was a Prussian officer and soldier during the Napoleonic wars. Based on his experience fighting the armies of the French Revolution under the leadership of their commander Napoleon, he wrote one of the enduring contributions to military theory. His most well known military dictum is that "war is . . . a continuation of political commerce [politics] . . . by other means."[2] Clausewitz's notion of war as a continuation of politics or a political activity has three facets. War is (1) the extension of state will, (2) an act of the state external to the affairs of the state, but for the benefit of the state, and (3) a historically causative force.[3] Of course, the correlation between teaching-research and war-politics is not exact. For instance, when a state opts to pursue war to achieve a political aim, war is perceived as the prudent or only way to attain it. In respect to the relationship between teaching and research, teaching is probably rarely the best and never the only way to achieve a

---

2. Clausewitz, *On War*, 1.1.24 (p. 119).
3. Echevarria, "War, Politics, and RMA," 77.

research goal. Moreover, I do not intend to convey the impression that the classroom is the academic equivalent of a Napoleonic battlefield. Nevertheless, Clausewitz's idea of war as a continuation of political activity can be applied to the relationship between research and teaching in the following way: teaching is the continuation of research by other means. The following details the ramifications of this dictum according to the three nuances of Clausewitz's military axiom.

First, war as a political activity means that war is an extension of state will. War is a political activity because in it the state exerts its political will to accomplish something that less martial means will not procure. Applied to the research-teaching relationship, this means that teaching, as a continuation of research, is an act of the will of the scholar. What I mean is that one must make a concerted and determined effort to use teaching to pursue a research agenda. Research, for the most part, will not happen of its own accord, but requires the concerted and determined effort of the professor. Sure, one will always have periodic serendipitous flourishes of insight. However, one should not rely on these events, but rather intentionally use one's teaching opportunities for the service of research programs. This recommendation does not mean that lectures should be a thinly veiled pretext to parade one's most recent scholarly investigations. Being a responsible teacher means teaching what the course description requires and the students need, pursuing not just the narrow interests of the teacher. Notice that I said, "*not just* the narrow interests of the teacher." In most, perhaps not all, teaching assignments one can, through creativity, bring one's area/s of interest/s into the classroom.

For example, when I taught New Testament History and Literature, I covered the material that was necessary for an undergraduate introductory course in New Testament studies. However, I also devoted significant energy in course preparation and lecture presentations to areas of the New Testament that cohered with my research interests in the doctrines of the Holy Spirit and grace. This strategy was beneficial both to me and to the students—to me, because I was able to harness that time spent in course preparation for my research and writing projects. To the students, because I was able to lecture and lead discussions on topics that reflected my strengths, which meant that the students received superior course content. The application of Clausewitz's principle to the teaching-research relationship means that achieving synergy between what appear to be disparate teaching and research goals requires intentionality. Teaching, as research by other means, requires the professor's exertion of will.

Second, war is an act of the state external to the affairs of the state, but for the benefit of the state. Teaching is an activity distinct from research and in this sense it is an activity that is external to the affairs of research. Research, unless one is writing a textbook, has an academic audience in mind. Research focuses on very specific topics and treats them with nuance and sophistication that other specialists in the field will respect and find persuasive. Teaching has a different audience in mind—the undergraduate and seminary classroom. The classroom calls for the teacher to condense vast amounts of information and to present it in a way that is digestible by people who often have little background and interest in the material. Thus, teaching is an act of the professor that is external to the research affairs of the professor. However, teaching can be pursued in the interests of and for the benefit of research.

Let's reconsider my example of teaching New Testament Literature and History. While I was teaching this course, I was in the thick of research on the implications of Puritan Jonathan Edwards' and Roman Catholic David Coffey's trinitarian theology for their respective doctrines of Christ, the Holy Spirit, and redemption. I, of course, delighted in the devotional reading of the New Testament, but had little interest in the scholarly nuances of New Testament scholarship (just as I am sure that most New Testament scholars have little time for the esoteric sophistries of trinitarian theology!). The point is that teaching New Testament was an activity that was external to my research interests. Nevertheless, as indicated earlier, I discovered a way to conduct this external affair in such a way that it benefited my research program.

Third, war is a historically causative force. What this means is that war is an activity that has historical consequences and especially historical consequences for the state that wages war. Teaching, as the continuation of research by other means, is a causative force that can have consequences for research too. If you choose not to pursue research by the other means of teaching, the dilution of the yield of research by the time spent in preparation for teaching assignments is the consequence. On the contrary, if you pursue research by the means of teaching you will increase your scholarly output. This result is due to the simple fact that you will give your research agenda more attention and energy. Teaching obviously will not pay dividends equal to time spent in research in your area of specialization. However, it will contribute to it and in this sense it is a causative factor in your long-term contribution as a scholar. An additional beneficial consequence of the pursuit of research by teaching is that you will supplement your research and scholarly contribution with broader areas of scholarship. The causative effect of teaching on research has a connection with the intentionality of pursuing research through the means of teaching too. Your teaching will augment your research most effectively when done deliberately. For instance, while teaching through the New Testament, I was looking for and thus uncovered significant passages in the Gospel of John, Romans, and Ephesians that directly deepened my constructive work in the areas of pneumatology and grace.

TEACHING IN THE CONTEXT OF CONFESSIONALISM

Professors who teach in confessional schools face a difficult quandary: how do they fulfill legitimate academic standards and retain confessional faithfulness to the institution? Professors face this twofold difficulty particularly in the selection of texts and teaching methods. Texts that present the best scholarship frequently reflect viewpoints inconsistent with the school's denominational identity. Conversely, books that comport with denominational views often miss the mark of credible academics. Responses to the conundrum tend to be parochial and/or apologetic. I propose *critical confessionalism* as a means to avoid these two alternatives and to achieve academic and confessional integrity in text and teaching style decisions. In order to develop the case for critical confessionalism, the following (1) describes the challenge of teaching in a confessional context, (2) outlines the meaning of critical confessionalism, and (3) sets forth several benefits of critical confessionalism.

The chief challenge for teaching within a confessional context is that a confessional school has a clear denominational affiliation. It often receives financial support from a denomination, adheres to a clearly defined theological and religious tradition, and bears the explicit purpose of transmitting that tradition to students. The latter purpose is particularly the case for schools that train ministerial students. My first full-time position was at a confessional school in the Wesleyan-Holiness and Pentecostal traditions—i.e., it affirms three works of grace: conversion, sanctification, and baptism in the Holy Spirit (in other words, the confessional minefield was dense). In all of my classes, the texts had been pre-selected and the broad content framework of the courses predetermined. The point is that in a confessional context, professors must tacitly and often explicitly endorse and promote a historically and theologically specific tradition of Christianity.

The ethical dilemma for the professor in a confessional context is to select texts and teaching methods that meet credible academic criteria and also conform to the tradition of the school. In the face of this challenge it is easy to pursue one goal and neglect the other one. On the one hand, teachers choose a parochial approach. They adopt texts and methods that embed students in the tradition, but deprive them of a proper orientation to the field of study. On the other hand, professors select readings and methods that meet academic standards, but diverge from the institution's confessional identity. The result of the latter decision can be twofold. The professor assumes an apologetic posture that negates other viewpoints and defends those of the institution. Thus, the professor must constantly defend the school's tradition vis-à-vis the textbook. The apologetic approach is problematic pedagogy because it lends itself to misrepresenting the alternative views. Caricaturing is a disservice to students because it does not provide them with an accurate presentation of the other view(s). A second consequence is that the class implicitly undermines the denomination's doctrines or viewpoints by overtly teaching ideas at variance with the school's confessional identity. The ethical conundrum is that these options violate either the ethics of academic responsibility or loyalty to the institution's mission; which, particularly in the case of the latter, may jeopardize the professor's longevity at the institution.

A solution must provide a way for the professor to fulfill the call of academic responsibility and institutional fidelity. Critical confessionalism is a teaching style that enables the professor to meet academic and institutional responsibilities and it is therefore academically and institutionally ethical. In this section of the essay, I use my experience teaching within a confessional context and the specific course "Pentecostal History, Theology, and Polity" to illustrate the proposed method. Moreover, I approach this issue from the perspective of teaching historical theology.

The method reflects *confessionalism* because it assumes a commitment to a particular tradition of Christianity. As indicated, my teaching context was a confessional school that represented the Wesleyan-Holiness and Pentecostal traditions. The college embraces students from diverse Christian backgrounds and does not seek to proselytize, but at the same time it expects its professors, particularly in the disciplines where theological issues become explicit, to teach from the perspective of its representative traditions. Teaching at the college requires at times only an implicit, but at other times a clear, affirmation of those traditions. The school employs professors from other traditions, but they are expected to refrain from overtly criticizing the traditions of the school and promulgating the perspective(s) of their traditions. A confessional teaching method therefore assumes a positive posture toward the theological tradition(s) of the school.

The teaching method is also *critical*. A critical method has several characteristics.

First, it strives for comprehensiveness. For example, when I took a similar course as a student in a Pentecostal college I received a selective history that narrated the positive and ignored the negative aspects of the movement. The course reflected a rose-colored-glasses method of teaching Pentecostalism. However, early Pentecostal history is not entirely positive and flattering. Racism, segregation, anti-intellectualism, and spiritual elitism characterized some aspects of early Pentecostalism. When I approached teaching the course titled "Pentecostal History, Theology, and Polity," I decided that if I avoided these unseemly aspects, I would fail to introduce students to the history of Pentecostalism. Thus, I strove to give a comprehensive account of the Pentecostal movements and not only one that complimented the sponsoring denomination. At the same time, however, I made sure to highlight the positive nature of Pentecostalism.

Second, a critical method is comparative. In the course on Pentecostalism, I could have taught it as an apologetic for the sponsoring college's historical and theological self-understanding. However, that approach would deprive students of other Pentecostal and non-Pentecostal interpretations that can supplement and enrich their appreciation of the school's history, theology, and contemporary direction. Academic credibility required that my teaching method include interpretations of Pentecostalism that differed from and might question the institution's and denomination's self-interpretation. Teaching the denomination's self-understanding is appropriate because it is one of the versions, but to neglect alternative accounts is academically irresponsible. Nevertheless, course content and methodologies should be consistent with the institution's theological outlook.

Third, critical teaching introduces students to materials that reflect the best scholarship in the given field appropriate to the course level. In an important way, the text book/s is/are the measure of the scholarly level of the course. Critical teaching calls teachers to use the best texts in the field. When I began to investigate possible course texts for "Pentecostal History, Theology, and Polity," I discovered that many texts cover the theological history of Pentecostalism, but that most of these are denominational or movement hagiographies. I also found that a non-Pentecostal had written the best historical-theological account of the movements and so I assigned it as required reading in the class. Some of my colleagues believe that it is problematic to use a non-Pentecostal's (i.e., an "outsider's") interpretation of the movement to teach a course on Pentecostalism at a Pentecostal college, but it was the most thorough treatment of early Pentecostal theology and history. My goal was to provide students with the best scholarship available. A non-Pentecostal scholar's work was at that time the best text available on early Pentecostalism, so I assigned it for the course. However, I also used the prescribed text that covers the early and contemporary history of the movement composed by a credible historian who is also part of the school's tradition. Nevertheless, I decided that if I omitted the former text, I would fail to introduce students to the best scholarship on the subject, which is academically unethical because they are paying for the best I can give to them.

Fourth, higher education should involve self-analysis. Every tradition, school of interpretation, theory, etc. has internal problems and data that suggest a view alternative or even contradictory to its own. A teaching method that ignores these issues fails to genuinely introduce students to the subject matter. Critical teaching avoids the hubris of thinking that we and our particular tradition of Christianity are always correct and are without need of revision and correction. Additionally, self-criticism is not equivalent to self-deprecation. In the course on Pentecostalism, the examination of early Pentecostal thought illuminated deficiencies in contemporary Pentecostal spirituality. Both Richard G. Spurling's communitarian vision of love and Charles F. Parham's emphasis on the missional understanding of the purpose of the Pentecostal experience critique and correct the self-absorbed spirituality that characterizes elements of contemporary Pentecostalism. Thus, the role of critical self-analysis is constructive.

Fifth, course content should reflect the course title and description. For instance, a course titled American Christianity and described as an introduction to the various forms of American Christianity should not primarily tell the story of the sponsoring denomination. Thus, the course on Pentecostalism needed to cover the broad contours and diverse forms of the movement. Critical teaching keeps the focus on the purpose of college education. Colleges exist to educate students and not to indoctrinate them with a set of pre-conceived questions and answers.

Critical confessionalism also has several benefits. The first benefit is that critical confessionalism is ethical. The professor meets academic standards and remains faithful to the institution's identity. The professor rejects parochialism because it is a disservice to his/her students. Critical confessionalism also avoids the apologetic posture, which uses the right resources, but then assumes a defensive posture vis-à-vis the sources and the school's confessional distinctiveness. The critical confessional method provides students with a sound education and at the same time retains its confessional fidelity. Thus, the method offers a way to transcend the polarities of being either academically respectable or institutionally faithful by uniting both concerns.

Critical confessionalism is also constructive. It recognizes that critiquing the confessional tradition can be positive when its goal is either growth or retrieval of an earlier insight that is lost to the current generation. Engagement with alternative views also enriches the students. To affirm the positive in another tradition or viewpoint is not to stand against our own tradition. Nor do we need to list all the problems with another view if we speak positively on certain of its aspects. Critical teaching enables students to develop a mature understanding of their tradition. Additionally, it equips them to dialogue with other viewpoints and to integrate appropriate insights from other traditions.

CONCLUSION

The transition from doctoral research to teaching presents significant challenges. It entails contexts that have different cultural values and expectations and requires different skill sets for success. The demands of teaching in an undergraduate and seminary context can also divert new professors from developing their research programs. Moreover, schools often have clear confessional contours, which can stand in tension with the ecumenical and critical approach to issues the teacher was used to in graduate school. This essay encourages new professors to embrace the unique values of the classroom, suggests ways to persist in pursuing a research agenda, and recommends a strategy to negotiate the terrain between credible academics and institutional fidelity.

QUESTIONS TO ASK YOURSELF

1. What are some of the challenges you face in the transition from graduate school to teaching?
2. What are some of the ways you can make your classes academically credible, relevant, and accessible to your students?

3. What is the culture of your teaching context in terms of research and teaching ethos?
4. What are several ways that you can integrate your teaching assignments and research interests?
5. What is the confessional make-up of your teaching context?
6. What are some of the challenges your context poses and how might you address them?

BIBLIOGRAPHY

Clausewitz, Carl von. *On War*. Edited with an introduction by Anatol Rapoport. New York: Penguin, 1968.

Echevarria, Antulio J., II. "War, Politics, and RMA—The Legacy of Clausewitz." *Joint Force Quarterly* 10 (Winter 1995–96) 76–80.

Stackhouse, John G., Jr. "The Christian Church in the New Dark Age: Illiteracy, Aliteracy, and the Word of God." In *Evangelical Landscapes: Facing Critical Issues of the Day*, by John Stackhouse, 89–102. Grand Rapids: Baker Academic, 2002.

———. "Perpetual Adolescence: The Current Culture of North American Evangelicalism." In *Evangelical Landscapes: Facing Critical Issues of the Day*, by John Stackhouse, 13–23. Grand Rapids: Baker Academic, 2002.

10

The Upside-Down Professor
The Professor in a Christian Institution

GORDON L. HEATH

There are at least two popular stereotypes of professors, and both are not very positive. The first can be seen in the movie *Nutty Professor* (1963), with Jerry Lewis. For many, professors are exactly what Lewis portrayed: nerds, geeks, awkward misfits, and loners. The second can be seen in the more recent made-for-TV movie *Wit* (2001), with Emma Thompson. In that movie, Vivian, professor of English, is dying of cancer. Throughout her harsh and dehumanizing treatment at the hands of the hospital staff she is reminded of her own cold and brutal treatment of her students. As her demise approaches, she slowly realizes that humility, compassion, and sensitivity were superior to the arrogance, aloofness, and inhumanity that marked her own academic career.

The problem of geekiness in the academy will have to be dealt with by someone else. This brief chapter will deal with the other problem, that of arrogance, insensitivity, and abusive power. More specifically, it will propose a radically different approach to being a Christian professor, especially for those who train leaders in Christian colleges or seminaries. Sadly, as my students will attest, I do not live up to everything that I propose.

My issue is not with the need for a Christian mind, as Mark Noll calls for in *The Scandal of the Evangelical Mind* (1994), or with the integration of a Christian worldview with one's research, as George Marsden exhorts us to do in *The Outrageous Idea of Christian Scholarship* (1998). I am a firm supporter of both. Rather, my particular concern is with the disposition of Christian professors and how it relates to training people for ministry.[1]

My title draws upon the decades-old book by Donald B. Kraybill, *The Upside-Down Kingdom* (1978). Kraybill's central thesis is that "the shape and form of the new kingdom contrasts sharply with the old social order."[2] He writes,

> The Gospels suggest that the kingdom of God is inverted or upside down when compared with the conventionally accepted values, norms, and relationships of ancient Palestinian society and of modern culture today.... It's a different game played in the middle of the old ball park. Kingdom players follow different rules and listen to a different coach. Patterns of social organization which are routinely taken for granted in modern culture are questioned by kingdom values.[3]

Kraybill compares society's view of greatness with Jesus', and notes how they are dramatically different:[4]

Greatness in Society	Greatness in the Kingdom of God
top, powerful, master, first, ruler, adult	bottom, servant, slave, last, child, youngest

Jesus washing his disciple's feet is a poignant example of such a radical reorientation.[5] Leaders in the kingdom are to be humble and serve their followers; they get down on their own knees rather than force others onto theirs. Everything that we know about leadership in the world (e.g., power, exploitation, arrogance, entitlement) is to be abandoned for a new way. In the words of Kraybill, following "Jesus means not only a turning around

---

1. My target audience in this chapter is professors in confessional institutions where speaking and living the Christian faith can be overt—and is expected. Parker Palmer's attention to the "inner life" of the teacher relates to my emphasis on the "disposition" of a Christian professor. See Palmer, *Courage to Teach*.

2. Kraybill, *Upside-Down Kingdom*, 21–22.

3. Ibid., 24.

4. Ibid., 276.

5. Ibid., ch.12.

in some personal habits and attitudes, but most fundamentally it means a completely new way of thinking—a new logic."[6]

While I do not agree with every aspect of Kraybill's book, I do think that he is right when he notes that the kingdom of God was central to Jesus' life and ministry, and that there are social implications to citizenship in that kingdom. The upside-down imagery is also helpful, for it provides a vivid mental picture of just how radical kingdom living should be: everything that we assume about power, prestige, privilege, and status is turned on its head. This brief chapter does not pretend to offer much by way of innovation, for others greater than I have already noted the importance of upside-down leadership, or what others have coined "servant leadership."[7] Nor is this a blueprint for "one-size-fits-all" institutional changes. However, what it does intend to do is remind Christian professors—especially those teaching at seminaries—of what they should already know. And in recalling such truth, hopefully a vision for new ways of professoring will be birthed.

THE PRESENCE AND PERILS OF PRIDE

Wayne Clark's sage advice to ministers includes a warning about the problem of conceit.[8] He claims ministers often become afflicted with what he coined the "God complex." But where did they get such an idea? Do you ever wonder where we get arrogant pastors and Christian leaders who pride themselves on their titles, status, and knowledge? Who abuse power? Who seem to know everything, or at least speak authoritatively about everything? Who make people feel small? Who wield power like a club? Perhaps they learned it from their professors.

This is not meant to be a jeremiad against the academy, for there are many outstanding professors. In fact, the majority of my professors were gracious women and men of faith who treated their students with respect and modeled humility. Nevertheless, the academy is a breeding ground for arrogance and misuses of power that can insidiously work their way into the classroom.

---

6. Ibid., 302.
7. For instance, see Agosto, *Servant Leadership*.
8. Clark, *The Minister Looks at Himself*, ch. 6. Of course, anyone familiar with early church history knows that ancient leaders like Chrysostom or Pope Gregory the Great warned of the dangers of pride.

Kraybill notes that the academic environment is particularly prone to very noticeable and inflexible social stratification.

> In colleges and universities the stacking and ranking of persons is obvious and rigid. At the top is the president or chancellor, followed by academic deans. Frequently there are division heads such as the chairman of the humanities. Then come departmental chairmen and three kinds of professors: full professors, associate professors, and assistant professors. Next are instructors, paraprofessionals, secretaries, maintenance personnel, and housekeepers. Students come somewhere near the bottom—a bit above housekeepers.[9]

This stratification in the academic world is reinforced by location and size of offices, degrees on walls, numbers of books, and official regalia during ceremonies. The need for structure in any organization is obvious; however, the danger is that those in the structures forget the nature of the upside-down kingdom.

That well-meaning professors often fall prey to the lure of power and pride should be no surprise. Professors are mere mortals like everyone else, and the trappings of the academic world only make the temptation more appealing. Besides the organizational structures that reinforce a pecking order, there are a few other reasons why the requirements of the upside-down kingdom can be eclipsed. First, students tend to place professors on pedestals (hard to resist the lure of that adulation!). Second, teaching a class comes with significant power. And if "power corrupts and absolute power corrupts absolutely" then professors are in great danger. Third, the educational paradigm that most professors were trained in is one where knowledge and publications are power, and the social order is very clearly delineated. What was learned in their doctoral program simply becomes transferred to the classroom. In short, there are many reasons why professors can fall victim to the lure of power and pride. In fact, with the odds stacked against them, it is a testimony to the character of those professors that they managed to be upside-down at all.

Much of my concept of seminary comes from Pietism. Pietism began around the work of Philipp Jacob Spener (1635–1705), a Lutheran who was concerned about the spiritual condition of his church. He felt that Lutheranism had become focused on doctrines, or confessions, and had become too formal, professional, and lifeless. Spener was convinced that right belief needed to be accompanied with true piety (sincere devotion and acts

---

9. Kraybill, *Upside-Down Kingdom*, 260.

of love). In other words, right doctrine was not enough (although it was important)—one needed to have a personal and living faith. The name "pietism" may have come from Spener's written work entitled *Pia Desideria* (1675) ("Devout Wishes" or "Pious Desires"). This was a guide to increase devotion, godly living, Bible study, and prayer. Another important figure in the movement was August Hermann Francke (1663–1727). Like Spener, he was a Lutheran concerned about the spiritual vitality of Lutheranism.

The movement spread through personal Bible studies, preaching, and lay-people exercising their gifts. It also spread through the University of Halle, where Francke taught, and which turned into a center for the spread of Pietism (hundreds of young people were trained in the ways of Pietism and placed into pastorates around Germany). He was convinced of the importance of *praxis pietatis*—a practicing piety, a living faith, and theological study rooted in the need to minister. Through his work at Halle the term "seminary" came into use for the training of pastors (*seminarium*—a hothouse for young plants). The problem with Christian professors who take the worst of the academy into the classroom is that they are poisoning the growth of future leaders—ironically, in the very place that was supposed to be a hothouse built for healthy development.

Unchecked pride leaves a wide swath of destruction. First, it damages self. The famous Baptist preacher Charles H. Spurgeon (1843–1892) made the following observation about the dangers of pride:

> It has too often happened that *prospering* professors have become *proud* professors and have forgotten God. When they were poor they associated with Christian Brethren whom they felt pleasure in recognizing. But now that they have gotten a large estate they no longer know the poor people of God and they spend their Sabbaths where they can meet with a little "society," and move among their "equals," as they call them—they, being so very much superior to the holy men and women whom once they held in honor! Such folks become high and mighty like Nebuchadnezzar—and as they walk their grounds or sit in their painted chambers they say, "Behold this great Babylon which I have built." A "self-made man," risen from the ranks, comes to have a name like the name of the great men that are upon the face of the earth—is not this something? Oftentimes has it happened that these things have turned away the hearts of professors from the God who loaded them with benefits.[10]

---

10. Spurgeon, "True Prayer." By "professors" Spurgeon generally means "those who profess to be Christians," but the quotation is also apt for academic professors.

Even if pride does not eventually destroy one's faith, it does make life miserable. Clark observed that a person filled with pride "is constantly tormented by the fear of being shown to be inadequate . . . he fears detection and demotion."[11]

Second, pride infects others and damages the church. It is axiomatic that we learn from example—seminarians being no exception. And the church will suffer if ministers-in-training learn from their professors a misuse of power and an inflated vanity. The following anonymous poem, *A Church Perish*, makes a simplistic but witty connection between a pastor's pride and the demise of the church:

> There is a pastor, himself he cherished,
> Who loved his position not his parish
> So the more he preached
> The less he reached
> And this is why his parish perished.

AN UPSIDE-DOWN PROFESSOR

What does an upside-down professor look like? What it does *not* mean is a free-for-all with no standards. There is nothing necessarily wrong with professors being trained in the academy, having degrees that enable them to have an expertise in what they teach, or being scholars who engage in world-class scholarship. In fact, rigorous training and high standards should be expected for professors. Classrooms should maintain painstaking standards and expectations, for the upside-down kingdom does not require, nor encourage, a closing of the mind. This model for education is also not just a technique to get things done.[12] An upside-down professor is that way because it is the way of the kingdom, not a means of manipulation.

Upside-down professoring relates to at least two obviously related issues, claiming privilege and exercising power. In both cases, vocation must be fulfilled in a way that reflects the counter-cultural nature of kindom living.

In regards to claiming privilege, the well-known example of Booker T. Washington (1856–1915), author, educator, and civil rights leader, provides some clues for how to cope with the expectations of privilege.

---

11. Clark, *The Minister Looks at Himself*, 121–22.
12. Kraybill, *Upside-Down Kingdom*, 260.

Shortly after taking over the presidency of Tuskegee Institute, Alabama, he was walking in an exclusive section of town when he was stopped by a wealthy white woman. Not knowing the famous Mr. Washington by sight, she asked if he would like to earn a few dollars by chopping wood for her. Because he had no pressing business at the moment, Professor Washington smiled, rolled up his sleeves, and proceeded to do the humble chore she had requested. When he was finished, he carried the logs into the house and stacked them by the fireplace. A little girl recognized him and later revealed his identity to the lady. The next morning the embarrassed woman went to see Mr. Washington in his office at the Institute and apologized profusely. "It's perfectly all right, Madam," he replied. "Occasionally I enjoy a little manual labor. Besides, it's always a delight to do something for a friend."[13]

A great deal of privilege comes with teaching, but upside-down professors are very careful how they claim it. They see their role in the classroom as one of service to the students, even to the point of stooping down to do tasks that may require the abandonment of privilege. They have radically different conceptions of what they are willing to do and be subjected to. Rather than demanding to be treated a certain way, they serve regardless of status. Of course, the abandonment of privilege is humiliating for those who could demand much more, but kingdom living based on the self-emptying example of Jesus and modeled by Washington beckons us down a road that seldom leads to our own exaltation.

As for exercising power, the way is even more difficult, for power is a dangerous thing and professors have a lot of it. Postmodernism and postcolonialism have made us much more sensitive to the uses and abuses of power in education, Paulo Freire's *Pedagogy of the Oppressed* (1970) being one example of such concern. A problem, however, is that the use (and misuse) of power in the classroom can be so enticing. As Mary Stimming notes, St. Augustine identified in his *Confessions* this propensity among teachers to crave power.[14] St. Augustine admitted that when he first began to teach he sought "to excel from a damnable and conceited ambition, and

---

13. This story is repeated in numerous sermon illustration sources. For instance, see under "Humility" on the Sermon Illustrations website, http://www.sermonillustrations.com/a-z/h/humility.htm. The story appears to be true, and is briefly mentioned in Harlan, *Booker T. Washington*, 143.

14. Stimming, "*Confessions* from the Classroom."

in human vainglory."[15] And as Stimming concludes, the struggle remains for us today.

> So, to my regret, I find that Augustine's diagnosis of vanity as the primary sin of teachers remains accurate today. I see it in the jockeying for the most prestigious panels at conferences, in the pursuit of the most impressive journals in publishing. I see it infect the classroom. I know a variety of manipulative acts teachers have employed to win campus popularity contests and to boost their own standings in annual student evaluations.... Vanity in its more subtle forms seeps into teaching.[16]

Despite the dangers of vanity and power, there is still a legitimate role for power structures. Upside-down professors still have rules, and will, when necessary, deal with classroom disorders—even from the front of the class if necessary. However, humility, compassion, and redemption direct their actions. Upside-down professors still have incredible power in the classroom, but are circumspect in how that power is exercised. They will remember St. Augustine's advice, "amendment is in secret."[17]

Both claiming privilege and exercising power as an upside-down professor require a humility that seeks to model that of Jesus. Efrain Agosto has summarized well the need for Christ's followers to live as their Lord did:

> Jesus elaborated on the nature of their mission as one of sacrifice. They [the disciples], like him, must serve and not expect to be served. Indeed, several times Jesus suggested that such service might entail the ultimate sacrifice of death because the nature of their leadership went counter to business as usual in the Roman Empire. Otherwise, they risked repeating the same mistakes of their oppressors and becoming oppressors themselves. "Lording over" their charges was not the way of the gospel, but rather ser-

---

15. Augustine, *Confessions*, 3.4.

16. Stimming, "*Confessions* from the Classroom," 140.

17. The context of the quotation is Augustine's addressing of sin from the pulpit to the entire congregation, rather than to a specific person. He said, "Let the reproof in secret profit you now. I speak openly, but I am rebuking you in secret. I knock at the ears of all; but I address myself to the conscience of some in particular. Were I to say, You, adulterer, mend your ways, I would in the first place say what I did not know, or maybe only suspect from something chance heard. But I do not say, You, adulterer, mend your ways, but what I do say is this: Let each one of you in this congregation who is an adulterer mend his ways. The rebuke is public; amendment is in secret. He who fears God will, I know, amend his life." See Augustine, "On Correcting One Another," 100.

vanthood was. To be first, to be a leader, entailed the sacrifice of service on behalf of those most in need.[18]

Perhaps one helpful guide to upside-down professoring is to ask the following types of questions related to privilege and power. What if my students took what they saw regarding leadership in the classroom and applied it in their ministries as church leaders? How would their pastoring go if they publicly shamed people, or drew attention to their congregant's sins in public? What would happen if they let it be known that their favorites were the smart ones, and the not-too-bright ones were somehow less than worthy of their attention? If they punished failure, rather than sought to bring redemption and healing? If they paraded their knowledge, and tried to act like they knew everything about everything? If they were only available when it fit their own schedule? If they required recognition of their titles, and did not do "lesser" jobs deemed beneath their station in life? What would their church look like if they claimed privilege and exercised power the way they saw it done in the classroom?

BUT HOW DOES ONE BECOME UPSIDE-DOWN?

There is no easy way to becoming an upside-down professor, and no mathematical formula that automatically (and miraculously) transforms someone into a humble and gracious educator. Spiritual growth is a uniquely personal experience, and what leads to growth in one person may not in another. Nevertheless, the following are some of the ways that one could work towards being an upside-down professor.

Clarify Your Purpose

I previously stated that much of my understanding of professoring in a seminary comes from the Pietist view of seminary being a hothouse for theological students. Another component of my self-understanding of vocational teaching in a Christian seminary has been developed from Calvin's view of the teachers, or doctors, of the church being (along with deacons, elders, and pastors) officers of the church. Teachers, or doctors, were to study the Scriptures, to teach doctrine, and among other things, to train and educate new ministers.

In what way does your vocation as professor connect to the life of the church, and in particular, to the training of Christian leaders? And how

---

18. Agosto, *Servant Leadership*, 199.

does this vocational calling affect the way you carry out your responsibilities as professor, especially as an upside-down professor?

Remind Yourself of Your Failings and Frailty

There is much to be said for not taking yourself too seriously. In fact, the way to humility is often through some healthy, and humorous, self flagellation. For instance, on a 1952 trip to Washington DC, Winston Churchill was asked, "Doesn't it thrill you to know that every time you make a speech the hall is packed to overflowing?" "It is quite flattering," Churchill replied, "but whenever I feel this way I always remember that if instead of making a political speech I was being hanged, the crowd would be twice as big."[19]

Churchill's comments reveal an important factor in the development of humility: we need to remember our failings, frailty, and the fact that all do not love us. I remember one class where I was waxing eloquent on a subject that had everyone transfixed (so I thought). I saw a hand rise and I stopped to answer the inquiring mind—thinking that the student needed clarification on one of my amazing points. The question was simply, "Has the attendance sheet been passed around yet?" I have always tried to remember this brief—but painful—experience, for it reminds me that my own perceptions of my greatness are not always shared by people in the classroom. Such reminders are an important corrective to any visions of grandeur that I might be tempted to hold. They also keep me from the pride that can easily cloud my vision and keep me from being an upside-down professor.

Look to Christ

In his recent work on evangelicals and the life of the mind, Mark Noll has a chapter entitled "Jesus Christ: Guidance for Serious Learning." One of the points he makes in this chapter is that the example of Jesus is an "antidote to the moral diseases of the intellectual life," and one of those diseases he identifies is pride. He writes:

> The sins of scholars are mostly those common to humankind: the lust of the flesh, the lust of the eyes, and the pride of life. But the predispositions of intellectuals and the circumstances of formal learning also make a few temptations especially threatening. There is pride to be cultivated in degrees earned, books published, honors bestowed, or interviews granted; academic

---

19. McGowan, *My Years with Churchill*, 138.

> introversion can easily transform into callousness toward people of ordinary intelligence; cliquishness and partisanship can be exploited for promoting my faction, race, sex, or political persuasion at the expense of others; and there is an eagerness to view the gifts that are not congenial to scholarship as somehow less important. These and other sins of intellectuals are familiar to everyone with any experience in the academy. They amount not to an argument against scholarship, but to occasions for redemption. The redemption is found in Christ.[20]

He goes on to argue that intellectuals who are dependent on Christ's redemption realize that their own existence is finite and their intellectual endeavors limited. Faced with the mystery of the incarnation—specifically that Jesus himself confessed that during his earthly ministry there were things that he did not know—scholars are made aware that their own wisdom is certainly limited. They should also heed the blunt words of Jesus for every servant of God: "We are unworthy servants, we have only done our duty" (Luke 17:10).

Look to the Past

In his defence of academic studies during the Second World War, C. S. Lewis stated that a study of the past was necessary in order to hear properly and gain some perspective on the many and varied voices that demanded attention: "A man who has lived in many places is not likely to be deceived by the local errors of his native village: the scholar has lived in many times and is therefore in some degree immune from the great cataract of nonsense that pours from the press and the microphone of his own age."[21] He made a similar statement in his introduction to *On the Incarnation*, where he urged readers to read ancient writings in order to challenge our contemporary works and assumptions.[22] These exhortations to look to the past have a bearing on being an upside-down professor, for the past can be a source of guidance and inspiration for today.

One of Thomas Oden's unique contributions to the church in the latter part of the twentieth century was his birthing a movement that emphasized a return to the church's rich classical traditions for contemporary guidance. For instance, his call for leaders to draw upon the riches of the

---

20. Noll, *Life of the Mind*, 61.
21. Lewis, "Learning in War-Time," 50–51.
22. Lewis, "Introduction."

Church Fathers challenged ministers to model their pastoral counseling on the insights of those such as Pope Gregory the Great (c. 540–604) rather than on secular psychotherapy.[23]

In a similar way, seminary professors should look back at the Church Fathers, or Reformers, or other "greats" of the faith, to shape their pedagogy and identity. What difference would it make to model one's vocation as a professor on the ministry of Pope Gregory the Great, St. Dominic (1170–1221), St. Aquinas (1225–1274), St. Catherine of Siena (1347–1380), St. Teresa of Avila (1515–1582), Martin Luther (1483–1546), or John Calvin (1509–1564) rather than the secular academy? Studying the lives of such men and women from the past will not help us figure out modern technological issues like why the PowerPoint presentation will not work (again!), but it will create opportunities for ancient mentors to provide clues as to how to live in an upside-down manner today.[24] The task of looking backwards is not to "do education" the exact way these figures did in the past, but rather, as Andrew Purves writes, it is to "allow these classical texts to provoke us into critical thinking by disturbing our calm, culture-bound assumptions concerning ministry."[25]

Ask Tough Questions

Kraybill reminds us that the kingdom that Jesus inaugurated was unlike any other kingdom of the day, and turned upside down all notions of success, status, and power. Now, as then, those claiming allegiance to Jesus are required to live according to a radically new social order. What this means for professors is that the world of academia, one so often riddled with arrogance and power, needs to be rethought. What that looks like in every situation is difficult to say, for being an upside-down professor is first and foremost a matter of an inner disposition, rather than a series of techniques. As Kraybill notes, "Kingdom ethics, translated into our modern context, suggest how we 'ought' to order our lives. We certainly won't find answers in the Scriptures for all our ethical questions. The Gospels don't offer a cookbook solution for every modern ethical dilemma. But

---

23. Oden, *Care of Souls*. A more recent example of a call for returning to the classics is Purves, *Pastoral Theology*.

24. This admonition to study the history of Christianity echoes what I have said elsewhere. See Heath, *Doing Church History*, ch. 2.

25. Purves, *Pastoral Theology*, 3–4.

they do raise the right questions. They nudge us towards the big issues that undergird the meaning and purpose of our living."[26]

CONCLUSION

One of my collegues recently told me that he knew of a seminary that began the academic year by having professors wash each other's feet.[27] While this may not be a workable option for every seminary, the principle behind it is important. The night before his betrayal Jesus washed his disciple's feet, a powerful and clear example of what he had been saying all along about life in the kingdom of God. Do professors see themselves as servants to one another and to their students, giving up honor due and power available, or are they captivated by status and systems of power? Despite the reputation and reality of arrogant professors in the academy, the challenge for us who seek to serve and train Christian leaders is to model an upside-down perspective. While he never used the words "upside-down" kingdom, Thomas à Kempis (c. 1380–1471) knew that imitating Christ meant denying privilege and eschewing power. Let me close with his reminder to the educated leaders of his day who knew definitions, but had forgotten the way of the kingdom:

> What good does it do to speak learnedly about the Trinity if, lacking humility, you displease the Trinity? Indeed it is not learning that makes a man holy and just, but a virtuous life makes him pleasing to God. I would rather feel contrition than know how to define it. For what would it profit us to know the whole Bible by heart and the principles of all the philosophers if we live without grace and the love of God? Vanity of vanities and all is vanity, except to love God and serve Him alone.[28]

BIBLIOGRAPHY

Agosto, Efrain. *Servant Leadership: Jesus and Paul.* St. Louis: Chalice, 2005.
Augustine. *Confessions.*
———. "On Correcting One Another." In *Sunday Sermons of the Great Fathers,* edited by M. F. Toal, 3:94–104. Swedesboro, NJ: Preservation, 1996.
Clark, Wayne C. *The Minister Looks at Himself.* Philadelphia: Judson, 1957.
Freire, Paulo. *Pedagogy of the Oppressed.* New York: Herder & Herder, 1970.

26. Kraybill, *Upside-Down Kingdom,* 20.

27. Perhaps closer to the example of Jesus would be the faculty washing the feet of students.

28. Thomas à Kempis, *Imitation of Christ,* 1.1.

Harlan, Louis R. *Booker T. Washington: The Making of a Black Leader, 1856–1901*. New York: Oxford University Press, 1972.

Heath, Gordon L. *Doing Church History: A User-Friendly Introduction to Researching the History of Christianity*. Toronto: Clements, 2008.

Kraybill, Donald B. *The Upside-Down Kingdom*. Scottdale, PA: Herald, 1978.

Lewis, C. S. "Introduction." In *The Incarnation of the Word of God, being the Treatise of St. Athanasius on the Incarnation*, 5–12. London: Centenary, 1944.

———. "Learning in War-Time." In *The Weight of Glory and Other Addresses*, 43–54. Grand Rapids: Eerdmans, 1965.

McGowan, Norman. *My Years with Churchill*. London: Pan Books, 1958.

Noll, Mark A. *Jesus Christ and the Life of the Mind*. Grand Rapids: Eerdmans, 2011.

Oden, Thomas C. *Care of Souls in the Classic Tradition*. Philadelphia: Fortress, 1984.

Palmer, Parker J. *The Courage to Teach: Exploring the Inner Landscape of a Teacher's Life*. San Francisco: Jossey-Bass, 1998.

Purves, Andrew. *Pastoral Theology in the Classical Tradition*. Louisville: Westminster John Knox, 2001.

Spurgeon, C. H. "Where True Prayer Is Found." Sermon #1412, 3–4. Online: http://www.spurgeongems.org/vols22-24/chs1412.pdf.

Stimming, Mary T. "*Confessions* from the Classroom: Teaching with Augustinian Eyes." *Teaching Theology and Religion* 2 (1999) 137–42.

11

Spirituality of Teaching and Theological Integration

Phil C. Zylla

Thinking about what it means to live a spiritual life as a teacher in a theological school inspires me to the core. It's not that this vocation is more important or more fundamental than others, but it is the richness of the opportunity to spend time thinking about God as the basis of all that you are doing. This essay is written to explore some of the foundations of the spirituality of teaching. Others have written eloquently about this, but it is my hope that this short essay will evoke resonance in those who also feel God's call to the ministry of theological education.

Albert Einstein is known to have said, "Everything should be as simple as possible, but not simpler." This cautionary principle helps to orient us to the task of the spirituality of teaching and theological integration—two very important and profound themes that have been part of my own searching as a theological professor for the past number of years.

COMMUNION WITH GOD AS THE STILL POINT OF OUR VOCATION

For me the most important starting point for thinking about this topic is the simple recognition that before I am a teacher, before I am a theological student, before I am a theological anything, I am a pilgrim. This leads me to the first principle for the spirituality of teaching: Communion with God is your true vocation. When we look at teaching itself as our vocation, we lose sight of the very essence of spiritual ministry. At its root, theological teaching is first a calling to live faithfully in the presence of God—to commune with the Triune God. Everything depends on this and everything flows from this.

In his book *Invitation to a Journey*, M. Robert Mulholland identifies part of what this means when he states that, "holistic spirituality is a pilgrimage of deepening responsiveness to God's control of our life and being."[1] To teach theology requires a deepening responsiveness and a profound awakeness to God. From this vantage point we can say what we see—offering our perspectives and the insights that are being born in us as we attend to God's voice and to God's leading in our lives. Spiritual teaching requires giving God our undivided attention and, from the posture of a listener, bringing our thoughts about God to others in deep humility.

Spiritual teaching not only begins with communion but it requires constant abiding with God. Our gathered fragments of insight and perceptiveness are inconsequential if they are not born from a sincere encounter with the living God. Spiritual teaching requires a posture and a perspective (to use the language of James Gustafson) of one who has heard from God, who is responsive to God's promptings in our life and in the lives of those who join us as participants in our courses. Teaching, then, is first a posture—a posture of attentive listening to God's voice and a posture of waiting on God for insight and understanding. Everything hinges on this first step. If you want to be a good theological teacher, draw near to God.

This has certain implications for us, however. It implies, first, that we have cultivated transformational spiritual habits in our lives. If we are to begin with communion with God, our lives need to be marked by prayer, devoted reading of Scripture, the practices of spiritual retreat and sojourn with God, and other spiritual habits that guide us to a life of being attuned to God. A life with God requires embedded patterns of knowing God deeply and requires our full concentration. To abide in Christ, to live a life that is grounded in God, and to orient all that we are to God is the fountain from which our spiritual teaching flows.

Second, this implies that there are significant forms of spiritual accountability in our lives as teachers. We benefit greatly when we journey with others toward God. The spiritual life is not an isolated one but rather

---

1. Mulholland, *Invitation to a Journey*, 12.

one in which we sojourn with others to give our attention to the voice of God in our life together. Spiritual friendship and spiritual accountability heighten our capacity to hear from God correctly and we share what God is teaching us as we travel in the life of discipleship together.

A third implication of this first principle of spiritual teaching is that we must live what we teach. Authenticity is an important buzzword in the postmodern era. For those of us who are called to the ministry of spiritual teaching it must represent something more than a buzzword. It must represent our constant attunement to God as the spiritual still point of our lives, "for in him we live and move and have our being" (Acts 17:28).

All of this reminds me of Parker Palmer's reflections on grace in teaching. He states:

> [T]he spiritual concept of grace goes beyond "information" and "events" into the realm of relational mystery that is at the heart of the way of knowing and teaching... In receiving spiritual grace we understand that we not only seek but are sought, that we not only know but are known, that we not only love but are loved. Indeed, it is because we are sought, known, and loved by grace that we are capable of seeking, knowing, and loving.[2]

To be in communion with God is at the core of the ministry of spiritual teaching and is the foremost principle from which all the others flow.

CREATE A TEMPLATE FOR SPIRITUAL INTEGRATION

The longer I participate in theological education the more I am convinced of the importance of having a template that will guide the practice of spiritual integration. Few begin this work with a clearly developed framework from which the work of theological teaching begins. I think that one of the closest things we have to a virtue list for teachers is the depiction of integration given in James 3:17, which I would propose as a template for spiritual integration. James writes, "But the wisdom that comes from heaven is first of all pure; then peace-loving, considerate, submissive, full of mercy and good fruit, impartial and sincere." This evokes a certain perspective on the ministry of spiritual teaching as a wisdom from above.

There are several implications of this. First, teaching implicates our whole being. A virtue orientation to spiritual teaching means that every aspect of our life is involved: the way we treat others, the respect that we foster in our collaboration with others, the attitudes and fecundity of our

---

2. Palmer, *To Know as We Are Known*, 113.

lives as teachers, our capacity for fair judgment—these are grounded in who we are. This leads to a second point, namely that our being is fundamentally related to our knowing and our doing. There is a tendency to separate these dimensions of teaching. However, who we are cannot be separated from what we know or how we do what we are doing as theological educators.

This template invites fresh reflection on the nature of the task of the spiritual teacher. If our teaching is grounded in a way of being, then this will require corresponding practices in our educational paradigm. What practices promote *purity*? This is seen when we are citing the original work of others and give due credit for our ideas. What about *peace-loving* practices? This invites us to effectively deal with conflict in the classroom. *Consideration* is another virtue that can be practiced with the timely return of assignments and constructive feedback that participants in our courses are seeking from us. *Submissive* has connotations of being amenable and flexible, which make for the qualities of a good colleague in a complex educational environment and sometimes taking on tasks that are not in one's forte. *Full of mercy* queries our evaluation practices in education. Will they be punitive or redemptive? *Full of good fruit* is a call to have our scholarship bear good fruit in all that we are doing, especially as we enter the classroom and bring that fresh thinking to our engagement with students. *Impartiality* is another key virtue in the practice of spiritual teaching. We should not be showing favoritism but rather should treat each student with respect and careful guidance in their own educational journey. *Be sincere* corrects inflated perceptions of who we are as teachers. We should not only bring our successes to the classroom situation but also the areas of our life where we have been challenged and stretched. Integration requires a lifetime of concerted effort. The value of having a template like this is that it helps us to keep a measured picture of our growth in the spirituality of teaching.

CULTIVATE A LARGE VISION OF THE WORLD

If you think small, you will mentor small-minded people. Don't just stay in your discipline—read widely and explore all of the creative and interesting things this world has to offer. Travel and engage deeply in church conversations, mission trips, overseas projects. Open yourself up to the world—don't allow yourself to become narrow and regional and forgettable.

There is a tension built into the enterprise of teaching, especially at the graduate level. It is the tension of our disciplinary [subject] expertise within the complexity of the world itself. If we resign ourselves to simply present what we know, we limit the capacity of our classrooms to become places of authentic transformation. This calls for openness and a curiosity that makes for good integration. We must be willing to explore the connections, the touch points, and the possibilities of integration with other information, with other disciplines, and with other life experiences.

Cultivating a large vision of the world does not mean giving an illustration from a third-world context. It is rather bringing that third-world context, or some other world-disclosing perspective, to bear on the subject in some transforming pattern of theological reflection. Creating the conditions for serious theological reflection requires such a capacity to transform, through imaginative teaching, the very settings that appear to be limited into those in which every dimension of the world is brought to bear on the subject at hand. The worldview of the teacher can limit or expand the horizons of the learning situation. The spirituality of teaching demands that we are always deepening our understanding, integrating a wide variety of information, and offering wider horizons for those who journey with us in our courses.

There are implications of a larger vision of the world in the ministry of teaching. First, it is a reminder that world-disclosing perspectives require radical engagement with the world. We must challenge ourselves as theological educators to expand our own horizons and our worldview. Without a deeply embedded orientation to all of life, our classroom will inevitably be diminished, regional, and limited. Part of the challenge of being a theological educator is the life-long journey of our own radical involvement in a complex world. Second, this is a reminder to us that theological reflection is much more than simple application, however important that may be. Theological reflection involves a cycle of continual reassessment of perspectives that are constantly being framed in our own constellation of understandings. We model good theological reflection to participants in our courses when we ourselves are actively invested in this cycle. A final implication of this point is that complexity requires that we hold our conclusions lightly. This is not to say that we should not have clear and defined perspectives on our discipline. However, it is a reminder that our perspective is always limited, partial, and in process. We model to our students the humility of crystallized thinking when we are able to hold in check our presumptions about what we know. The spirituality of teaching at its core is a ministry of humble understanding.

CREATING SAFE AND HOSPITABLE DIALOGUE

Welcome your students. Offer them respect. Honor their decision to share in the context of the course you have designed. These fellow-pilgrims have come with many complex motivations, backgrounds, and capacities. If you begin with respectful listening, you will discover what I have started to refer to as "the richness of the room." There is a latent wisdom in the community of learning that requires a hospitable conversation. Part of the work you are called to do is to create a safe and hospitable conversation and to foster the environment for learning. This happens in many ways: in your careful marking of essays and book reviews, in taking a conversational tone, in the prompting of wise questions, and in the self-disclosure not only of your best ideas but of your worst moments and the failures, wounds, and lessons that you have experienced in life. In each of these ways we reaffirm the classroom as a safe place of learning and deepening.

Henri Nouwen combines the German idea of hospitality (*Gastfreundschaft*) as "friendship for the guest" with the Dutch idea of hospitality (*gastvrijheid*) as "freedom of the guest" when he states, "Hospitality, therefore, means primarily the creation of a free space where the stranger can enter and become a friend . . . Hospitality is not to change people, but to offer them space where change can take place."[3]

Part of the spirituality of teaching is to foster in ourselves this spirit of hospitality. As other essays in this volume have already mentioned, teaching takes concentrated effort and time. If we come to class preoccupied, rushed, and strained we will not be able to create the conditions for transformation to take place. Hospitality requires creative effort—establishing the gentle contours of a learning experience that allow others to safely enter and to experience their own growth.

The implications of this principle of hospitality are threefold. First, it reminds us that the teacher must himself or herself be hospitable. Whether we are prone to introversion or extroversion, the capacity to warmly welcome and invite students to a posture of mutual respect and listening can create the conditions for transformative learning. We need to be who we are as teachers but keep in mind that one of our key aims in creating a classroom is to be hospitable ourselves. Second, we are reminded here

---

3. Nouwen, *Reaching Out*, 7.

that teaching at its core requires disciplined attention to the conditions that foster mature dialogue. Respect for one another, honoring the ideas that are brought to the classroom, offering gentle guidance with thought-provoking questions—these are the patterns of the hospitable classroom. Finally, this is a call to self-disclosure and vulnerable truth-telling. We must remember that everyone in the situation of learning is intimidated in some measure by what is happening. The teacher wonders if they have mastered the concepts they are teaching. Students wonder if they will ever understand the foundations of the subject area. The process of learning is itself intimidating. The spirituality of teaching requires thoughtful attention to how this anxiety will be managed so that all find a safe place for transformative learning.

FINDING YOUR VOICE AS A TEACHER

Integration is ultimately about finding your own voice. This is not a simple matter. We must invest deeply in the search for our own voice as a scholar and a teacher. Sift through all the versions of yourself until you find the "true north" of your core identity. To find your voice means, in part, discovery of what is most important to you. That may not be so easy to find. If, at the core of integration, is the maxim, "Know yourself," one must then discover the pathways to self-understanding, meaning, and one's own fundamental orientation to life. Few of us are prepared to examine our blind spots, and frankly, education breeds a kind of arrogance that removes all the mirrors from the house. So what are some of the implications of this constructive precept?

First, finding your voice will involve courageous speaking. Carol Gilligan offers a perspective on finding your voice when she writes, "By voice I mean voice. Listen, I will say, thinking that in one sense the answer is simple. And then I will remember how it felt to speak when there was no resonance, how it was when I began writing . . . To have a voice is to be human."[4] We need to know who we are and how we come across. This demands self-reflection and mindful awareness of our own journey as a Christian person in the world. Our voice is related to our sojourn. Second, finding our voice requires examination of our blind spots. We all have them. What is required is that through creative exploration we reflect on those parts of our life that are not integrated with our teaching. The spirituality of teaching demands constant self-critical awareness that

---

4. Gilligan, *In a Different Voice*, xvi.

teases out the growth areas in our life and in our understandings. Finally, this principle reminds us that we do not speak alone. We are part of a community of scholars on the faculty. We are one voice in a wide variation in our field of inquiry. We need to point to other voices that are of equal importance to the education of our students. When we honor other voices, our voice is more clearly understood.

KEEP YOUR SENSE OF HUMOR

Part of living an authentic spiritual life as a teacher is to maintain a proper self-estimation and to keep our perspective light. I have long maintained that humor is an important dimension of spiritual teaching. I am not suggesting that we resort to entertainment or comedy as teachers but to that disposition of proper self-estimation (Rom 12:3) and to the constant perspective that comes from reframing situations in life in appropriate ways. Humor diffuses complexity and fosters solidarity with others. Humor does this in three ways: (a) by recognizing the common situation of all of our lives, (b) by empathizing with the situations of others as our own situation, and (c) by opening up the possibility of a different response than resentment, anger, or frustration.

The spirituality of teaching involves modeling light-hearted self-understanding. We need to demonstrate that we can laugh at ourselves, but without self-deprecation or subtle self-inflation. The correct self-appraisal is one that is able to take less seriously the foibles of life but to demonstrate confidence in the life of goodness given to us by God. Jolly laughter is a demonstration of the poise and confidence that one gains from having their true rest in God alone. "My heart will not fear" (Ps 27:3). "I am still confident of this: I will see the goodness of the Lord in the land of the living" (Ps 27:13).

It is also important to recognize that we can diffuse hostility and anger with lightheartedness and humor. The Scriptures invite this deeper integration when we are challenged in Hebrews, "See to it that no one misses the grace of God and that no bitter root grows up" (Heb 12:15). It is easy to miss the grace of God in many situations. We do not make light of the seriousness of life situations, but rather point to the outworking of God's grace even in situations of conflict, frustration, and blocked success. Rather than allowing people to become bitter and frustrated, we can use humor to appropriately point to the grace of God at work.

A good spiritual teacher can use humor appropriately to help others gain new perspective on the complexities of life. No one has all the wisdom. However, there is a parallel between true wisdom and light-heartedness. When we assist others to gain a fresh perspective on a situation, we are helping them to gain the "eyes of the kingdom." This new perspective often results in joy and laughter. When we are able to make others laugh without using derision or down-putting comments, we are helping them to see better.

CONCLUSION

In this brief essay I have shared from my own sojourn as a theological educator some of the core precepts that inform a deeper spirituality of teaching. These are not complete or exhaustive but rather illustrative of the creative work that teaching demands. Theological integration and spiritual profundity are not matters that one can master, but rather are aims of our aspirations in the theological classroom. When we aspire to commune with God, we invite our students to become true worshippers. When we follow a template for spiritual integration such as is proposed in James 3:17, we invite reflection on dimensions of our teaching that might otherwise go unnoticed or undeveloped. When we open ourselves to the wider horizons of the world, we invite a particular deep searching in our students and in our classrooms. Offering a hospitable environment for learning and assuming an attitude of hospitality creates space for transformative learning. Paying attention to our own journey, our own unique giftings, and our own voice assists in clarifying for ourselves and for others the exciting paths of educational growth. A spirituality of teaching finds ways and means to integrate, to deepen, and to hold lightly what we know in such a way that our classrooms become places of contrition, hope, and aspiration.

BIBLIOGRAPHY

Gilligan, Carol. *In a Different Voice: Psychological Theory and Women's Development.* Cambridge, MA: Harvard University Press, 1993.

Mulholland, M. Robert, Jr. *Invitation to a Journey: A Road Map for Spiritual Formation.* Downers Grove, IL: InterVarsity, 1993.

Nouwen, Henri. *Reaching Out: The Three Movements of the Spiritual Life.* New York: Doubleday, 1975.

Palmer, Parker. *To Know as We Are Known: A Spirituality of Education.* San Francisco: Harper & Row, 1983.

Modern Authors Index

Agosto, E., 194, 199, 200, 204
Allen, L. C., 83
Ardnt, W. F., 132, 134
Avery, P., 149

Baume, D., 58, 88
Baur, W., 132, 134
Beetham, F. J., 126
Benchley, R., 43
Black, D. A., 126
Bloom, A., 12, 37
Briggs, C. A., 156
Bromiley, G. W., 134
Brown, C., 134
Brown, D., 100
Brown, F., 143, 156
Broyles, C., 75, 82
Brueggemann, W., 75, 78, 82, 86
Bullock, C. H., 83

Clark, W. C., 194, 197, 204
Clausewitz, C. von, 183, 184, 191
Coffey, D., 185
Collins, R. F., 162, 176
Costin, C., 78
Countryman, L. W., 126
Counts, G. S., 17, 37
Crabb, L., 78
Craigie, P. C., 83
Crook, M., 78
Cross, F. M., 40
Croy, N. C., 126

Dahill, L. E., 42, 55
Damon, W., 15, 37

Danker, F. W., 132, 134
daSilva, D. A., 102
de Beer, J., 162, 176
Dewey, J., 14, 37
Dillard, R. B., 148, 156
Dobson, J. H., 126
Dörnyei, Z., 139, 156
Downey, D. E. D., 29, 37
Driver, S. R., 156
Duff, J., 126
Duke, J. O., 162, 176
Dunn, K., 58, 88
Dunn, R., 58, 88

Eaton, J. H., 83
Echevarria, A. J., II, 183, 191
Edwards, J., 182, 185
Escalante, J., 21

Firth, D. G., 83
Fleming, N. D., 58, 88
Foster, C. R., 42, 55
Fountas, I., 152, 156
Freedman, D. N., 40
Freire, P., 198, 204
Friedrich, G., 134
Futato, M., 75, 76, 82, 85

Gardner, R., 139, 156
Garrido, A. M., 176
Gee, J. A., 126
Gilligan, C., 212, 124
Gingrich, F. W., 132, 134
Goldingay, G., 83
Golemon, L. A., 42, 55

Graham, E., 49, 55, 162, 176
Grasha, A., 58, 88
Greenspahn, F. E., 142, 156
Griffin, P. W., 135, 146, 156
Gustafson, J., 207

Hadjiantoinu, G., 126
Halabe, R., 135, 142, 143, 146, 147, 155, 156
Halliday, M. A. K., 142, 156
Harlan, L. R., 198, 205
Hawk, T. F., 58, 88
Hawthorne, N., 29
Heard, C., 149
Heath, G. L., 203, 205
Hewett, J. A., 126
Hirsch, E. D., Jr., 12, 37
Hobbins, J. F., 136, 157
Hoffer, V., 150, 152, 156, 157
Holladay, W. L., 143, 156
Holt, J., 15, 37
Hull, J. M., 32, 34, 35, 37

Illich, I., 19, 37
Isbell, C. D., 141, 151, 155, 157

Jay, E. G., 126
Jeroski, S., 151, 157
Johnston, G., 109, 122
Johnston, P., 83

Kajiura, L., 121
Keener, C., 102
Kelsey, D. H., 38, 39, 55
Kenyon, K. M., 45, 55
Killen, P. O., 162, 176
Kinast, R. L., 49, 55, 162, 176
Kittel, B. P., 144, 150, 152, 157
Kittel, G., 134
Knight, G. R., 11, 12, 14–19, 37
Kolb, D. A., 108, 122
Kraus, H.-J., 83
Kraybill, D. B., 193–95, 197, 203–5
Kübler-Ross, E., 78
Kuhn, T., 31, 37
Kunjummen, R. D., 126

Lalonde, R., 156

Lamerson, S., 128
Lewis, C. S., 202, 205
Liddell, H. G., 132, 134
Long, G. A., 128
Louw, J. P., 132, 134
Luz, U., 46, 55

Machen, J. G., 126
Macnair, I., 126
Marsden, G., 193
McCann, J. C., 83
McCann, N. R., 83
McCartney, D. G., 126
McGowan, N., 201, 205
McKeachie, W. J., 68–70, 88
McLuhan, M., 25
Metzger, B., 130
Miller, P. D., 83
Mills, C., 58, 88
Moberly, R. W. L., 46, 55
Moorcroft, R., 156
Mounce, W., 126, 128
Mulholland, M. R., Jr., 208, 215

Nida, E. A., 134
Noll, C. A., 129
Noll, M. A., 192, 201, 202, 205
Nouwen, H., 175, 176, 211, 214

O'Donnell, M. B., 126
Oden, T. C., 202, 203, 205
Odlin, T., 147, 157

Palmer, P. J., 193, 205, 208, 214
Parham, C. F., 189
Pattison, S., 162, 176
Patton, J., 49, 55, 162, 176
Payne, D., 49, 55
Penner, E., 126
Peters, M., 19, 37
Petersen, D. L., 83
Pinnell, G., 152, 156
Pitts, A. W., 12, 37
Porter, S. E., 12, 29, 37, 126, 133
Pratico, G. D., 148, 157
Prevost, R., 11, 37
Price, G. E., 58, 88
Purves, A., 203, 205

Reed, J. E., 126
Reed, J. T., 126
Richards, K. H., 83
Robinson, H., 109
Ryle, G., 36, 37

Sawyer, T., 126
Schaefer, K., 75, 82
Schön, D. A., 48, 55
Scott, R., 132, 134
Shah, A. J., 58, 88
Shaw, G. B., 1
Skinner, B. F., 18, 37
Spener, P. J., 195, 196
Spurgeon, C. H., 196, 205
Spurling, R. G., 189
Stackhouse, J. G., Jr., 180, 191
Stimming, M. T., 198, 199, 205
Stone, H. W., 162, 176
Summers, R., 126

Thompson, J., 162, 176

Thompson, R., 176
Toffler, A., 18, 37
Tolentino, B. W., 42, 55
Treasure, J., 78

Vail, S. M., 142, 157
Van Pelt, M. V., 148, 157

Wain, K., 19, 37
Walton, H., 49, 55, 176
Ward, F., 49, 55, 176
Weimer, M., 119, 122, 136, 157
Wenham, J. W., 126
Westney, P., 146, 155, 157
Whitehead, E. E., 49, 55, 162, 176
Whitehead, J. D., 49, 55, 162, 176
Whiteley, S., 58, 88
Williams, T. F., 144, 157
Wilson, G. H., 83
Woodward, J., 176
Wright, R. A., 150, 157

Yount, W. R., 112, 122

www.ingramcontent.com/pod-product-compliance
Lightning Source LLC
Chambersburg PA
CBHW070255230426
43664CB00014B/2537